NEBENAN
AUSCHWITZ
NEXT DOOR

DIE NACHBARSCHAFTEN
DER LAGER AUSCHWITZ I–III

*THE NEIGHBORHOODS
AUSCHWITZ I–III*

Kai Loges und Andreas Langen (die arge lola)
Hartmann Books

Auschwitz ist ein vielfach ausgeleuchteter Ort, seit Jahrzehnten erforscht, von Millionen Besuchern jedes Jahr besichtigt. Trotzdem existiert im unmittelbaren Umfeld der ehemaligen Konzentrations- und Vernichtungslager Auschwitz eine fast unbekannte Sphäre: die Lebenswelt von Menschen, die aufgrund historischer und biografischer Fügung zu Nachbarn dieser Schreckensorte geworden sind.

Wir haben die Nachbarschaften der ehemaligen Lager in den Jahren 2012 bis 2017 intensiv bereist. Unsere Erkundungen konzentrieren sich auf das Umfeld der ehemaligen Hauptlager Auschwitz I-III: Stammlager, Vernichtungslager Birkenau und Arbeitslager Monowice/Buna-IG Farben.

Unsere Bilder und Texte sind eine Reflexion über den historischen Ort Auschwitz und die weiter reichenden Fragen, die er aufwirft: Wie leben Menschen im Schatten einer einstigen Mordstätte? Wie gestaltet sich das Zusammenleben angesichts historischer Traumata? Wie verhalten sich kollektives und individuelles Gedächtnis zueinander? Was ist das, der Geist des Ortes? Und vor allem: Was geht uns Auschwitz heute an?

Kai Loges und Andreas Langen

Much light has already been shed upon Auschwitz; it has been researched for decades and is seen by millions of visitors every year. Still, in the immediate area around the former concentration camp is a nearly unknown sphere of people who, owing to the coincidences of history and life, have become the neighbors residing near this site of death and horror.

In the period between 2012 and 2017, we traveled extensively through the communities surrounding the former camp. Our explorations were concentrated on the area around Auschwitz I–III: the main camp, the Birkenau death camp, and the Monowitz labor camp once operated by Buna-IG Farben.

Our pictures and essays reflect upon Auschwitz as a historical site, as well as upon the broader issues it raises: How do people live in the shadow of a mass murder site? What does community life look like in the face of historical trauma? How do collective and individual memory relate to each other? What is that thing known as the spirit of the place? And, most of all: Why should Auschwitz concern us today?

Kai Loges and Andreas Langen

AUSCHWITZ I – STAMMLAGER

Oświęcim / Auschwitz liegt im Westen von Polen, dicht an der ehemaligen Ostgrenze des Deutschen Reiches. Beim Überfall auf Polen, mit dem am 1. September 1939 der Zweite Weltkrieg begann, wurden die Stadt und ihre Außenbezirke sehr schnell von der deutschen Wehrmacht attackiert und besetzt.

In Auschwitz errichtete die SS ein System von KZs mit zuletzt 50 Außenlagern in der Region. Den Anfang machte sie mit einer Kaserne am südwestlichen Rand der Stadt, dem sogenannten Stammlager. Weithin bekannt ist dessen Tor mit dem Schriftzug »Arbeit macht frei«.

Hier wurden zunächst vor allem politische polnische Gefangene interniert. Die Anlage wurde stetig erweitert, zeitweise waren hier bis zu 18.500 Gefangene eingesperrt. Misshandlung, Unterernährung, Folter, medizinische Menschenversuche und Mord waren an der Tagesordnung. Die Zahl getöteter Stammlagerhäftlinge wird auf 65.000 geschätzt. Auch die Massentötung durch Giftgas wurde hier getestet, als Vorlauf für die industrielle Tötungsanlage im Vernichtungslager Birkenau.

Heute gehört der größte Teil des Areals zum Staatlichen Museum Auschwitz. Teile der Infrastruktur, z. B. eine Erweiterung im Raster der Kasernengebäude und Teile der Zwangsarbeitsstätten, die in der Nähe des Stammlagers errichtet wurden, sind heute nicht als ehemalige Lagerteile ausgewiesen, werden als Wohnviertel genutzt oder stehen leer.

AUSCHWITZ I—MAIN CAMP

Oświęcim (known as Auschwitz in German) is located in western Poland, close to the former eastern border of the German Reich. During the invasion of Poland, which began World War II on September 1, 1939, the city and its outskirts were quickly attacked and occupied by the German army.

In Auschwitz the German SS erected a system of concentration camps, which ultimately included fifty satellite camps in the region. They began with a barracks on the city's southwestern periphery, known as the Stammlager, or main camp. Its gate, with the inscription Arbeit macht frei, or "work makes you free," is widely known.

At first, most of those interned here were Polish political prisoners. The facility was constantly expanded; for a while up to 18,500 inmates were imprisoned here. Abuse, malnutrition, torture, human medical experiments, and murder were the order of the day. It is estimated that 65,000 prisoners died in the main camp. Here, they tested a method for committing mass murder by poison gas, a precursor to the industrial extermination camp at Birkenau.

Today most of the facility is part of the Auschwitz-Birkenau State Museum. Some of the infrastructure, such as an expansion of the grid of barracks buildings and some of the forced labor camps erected near the main camp, are no longer identified as part of the old camp but are now either residential areas or empty.

AUSCHWITZ II – VERNICHTUNGSLAGER BIRKENAU

Etwa zwei Kilometer nordwestlich des Stammlagers ließ die SS ab Frühjahr 1941 von Gefangenen das Vernichtungslager Birkenau errichten. Der Name, und teilweise auch das Baumaterial, stammten vom entvölkerten Dorf Brzezinka (deutsch: Birkenau), dass bis auf wenige Betongebäude abgetragen wurde. Der Zweck des Lagers war es, viele Menschen möglichst effizient zu ermorden und spurlos zu beseitigen. Dazu wurden Einheiten von Krematorien und Gaskammern entworfen und gebaut, in denen die SS bis zu ca. 2000 Menschen auf einmal tötete und von anderen Häftlingen (»Sonderkommandos«) verbrennen ließ. Die Asche der Ermordeten wurde von der SS in der Umgebung verstreut. In Birkenau wurden ungefähr 1,1 Millionen Menschen getötet, die meisten von ihnen Juden.

Nach der Befreiung im Januar 1945 kehrten die vertriebenen Einwohner von Brzezinka zurück und bauten ihr Dorf, das großen Teils direkt neben dem Lagergelände gelegen hatte, auf dem ursprünglichen Grundriss der Wege und Gebäude wieder auf, teilweise mit Material aus dem Lager.

AUSCHWITZ II—BIRKENAU EXTERMINATION CAMP

Around two kilometers northwest of the main camp the SS forced prisoners to begin building the Birkenau death camp in spring 1941. The name and some of the construction materials came from the vacated village of Brzezinka (Birkenau in German), which was demolished, except for a few concrete structures. The goal of the camp was to murder a great many people as efficiently as possible and to get rid of the bodies without a trace. In order to accomplish this, units of crematoria and gas chambers were designed and built. There, the SS was able to kill up to around two thousand people at once, who were then incinerated by other prisoners (Sonderkommandos, or "special units"). The SS then scattered the ashes of their victims in the surrounding area. In Birkenau around 1.1 million people were killed, most of them Jews.

After the liberation in January 1945 the displaced inhabitants of Brzezinka returned and rebuilt their village, much of which had been located next to the camp, using the original layout of roads and buildings and some of the materials from the camp.

AUSCHWITZ III - MONOWITZ/BUNA

Östlich der Stadt Auschwitz (polnisch: Oświęcim) ließ die deutsche IG Farben ab 1941 eine riesige Chemiefabrik errichten, vor allem für die Herstellung des kriegswichtigen synthetischen Kautschuks »Buna«. Für Bau und Betrieb des Werks bediente sich die SS ihrer Häftlinge, die sie an die IG Farben vermietete. Um den Einsatz dieser Arbeitskräfte zu optimieren, ließ die IG Farben unmittelbar südöstlich des Werksgeländes das Dorf Monowice einebnen und dort das Zwangsarbeiterlager Monowitz errichten. Es war das erste privat finanzierte deutsche KZ, maximal belegt mit ca. 11.000 Häftlingen. Sein Betrieb unterlag einem Paradox: Während die IG Farben die Arbeitskraft der Häftlinge maximal ausbeuten wollte, verfolgte die SS die so genannte »Vernichtung durch Arbeit«. Primo Levi hat die brutalen Bedingungen in Monowitz überlebt und in seinem Bericht »Ist das ein Mensch?« eindringlich geschildert. 22.500 der Häftlinge dieses Lagers sind umgekommen, fast alle Juden.

Die hölzernen Häftlingsbaracken waren in einem rechtwinkligen Raster angeordnet, auf Fundamenten aus Mauerwerk und Beton. Nach der Befreiung 1945 nutzen die zurückkehrenden Einwohner von Monowice diese Fundamente für ihre neuen Häuser. Heute existieren nur noch Teile von zwei hölzernen Baracken aus der Lagerzeit. Das Gelände ist nicht Teil des Staatlichen Museums Auschwitz.

AUSCHWITZ III—MONOWITZ/BUNA

To the east of the city of Oświęcim (now known as Auschwitz in German), the German company IG Farben had a gigantic chemical factory built in 1941, primarily to manufacture a synthetic rubber called "Buna," which was essential to the war effort. To construct and operate the factory, the SS rented out its prisoners to IG Farben. In order to optimize the use of this labor force, IG Farben leveled the village of Monowice, which lay to the immediate southeast of the factory, and there they built the Monowitz labor camp. It was the first privately financed German concentration camp, with a maximum occupancy of around 11,000 prisoners. Its operation was subject to a paradox: while IG Farben wanted to exploit the prison labor to the maximum extent, the SS pursued its policy of "extermination through work." Primo Levi survived the brutal conditions in Monowitz and in his memoir, If This Is a Man, *he vividly describes how 22,500 prisoners were killed there, nearly all of them Jews.*

The wooden prison barracks were arranged in a rectangular grid on foundations of masonry and concrete. After the liberation in 1945, the residents of Monowice returned and used these foundations for their new homes. Today only parts of two wooden barracks from that era still exist. This area is not part of the Auschwitz-Birkenau State Museum.

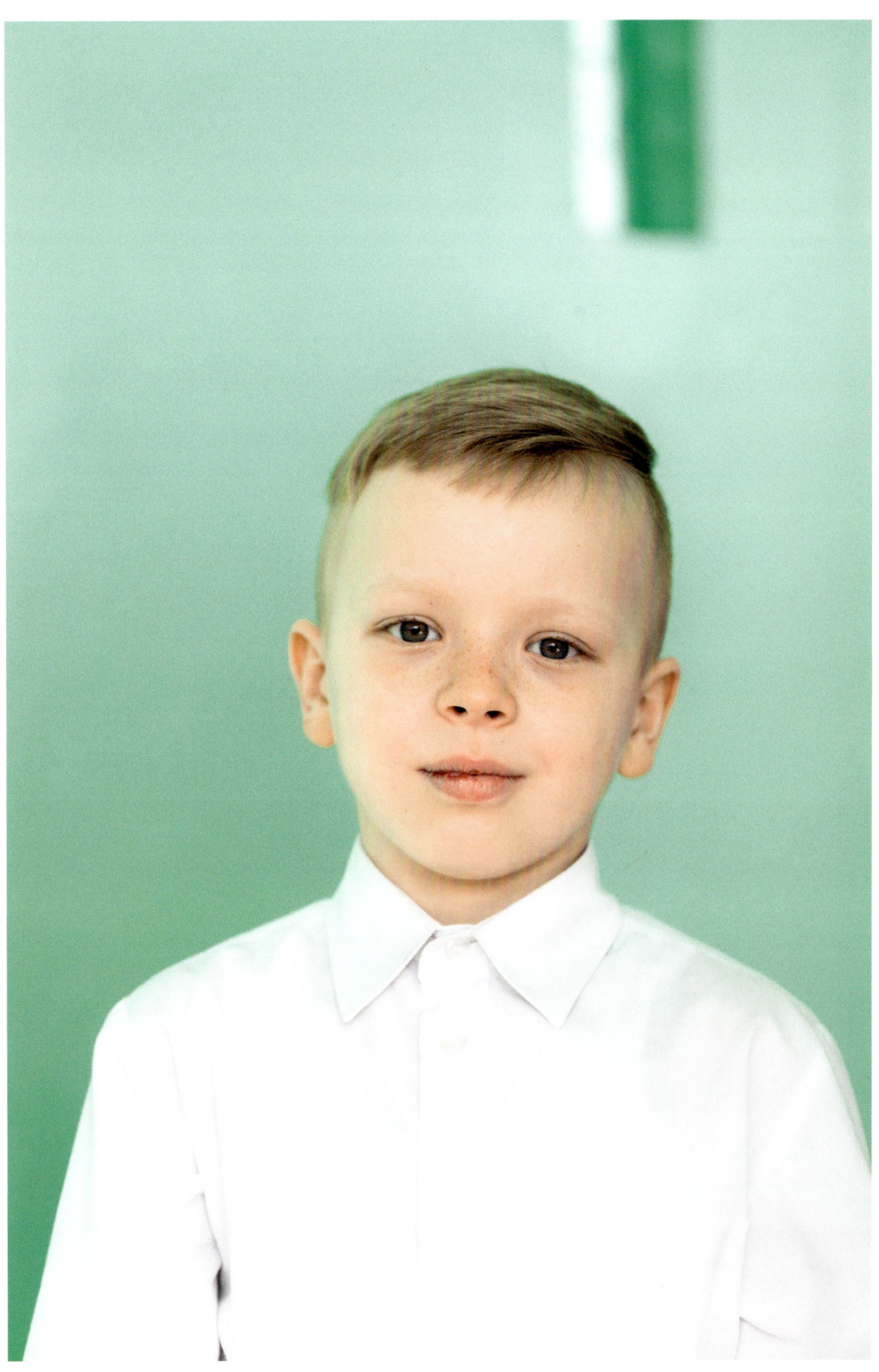

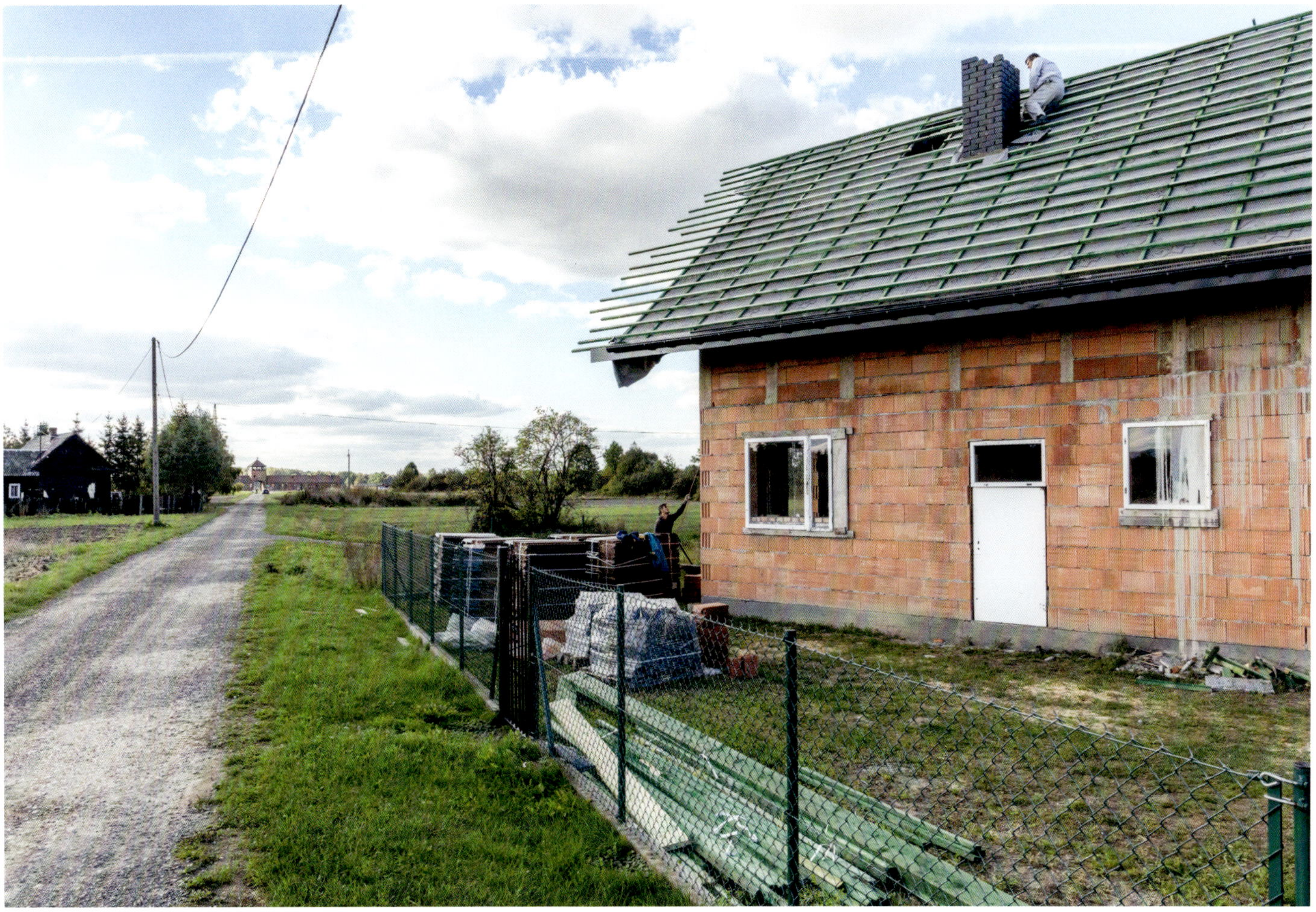

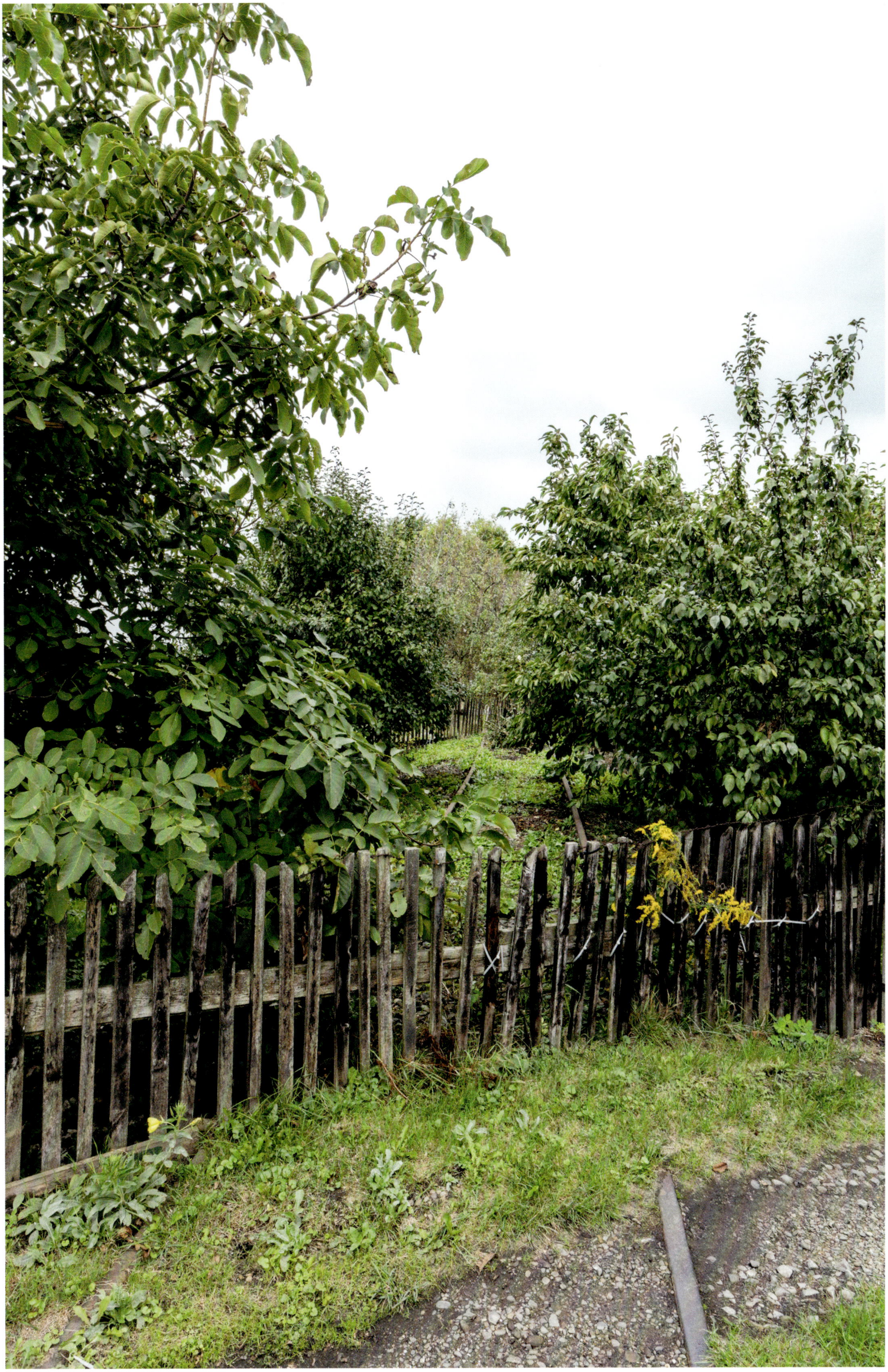

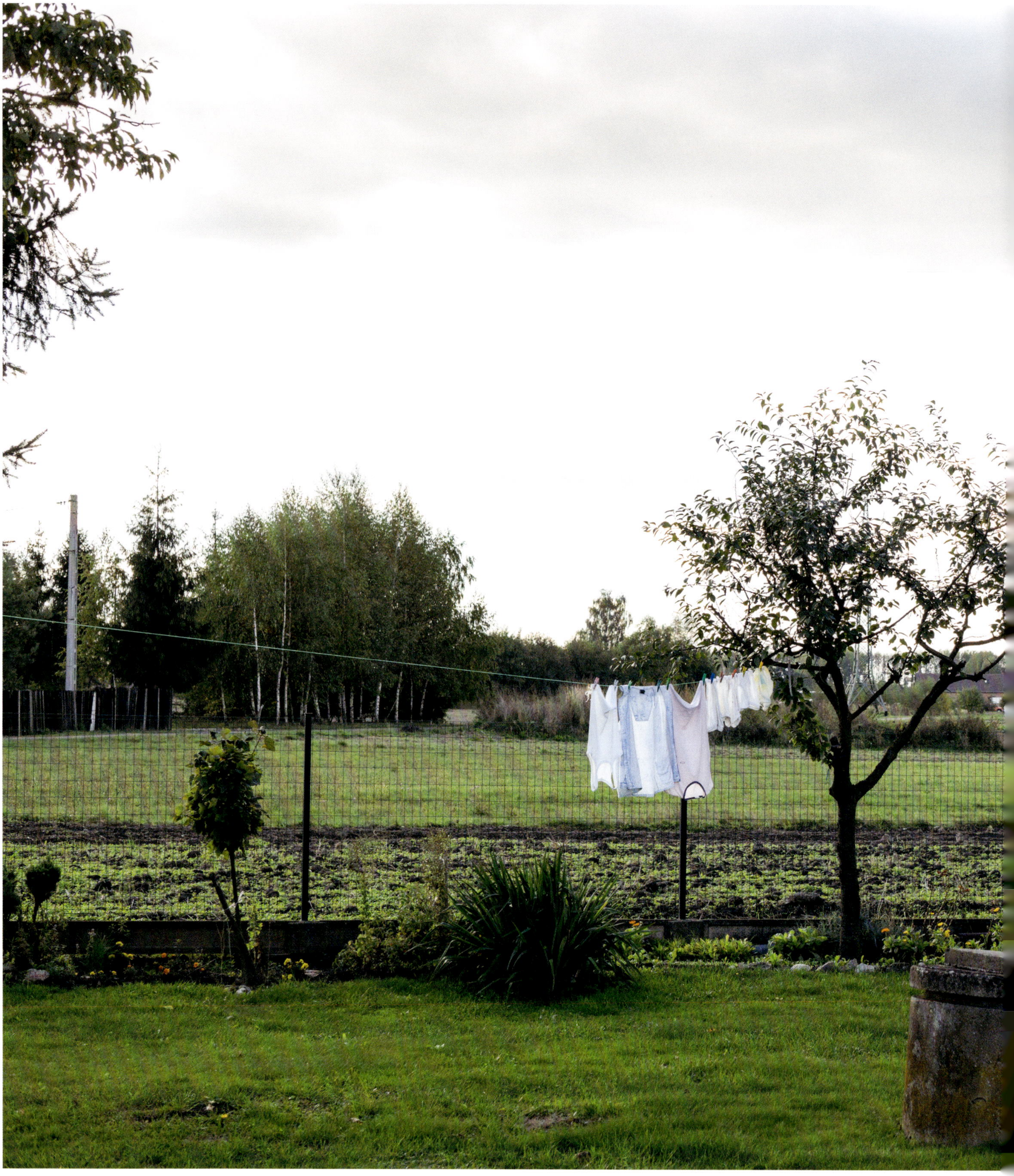

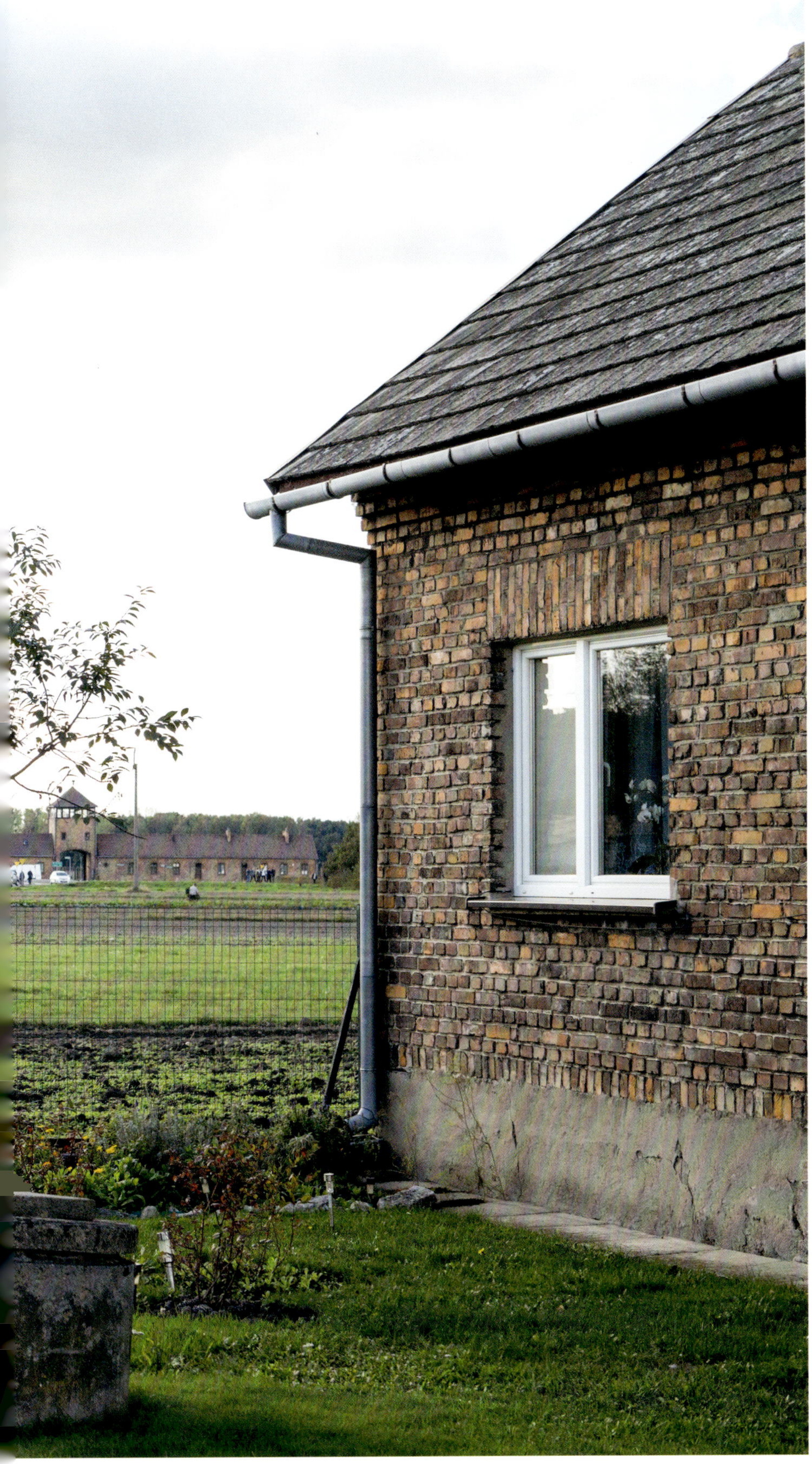

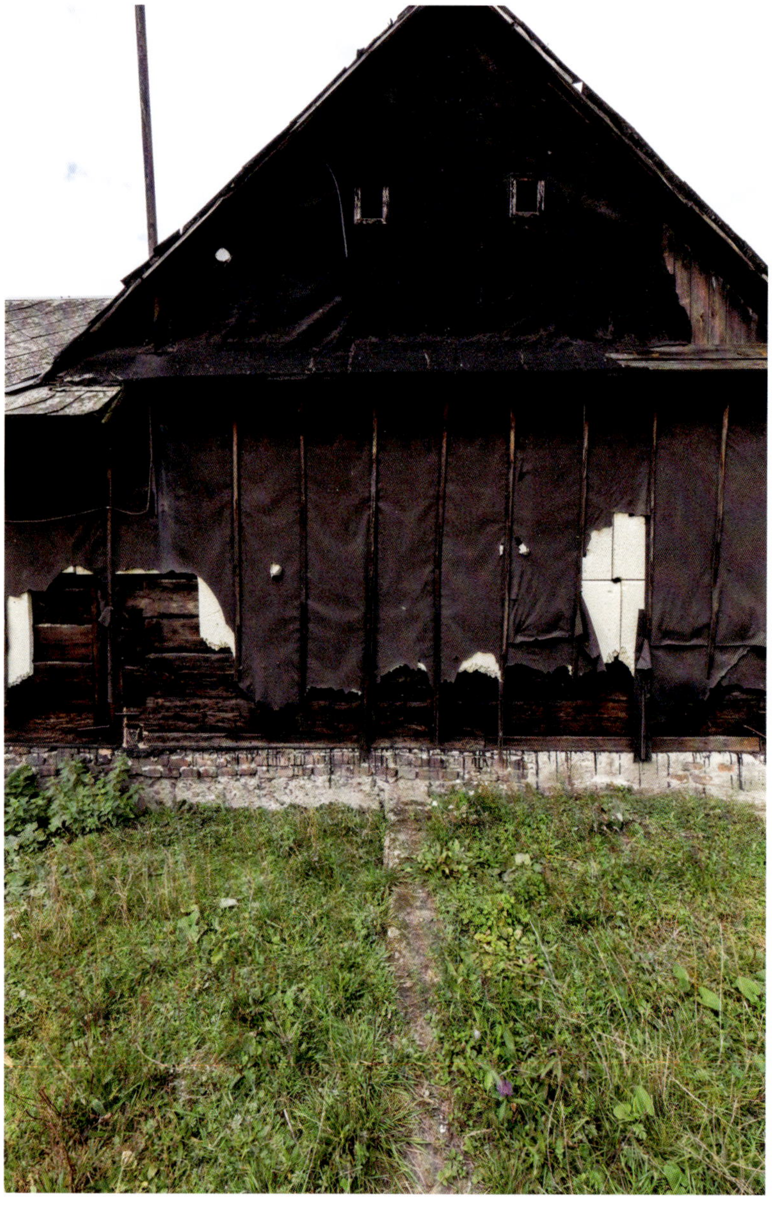

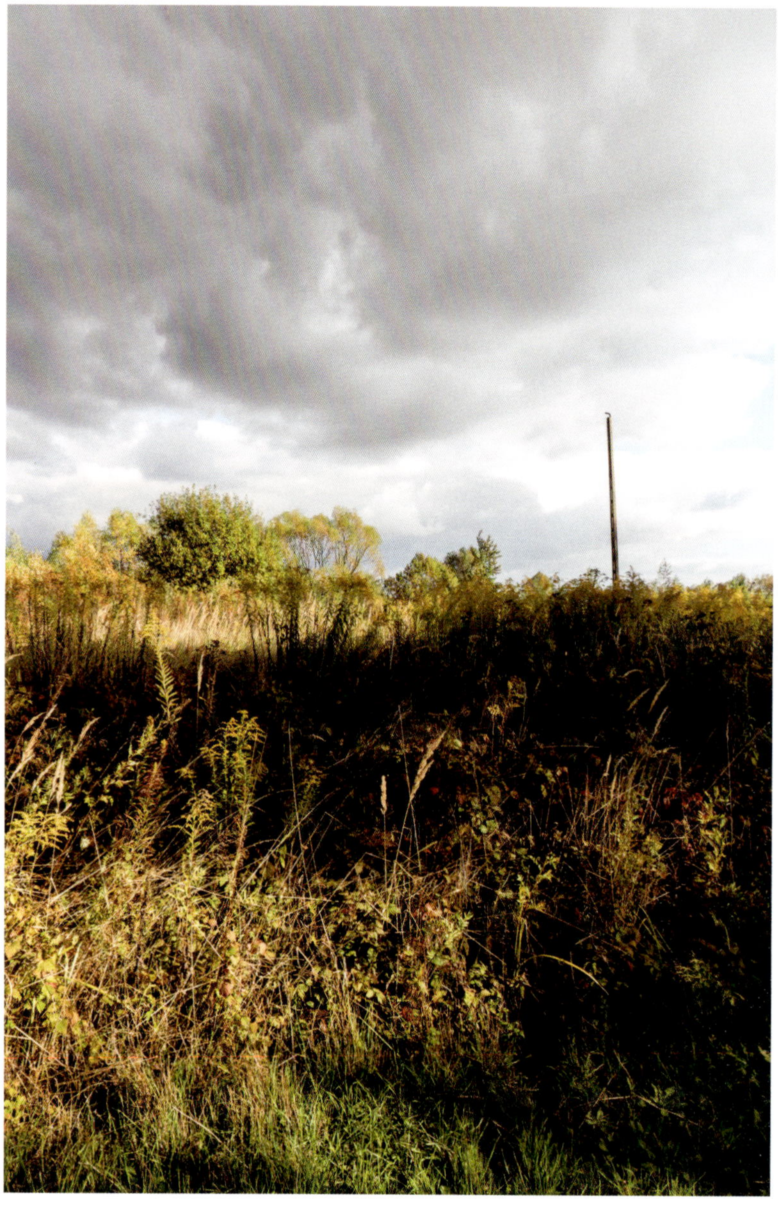

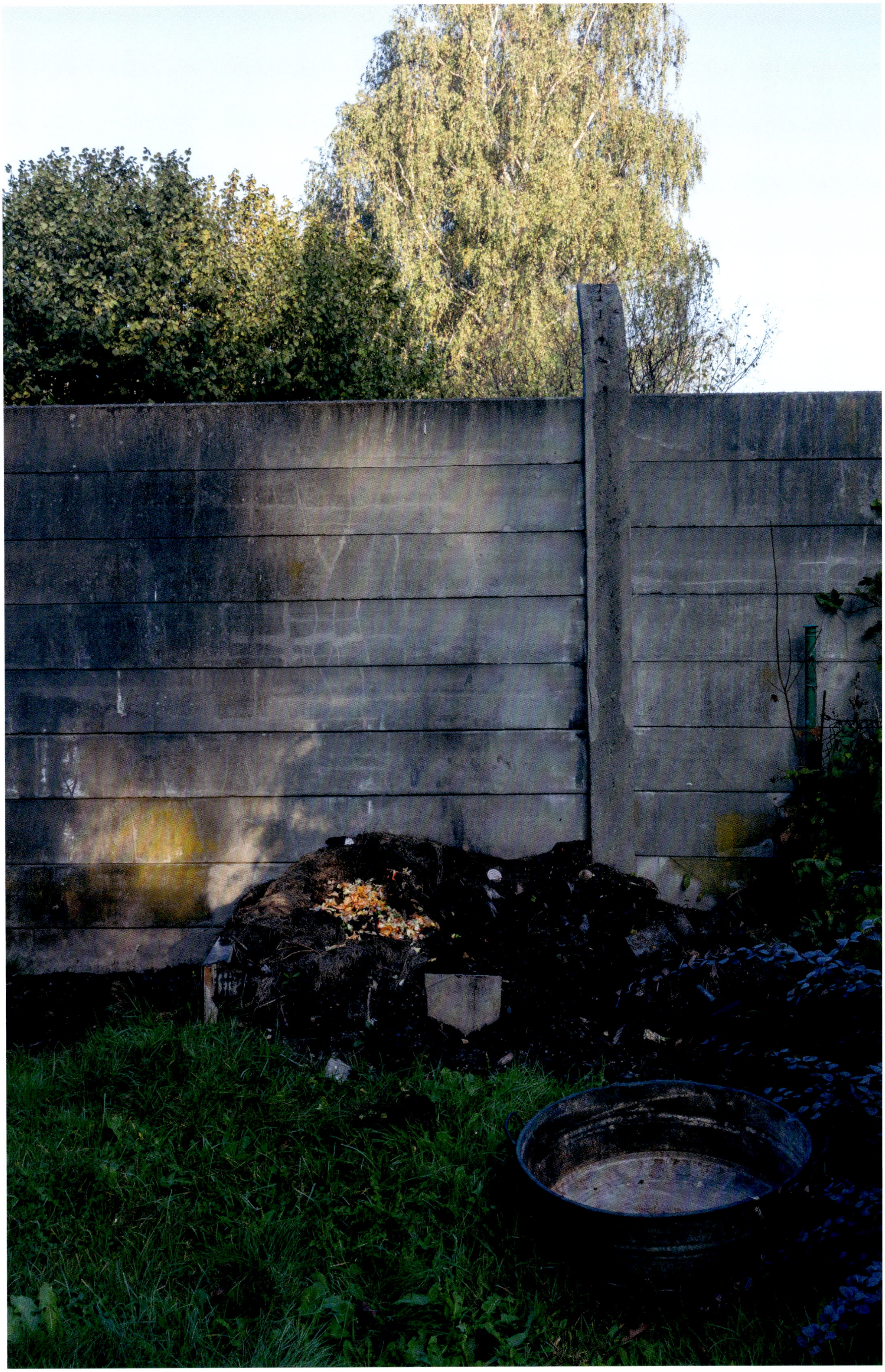

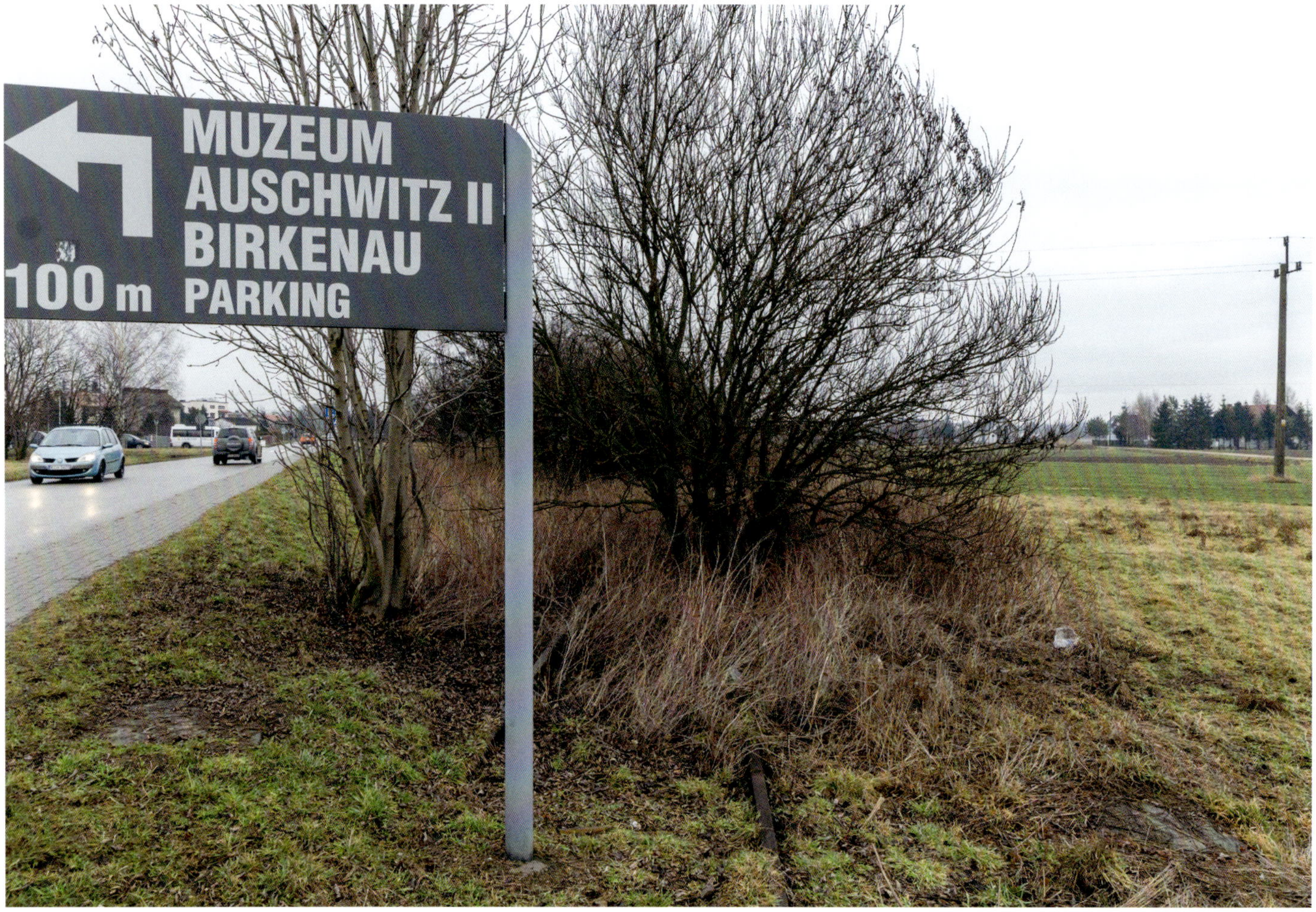
MUZEUM
AUSCHWITZ II
BIRKENAU
100 m
PARKING

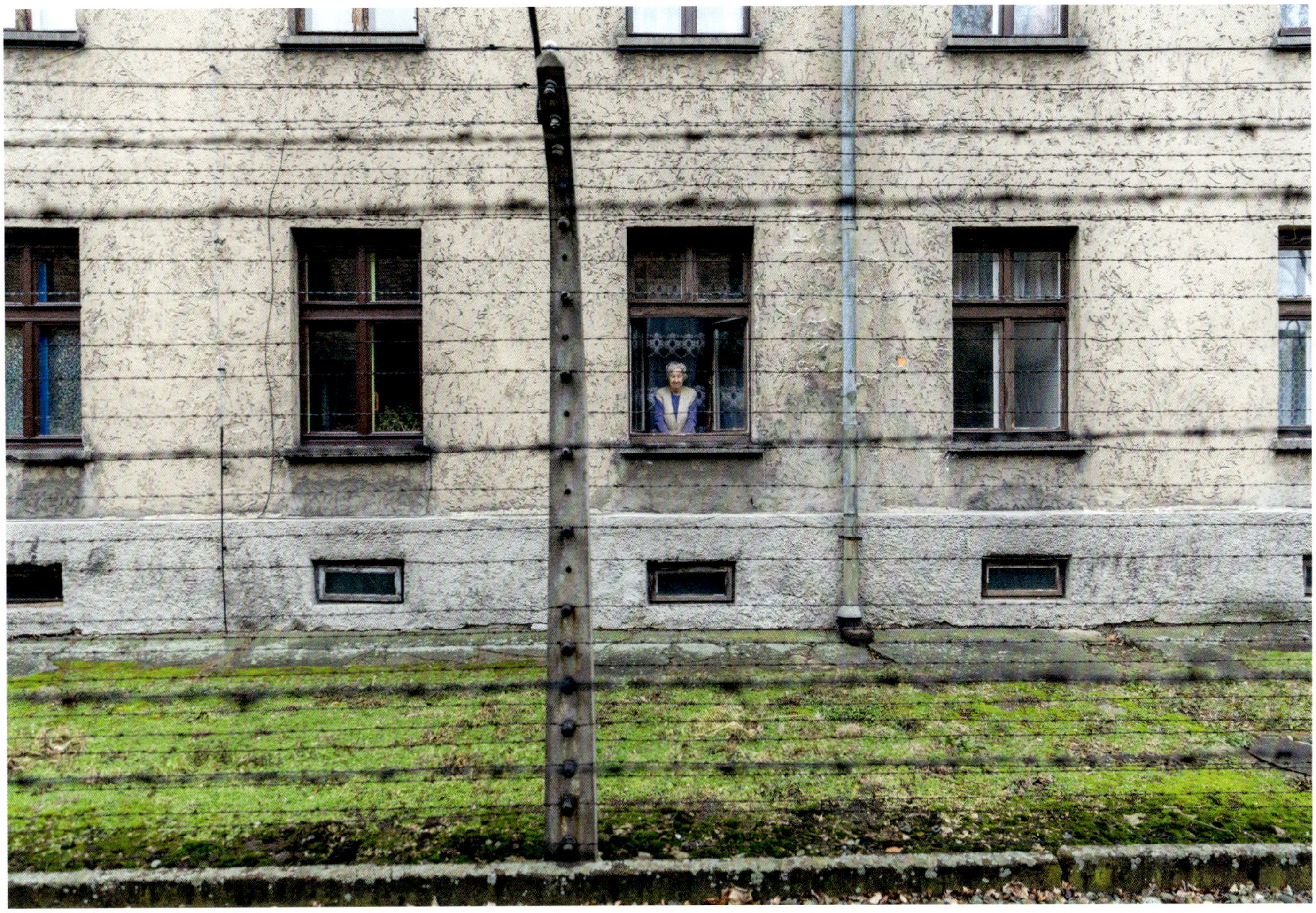

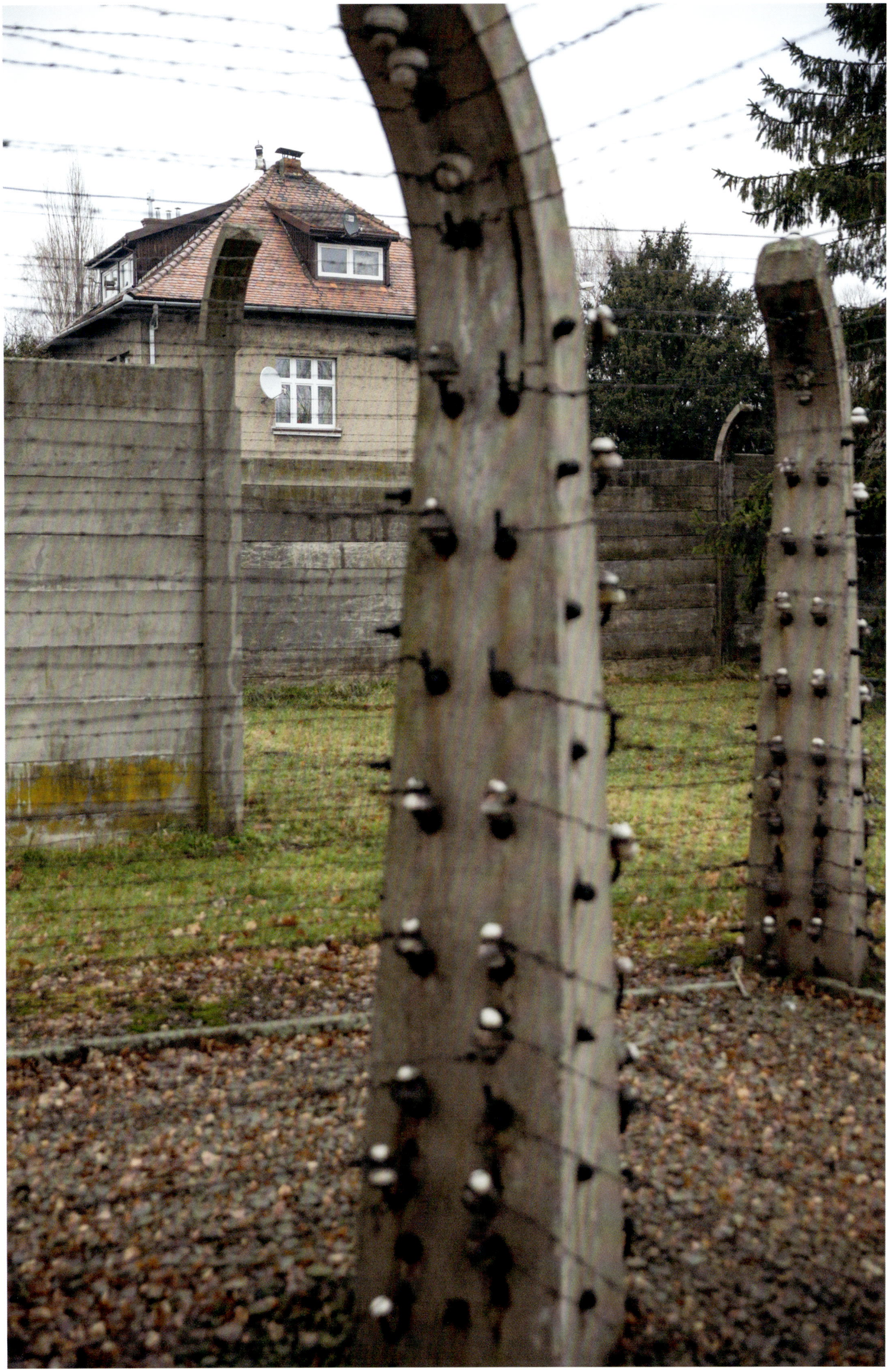

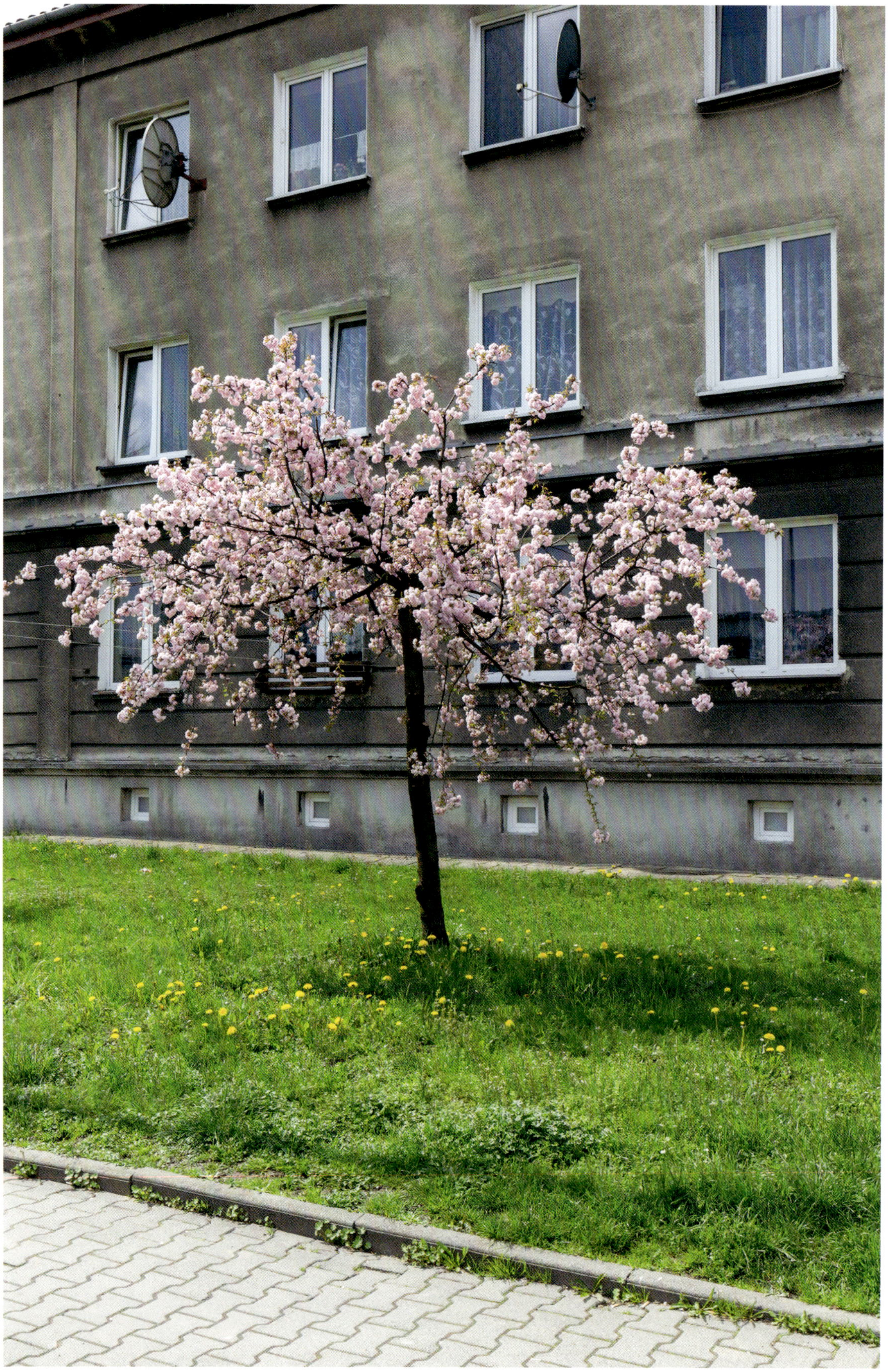

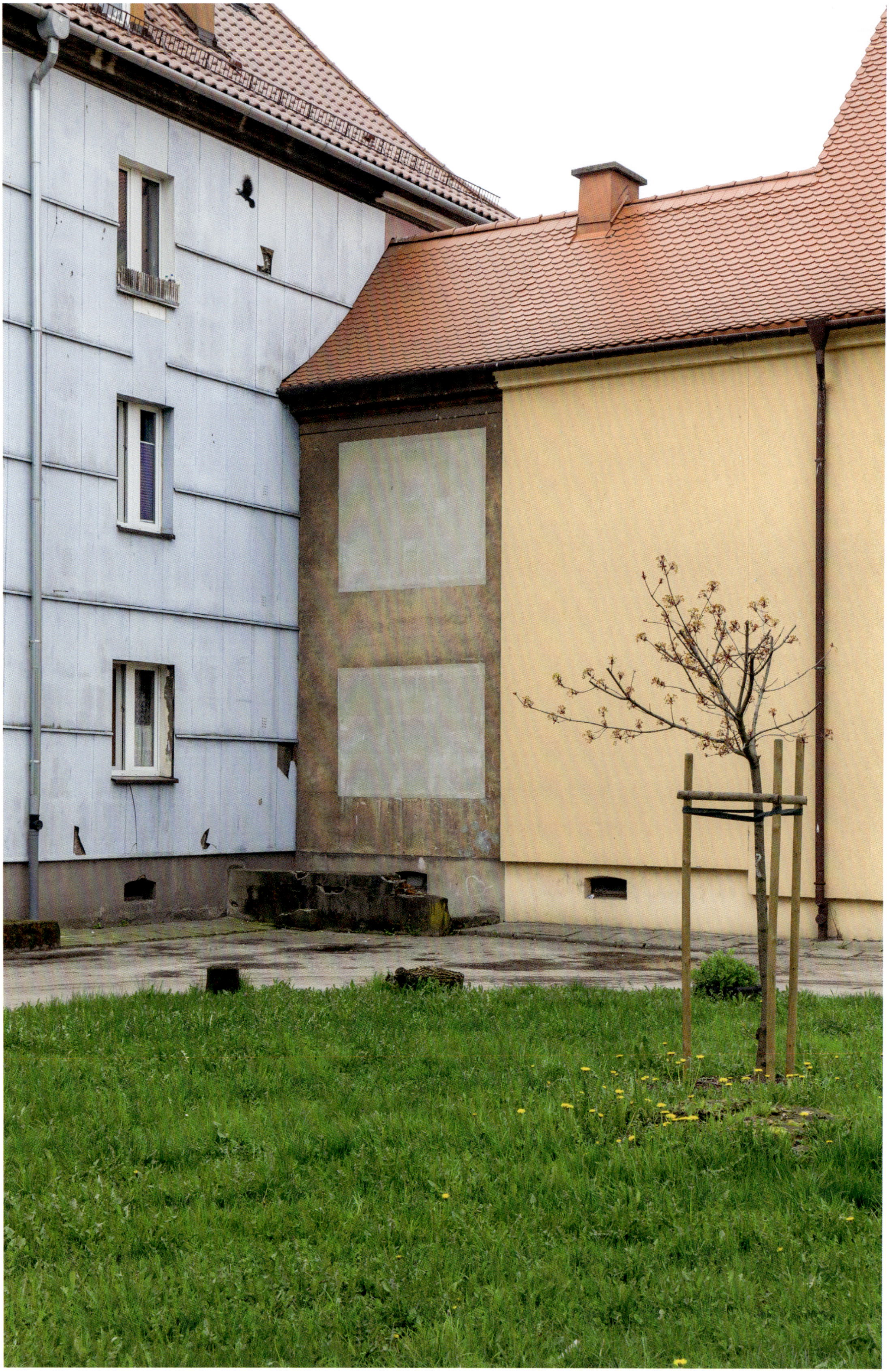

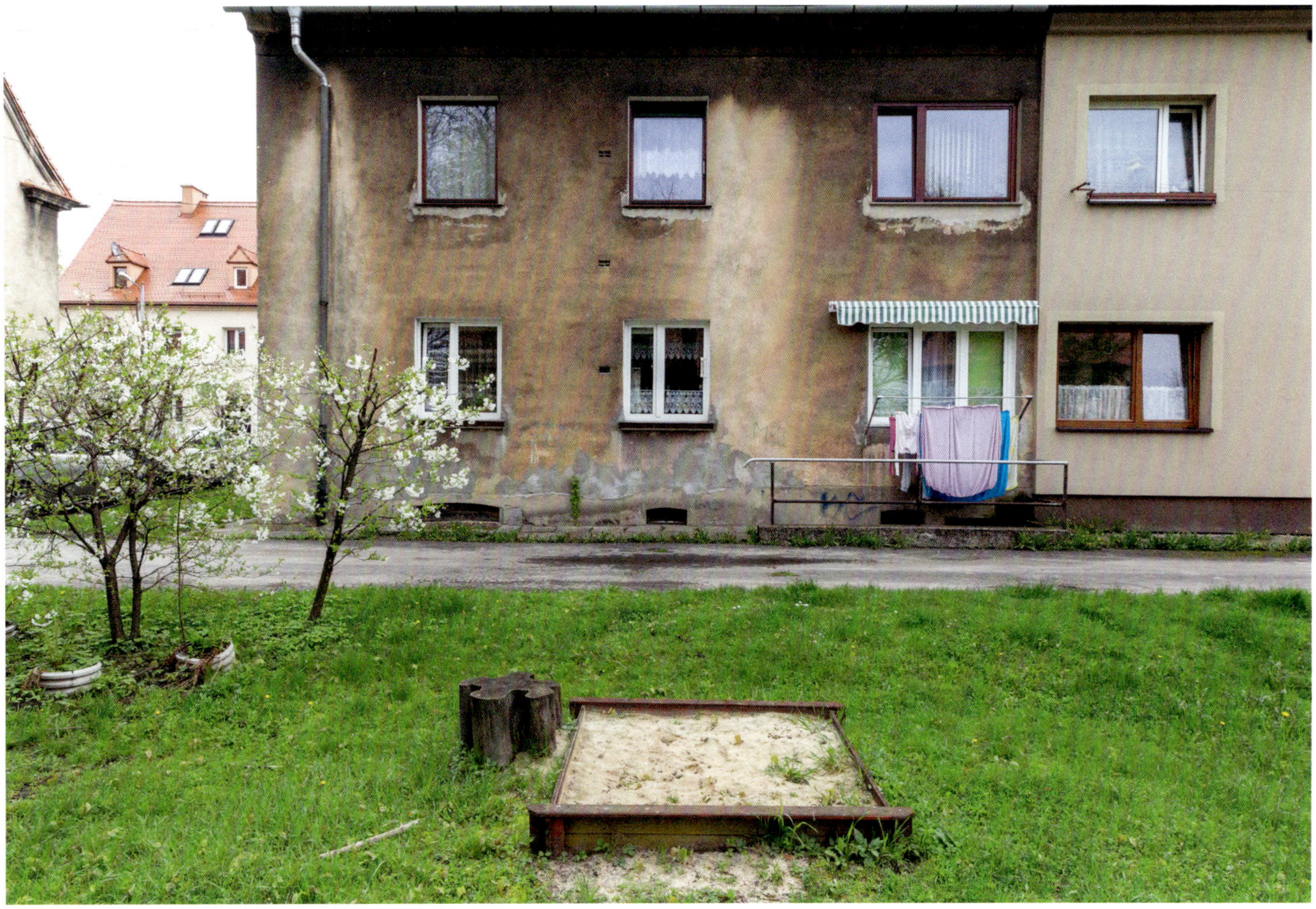

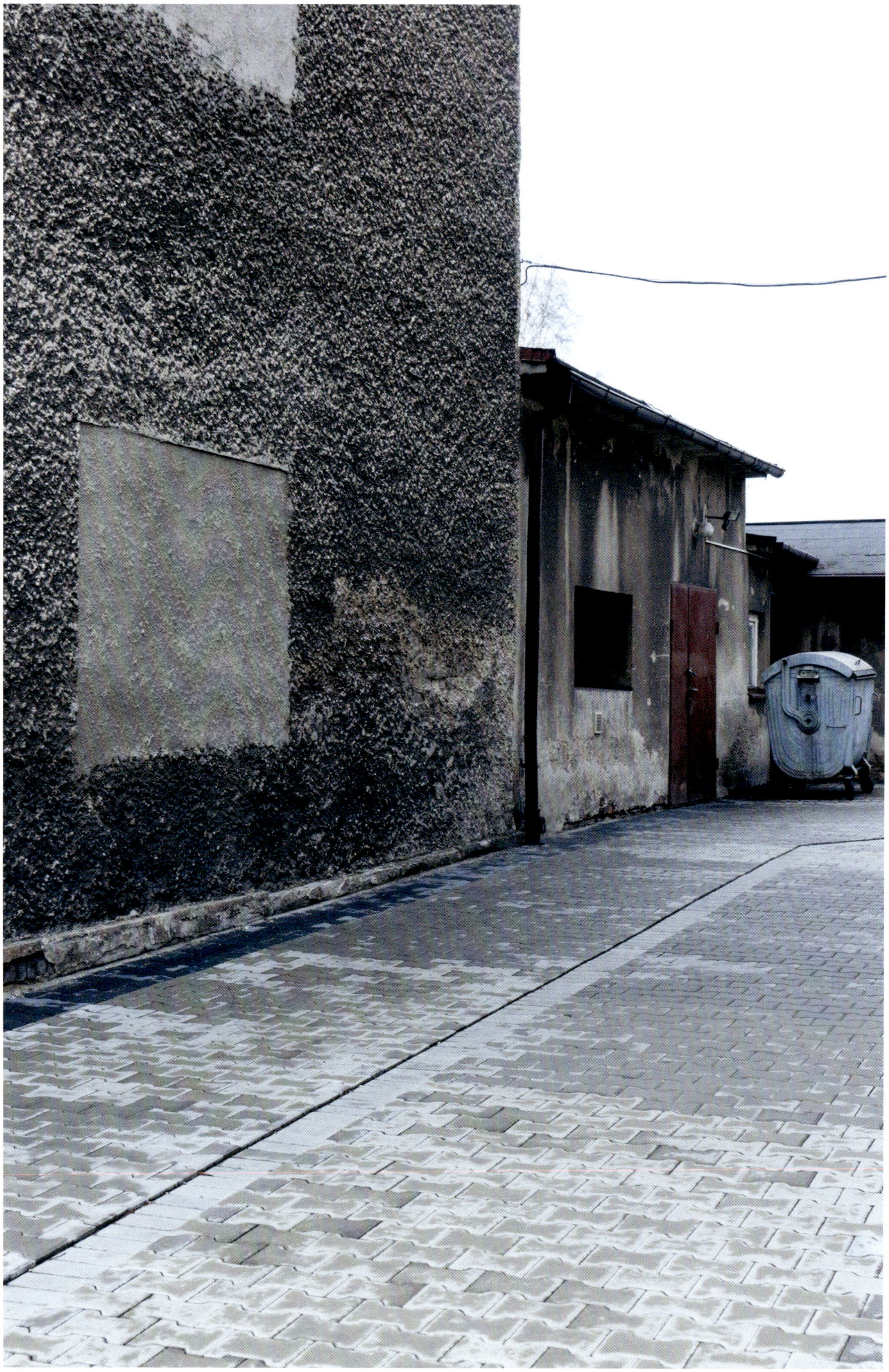

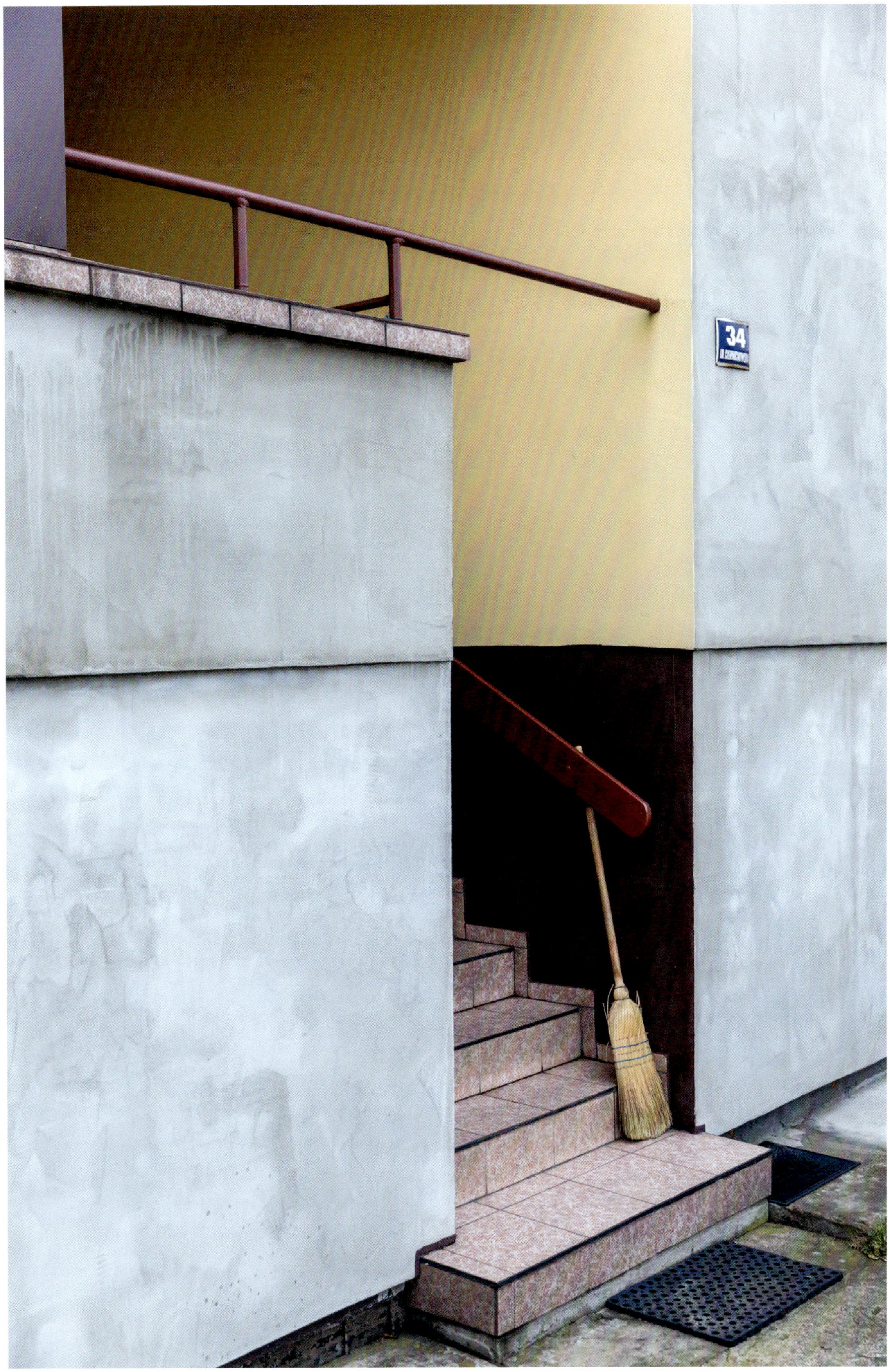
34

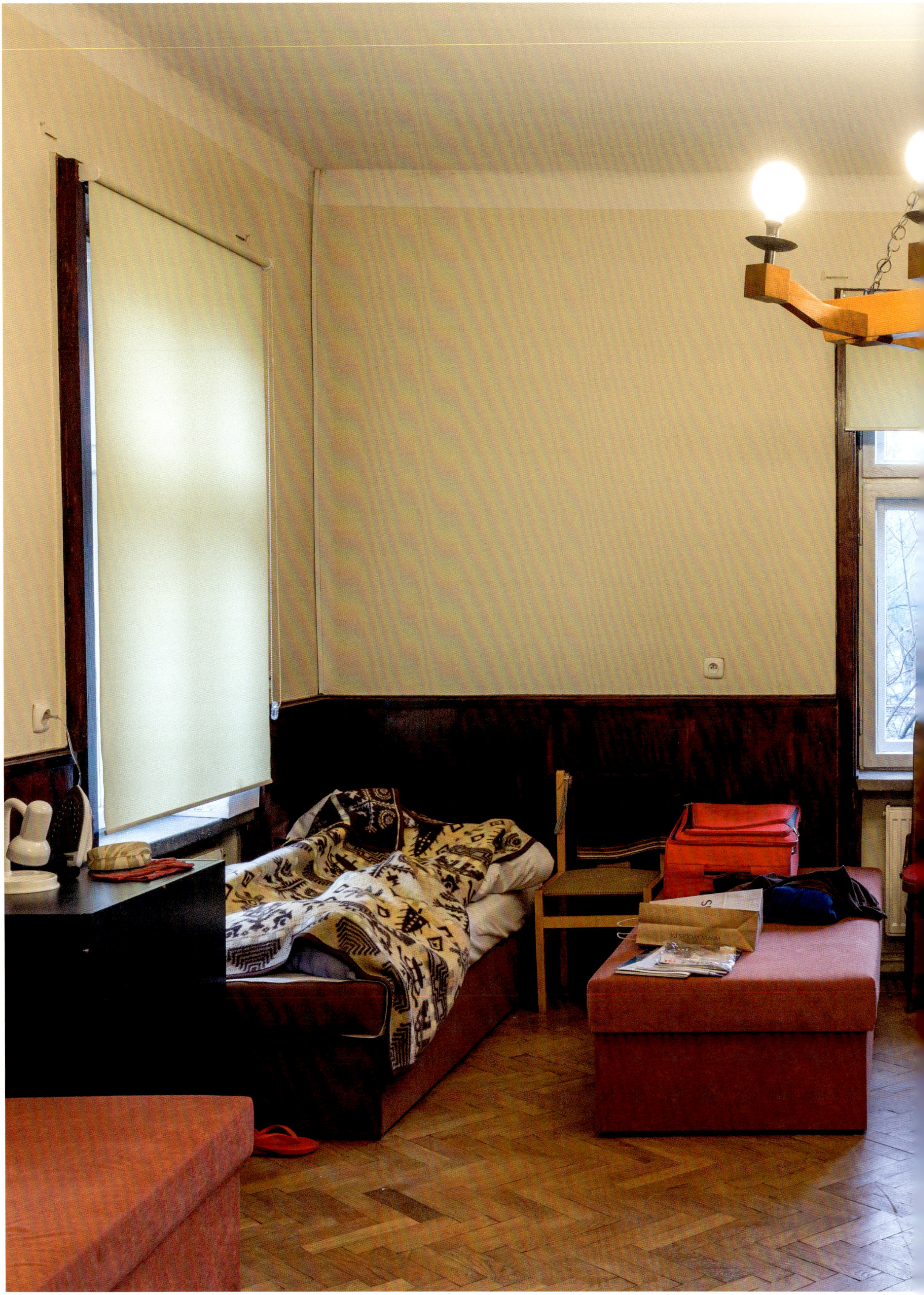

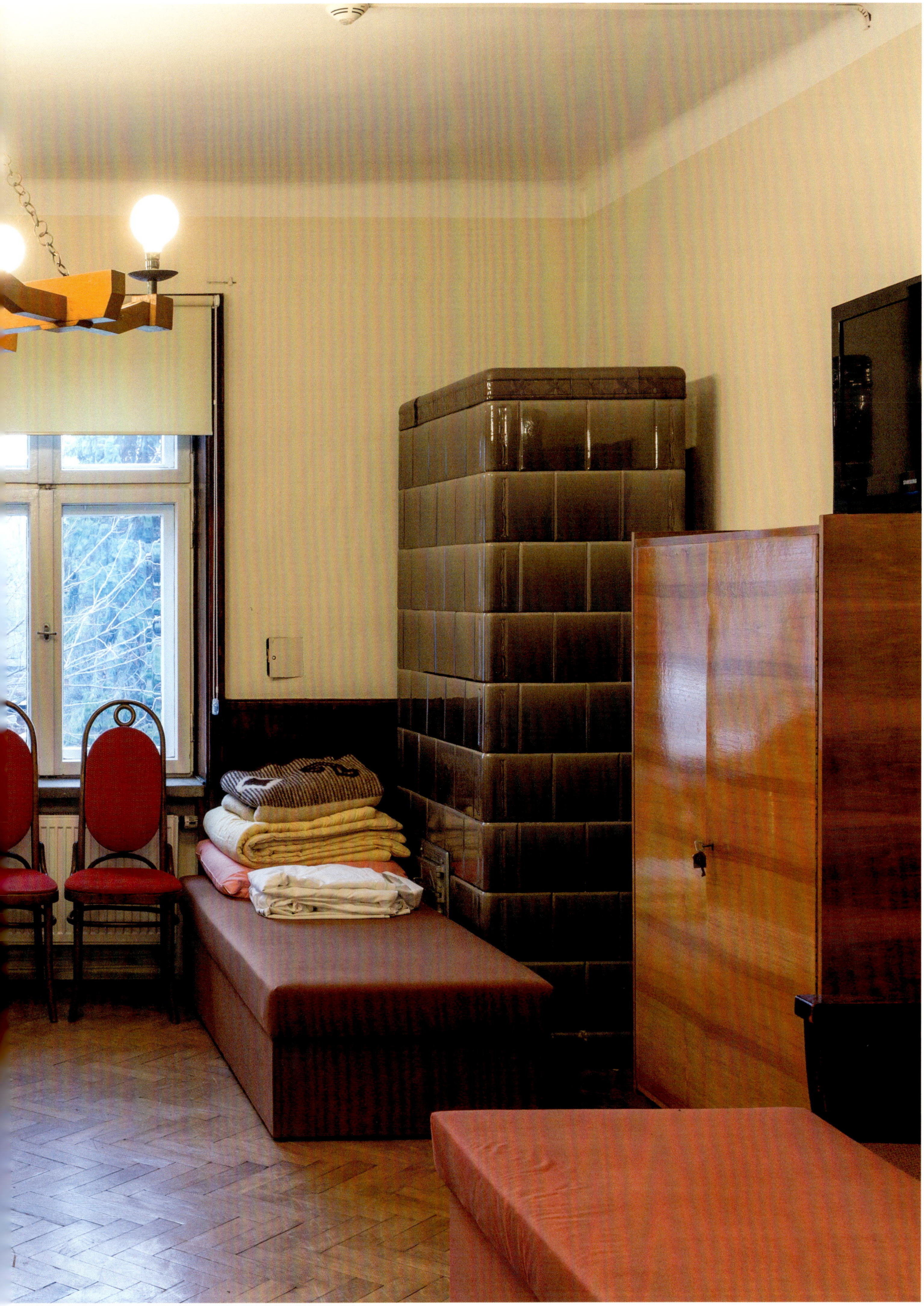

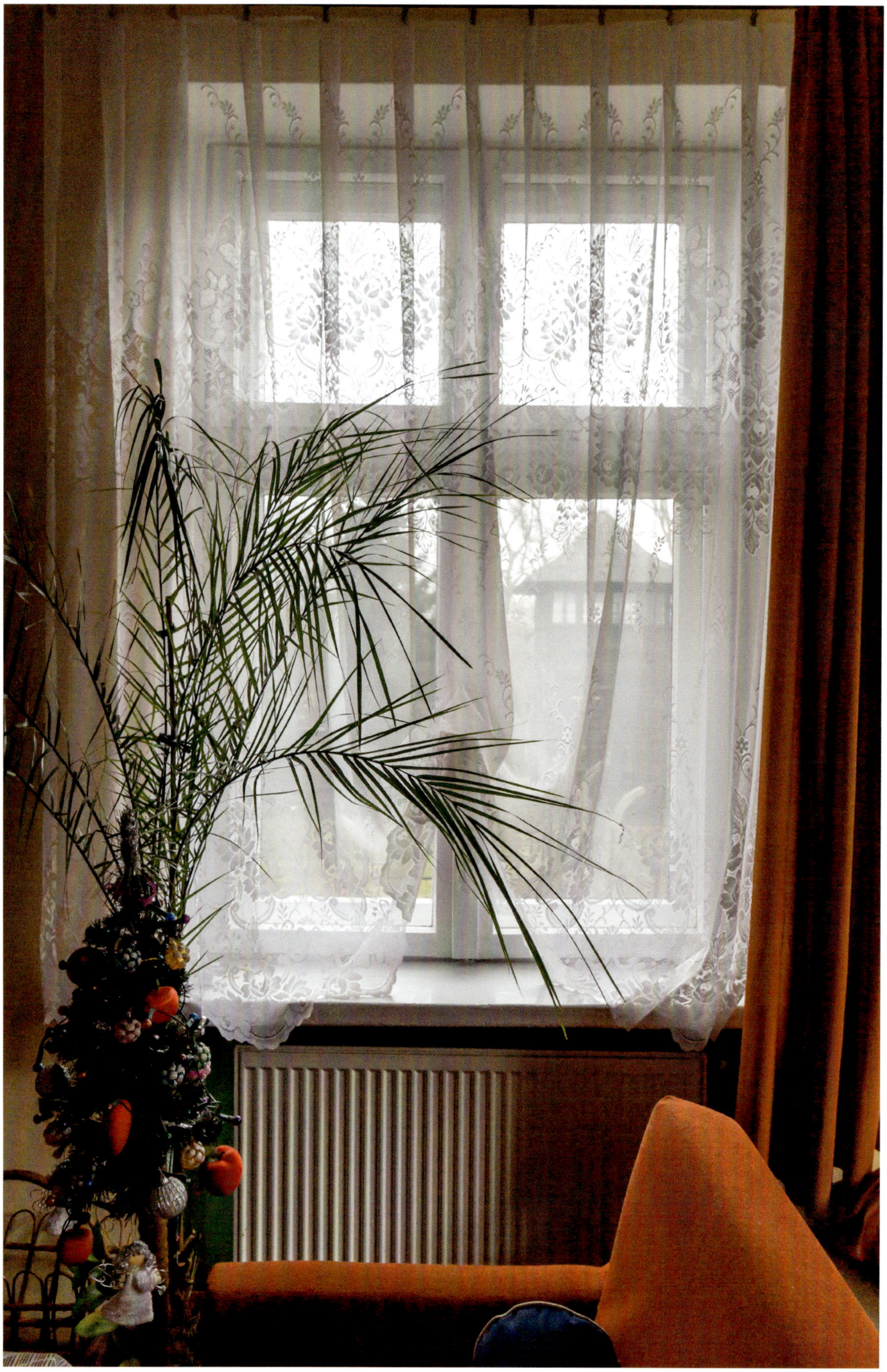

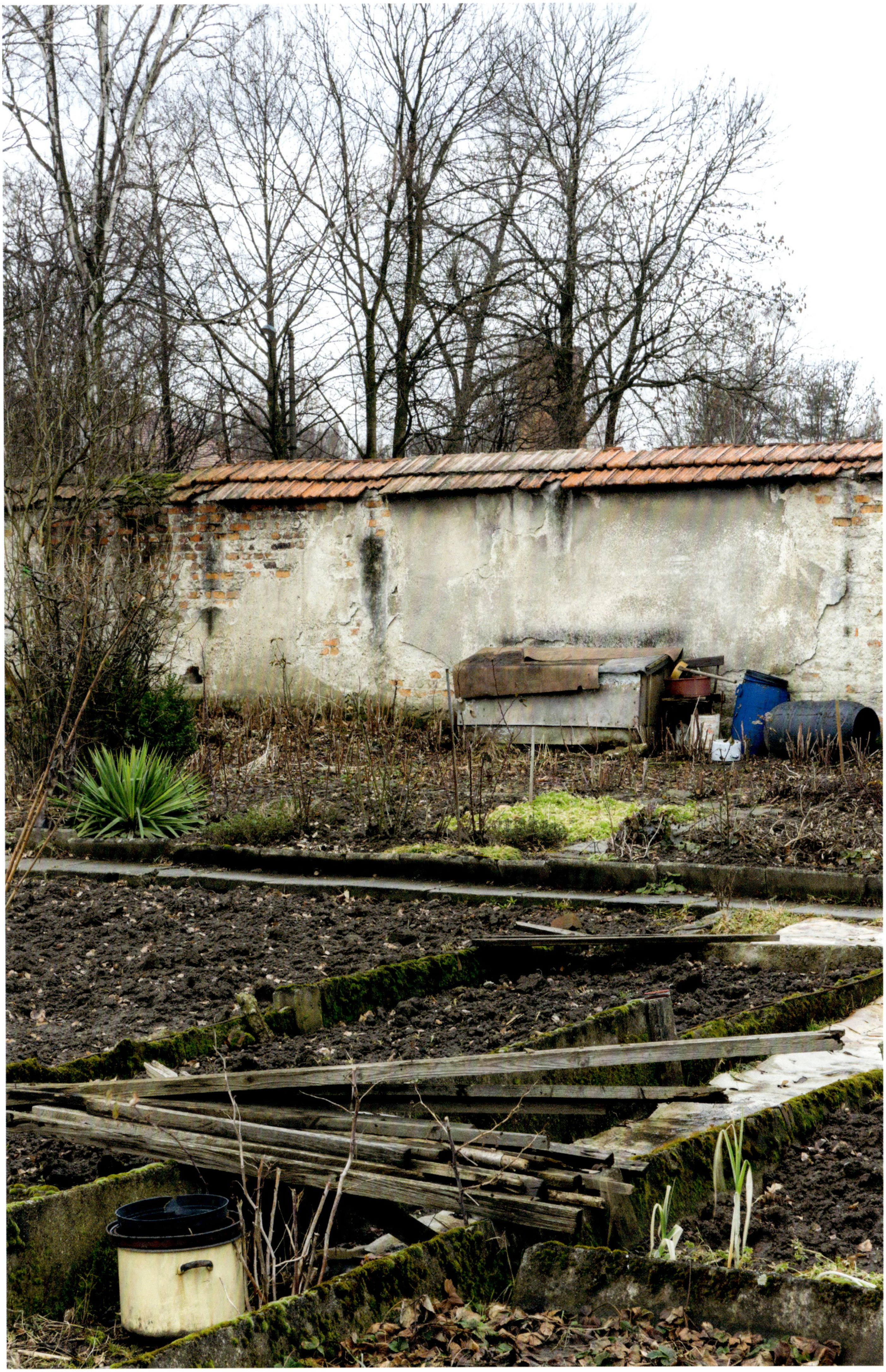

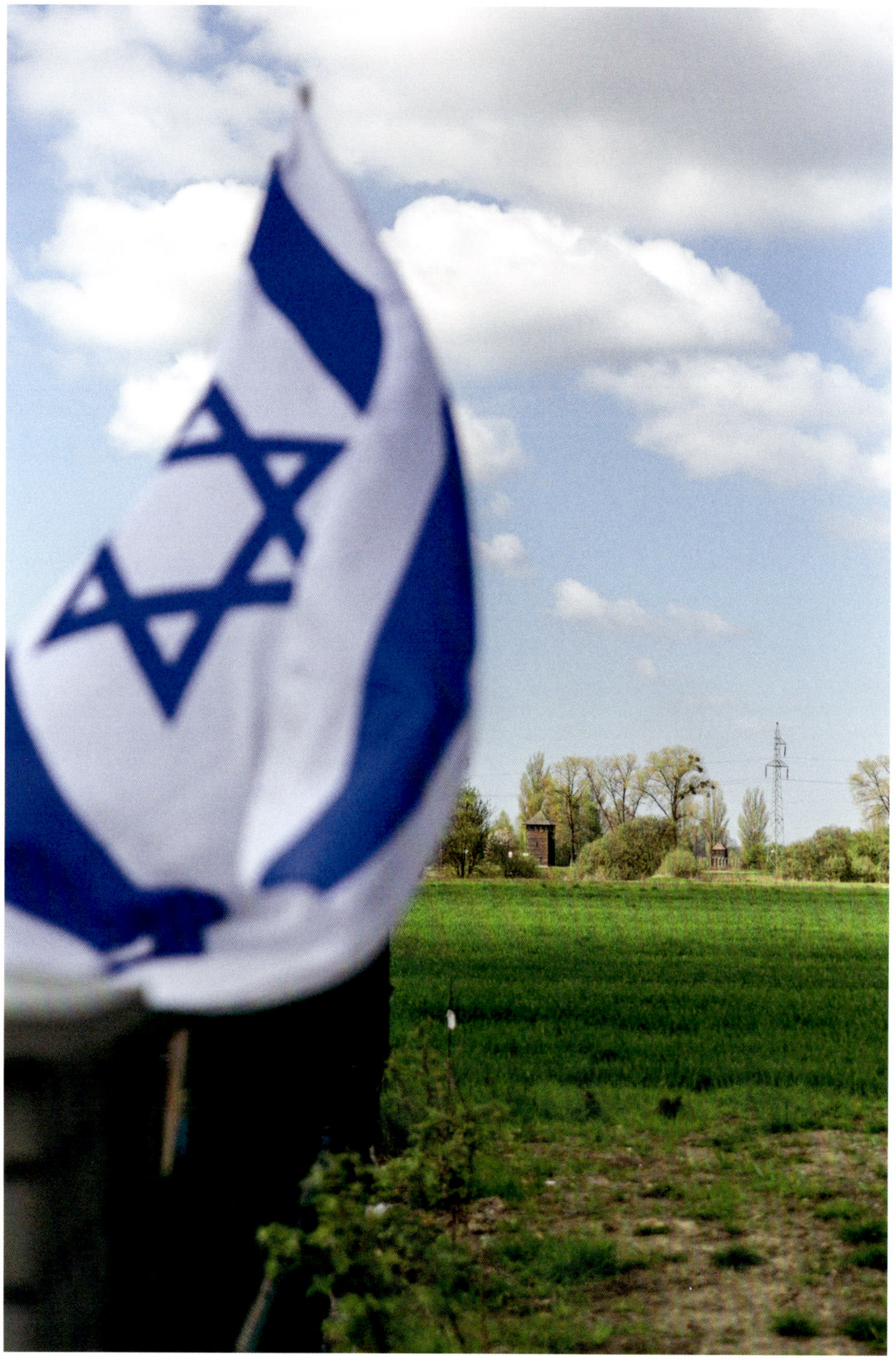

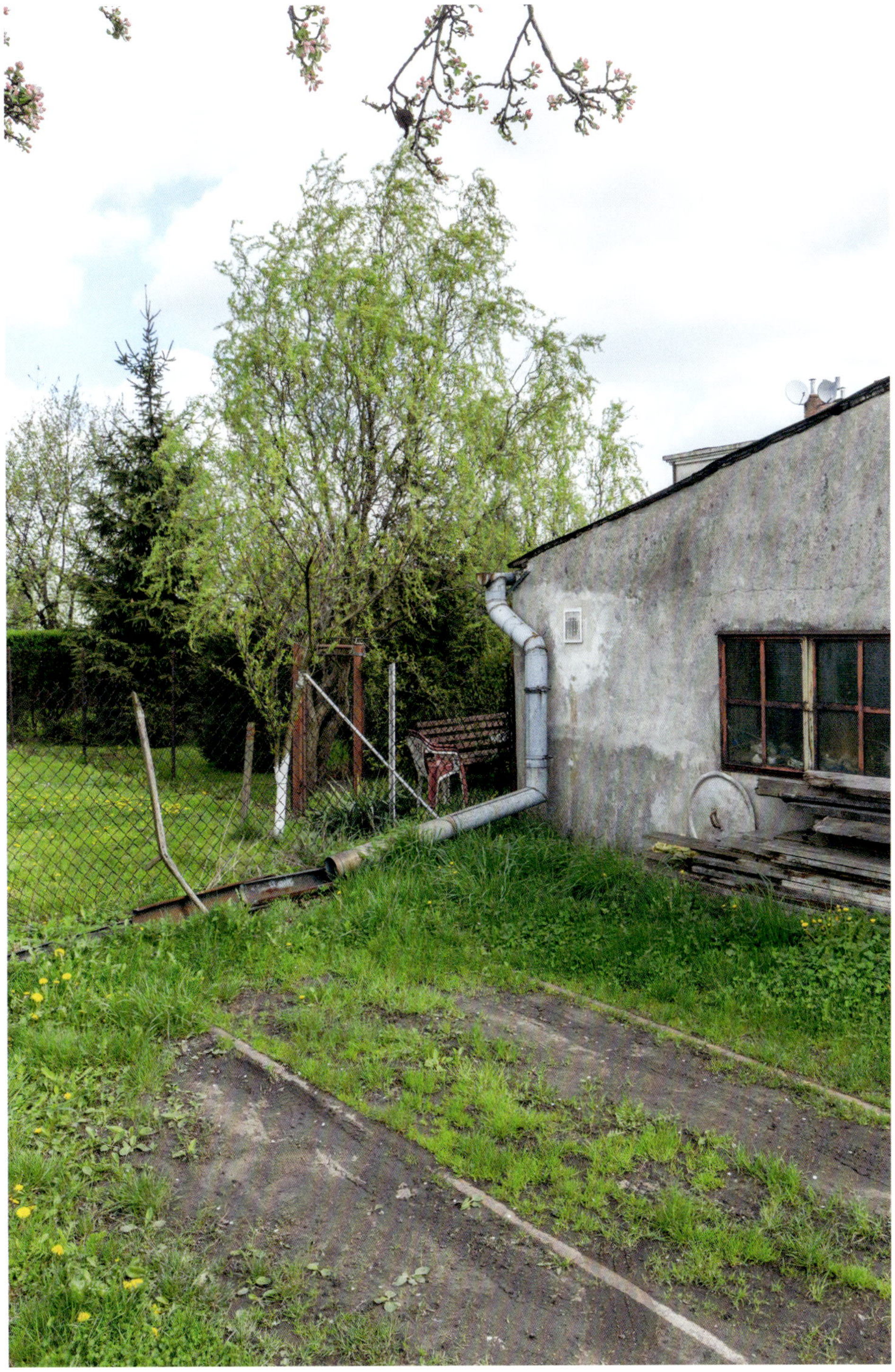

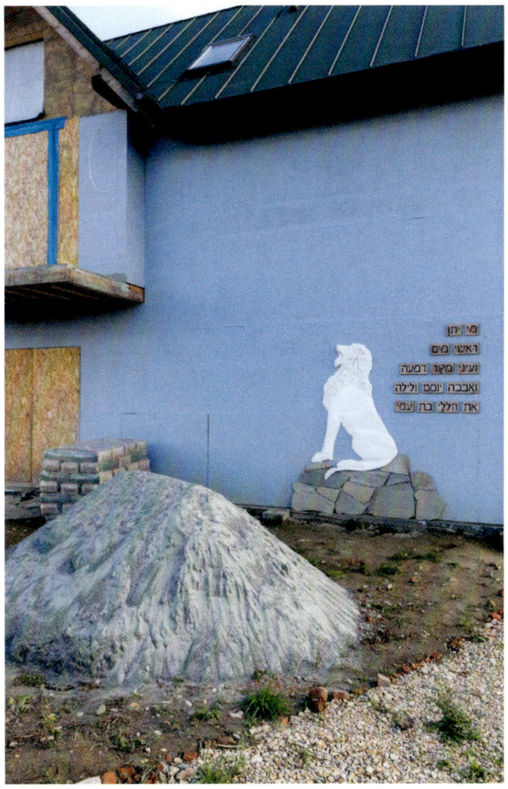

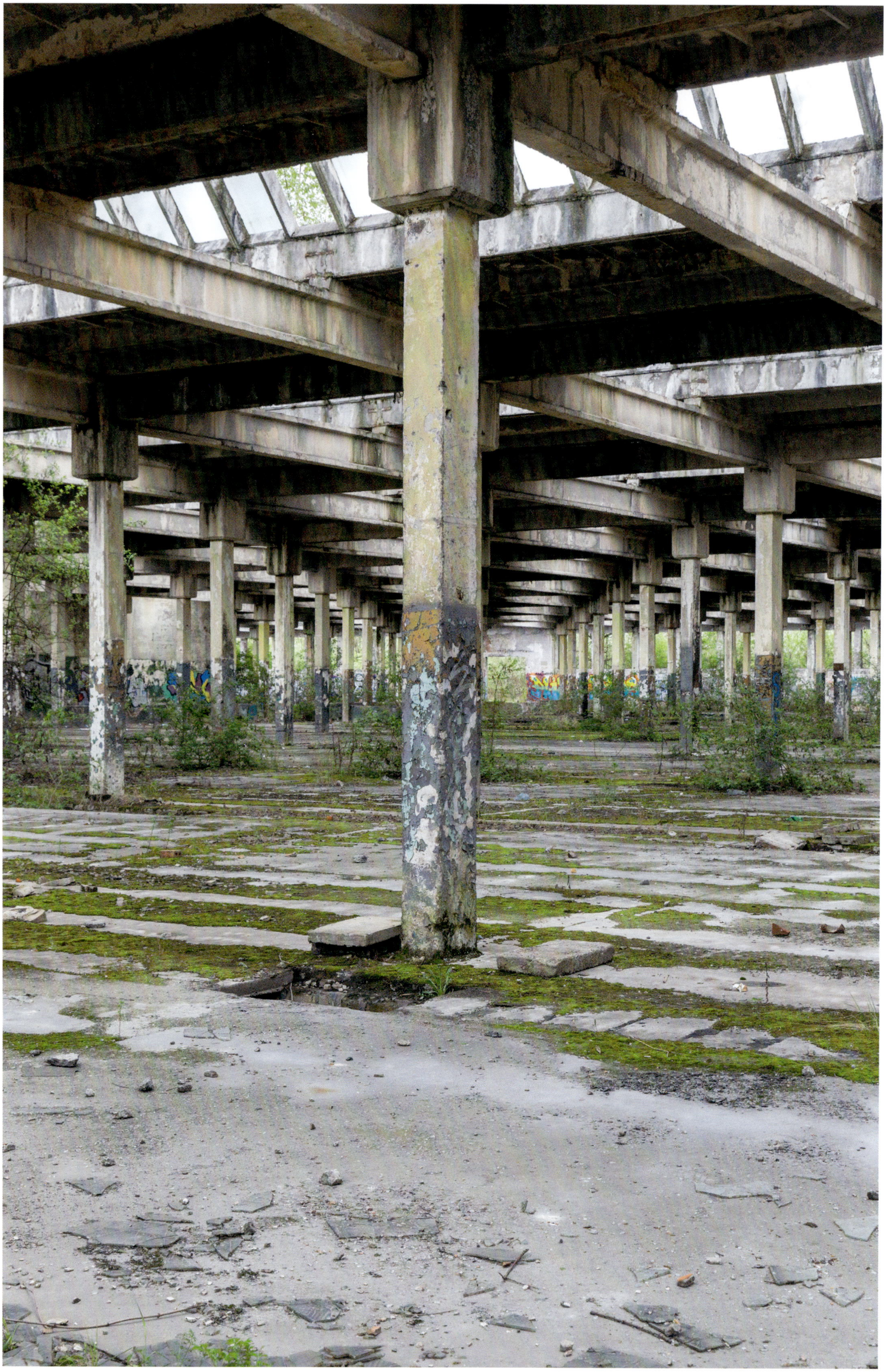

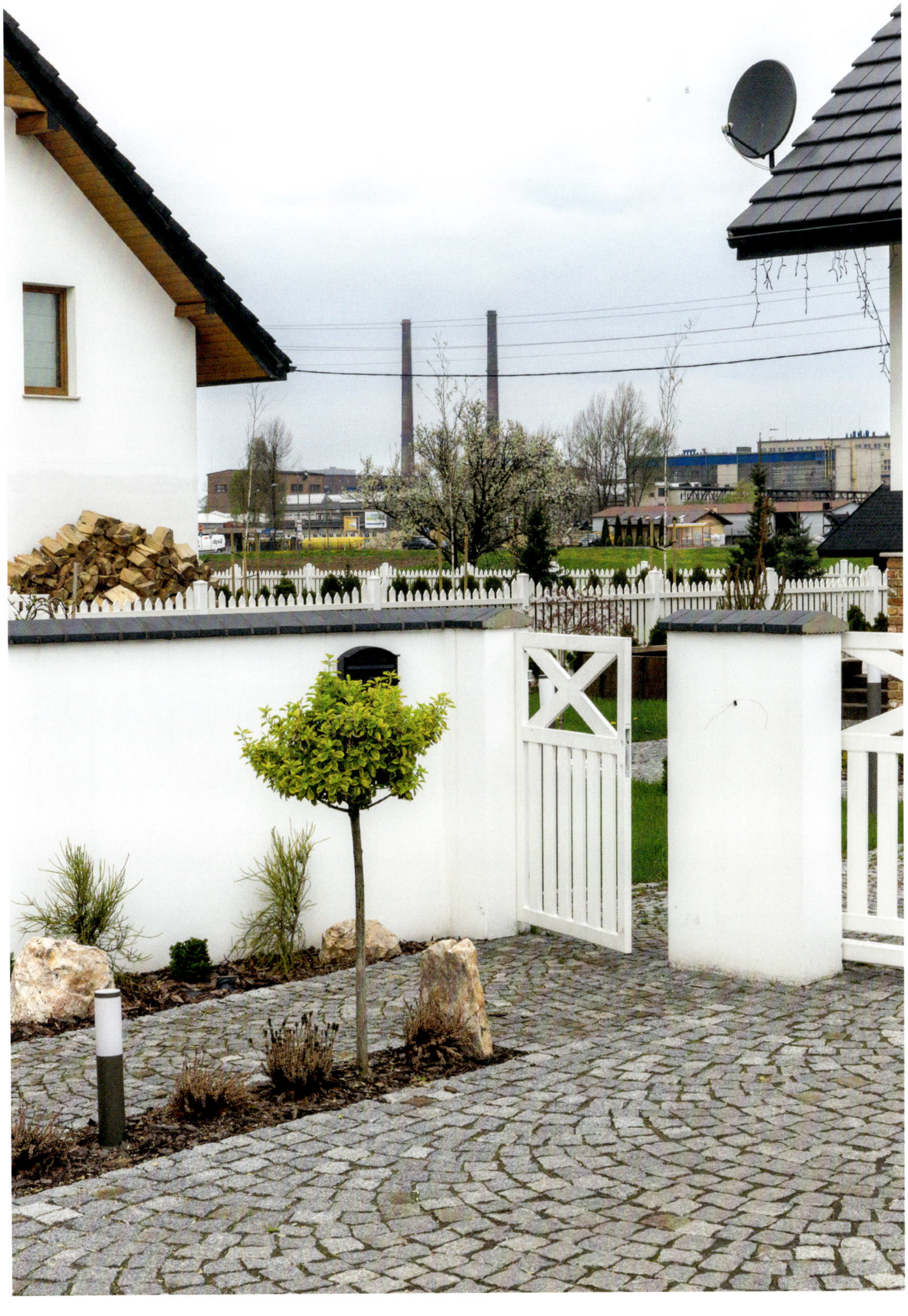

MIEJSCE PIERWSZEJ PROWIZORYCZNEJ KOMORY GAZOWEJ
SITE OF THE FIRST TEMPORARY GAS CHAMBER
MASOWA MOGIŁA RADZIECKICH JEŃCÓW WOJENNYCH
MASS GRAVE OF SOVIET PRISONERS OF WAR

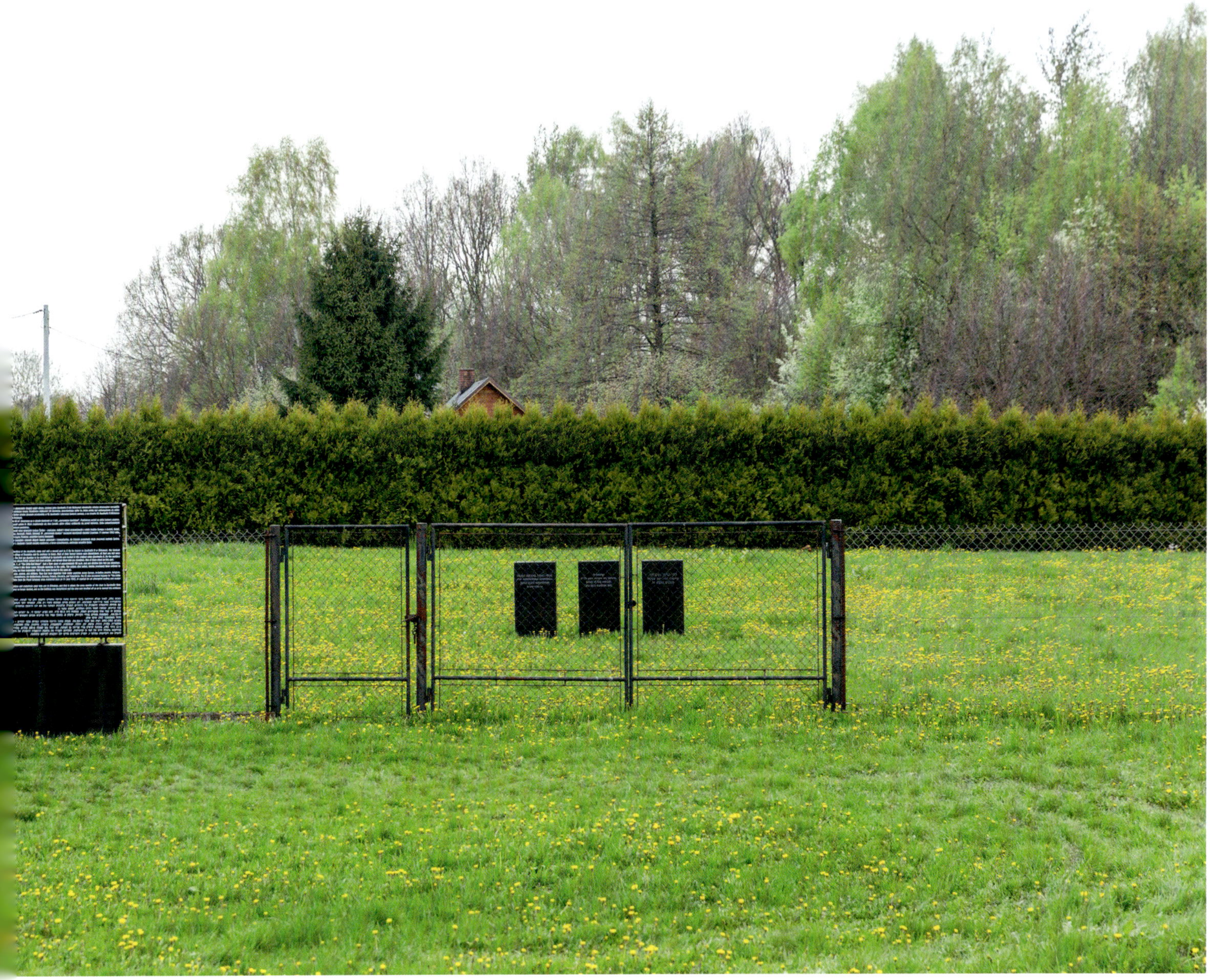

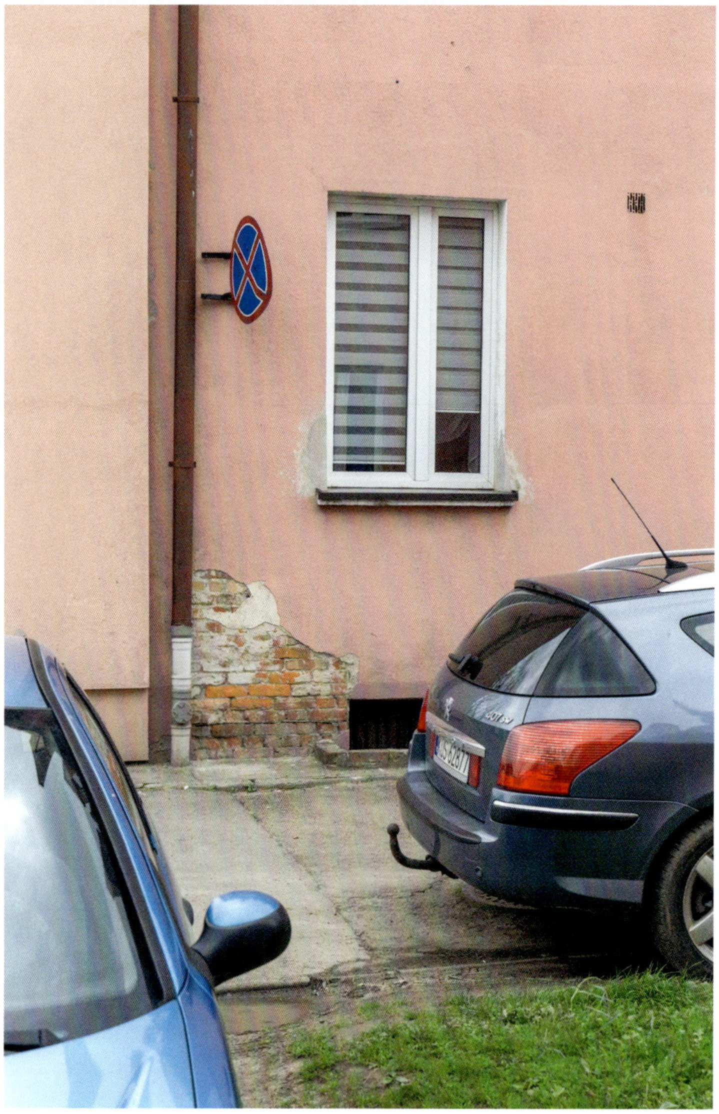

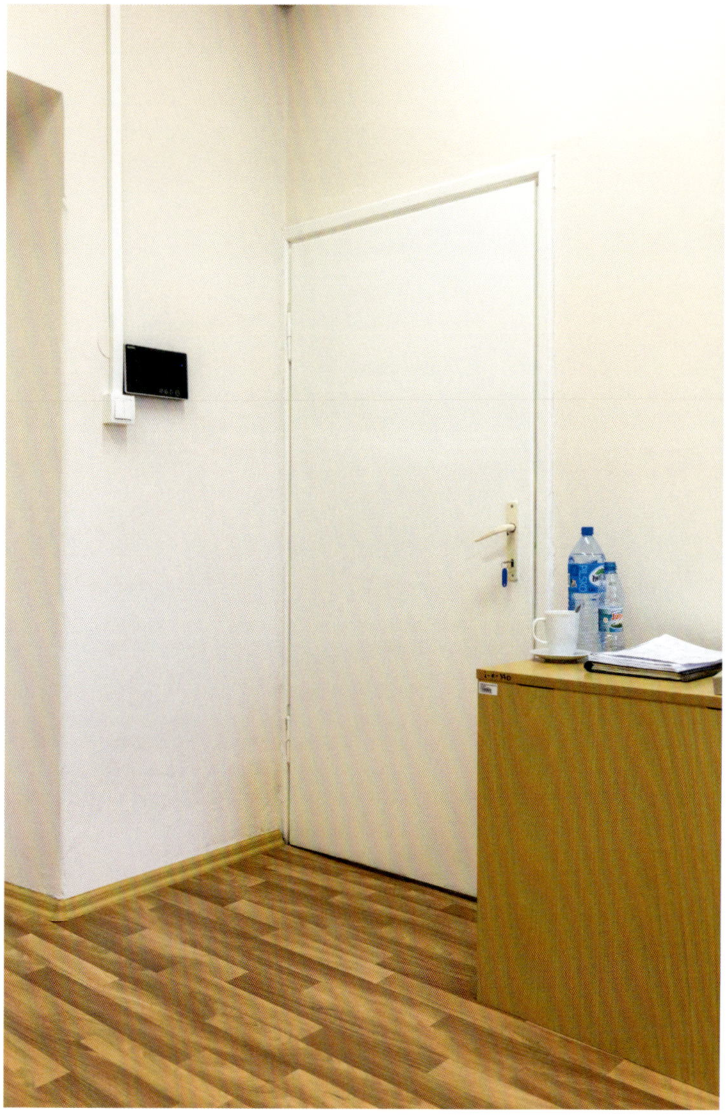

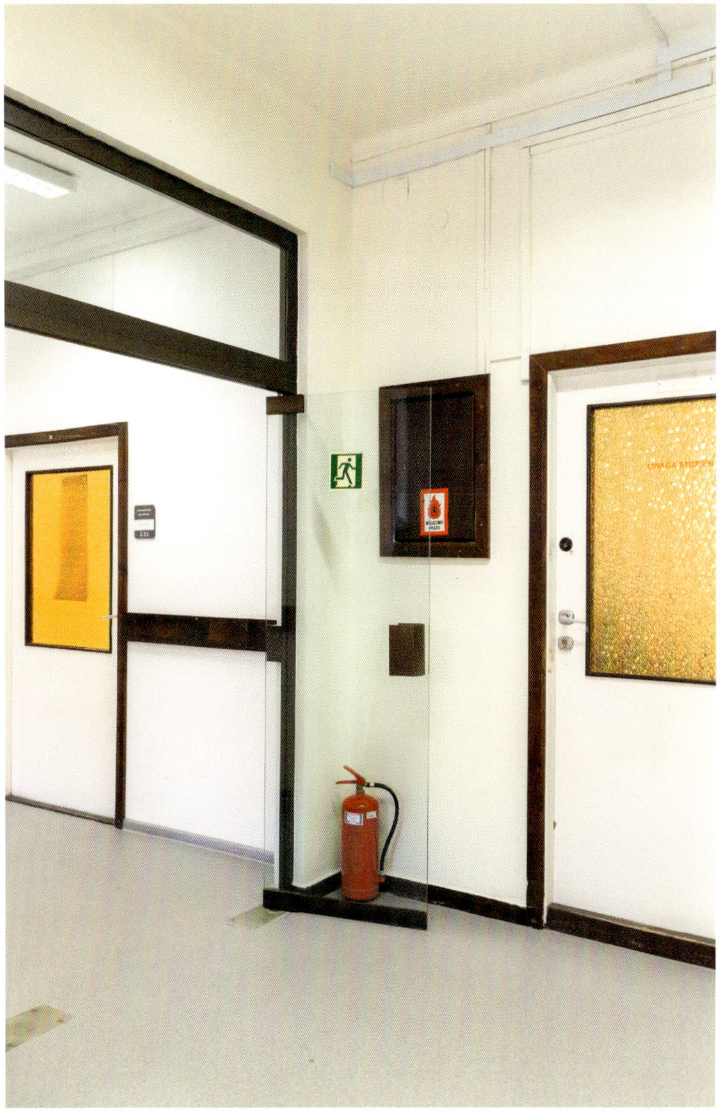

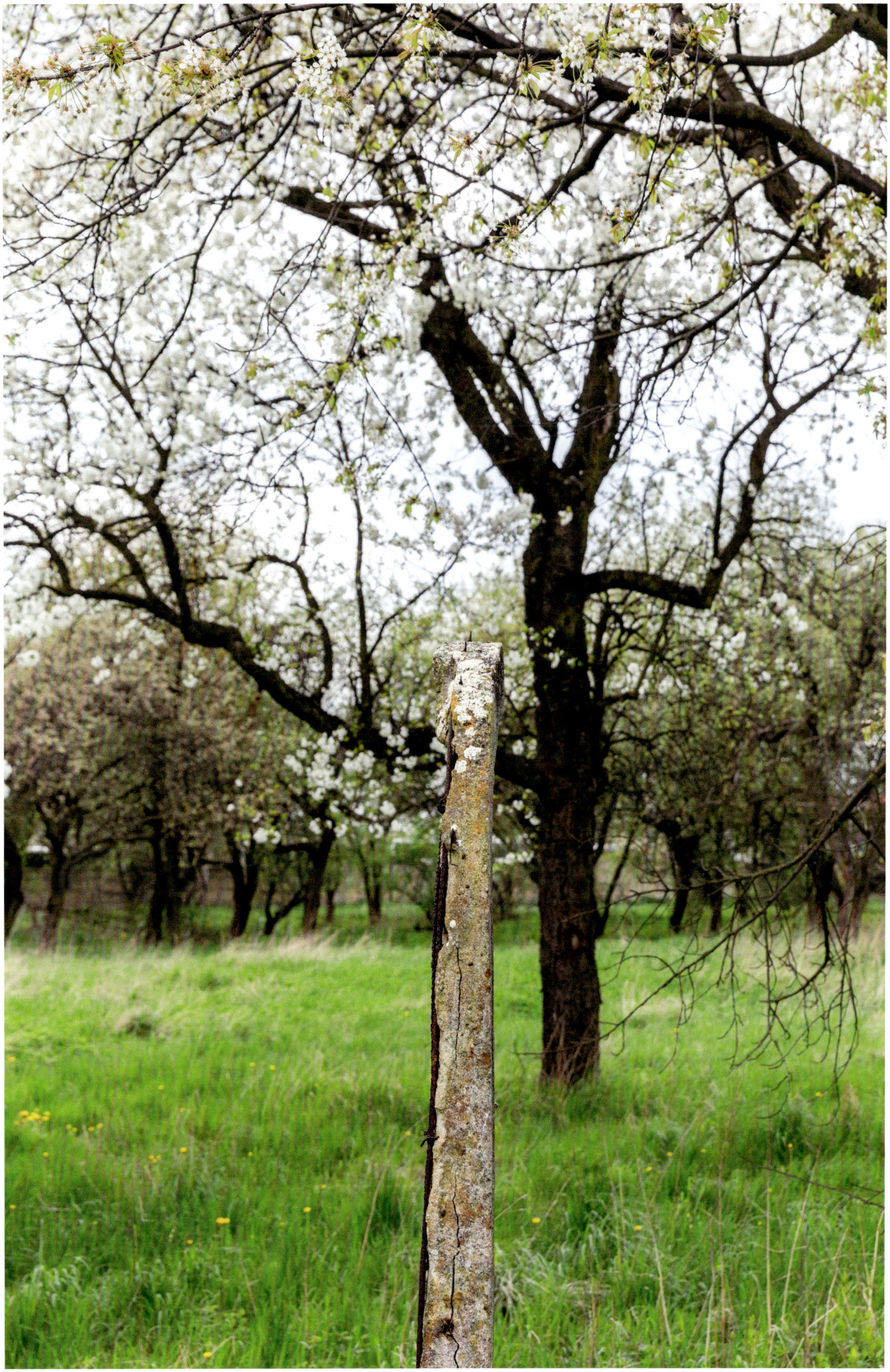

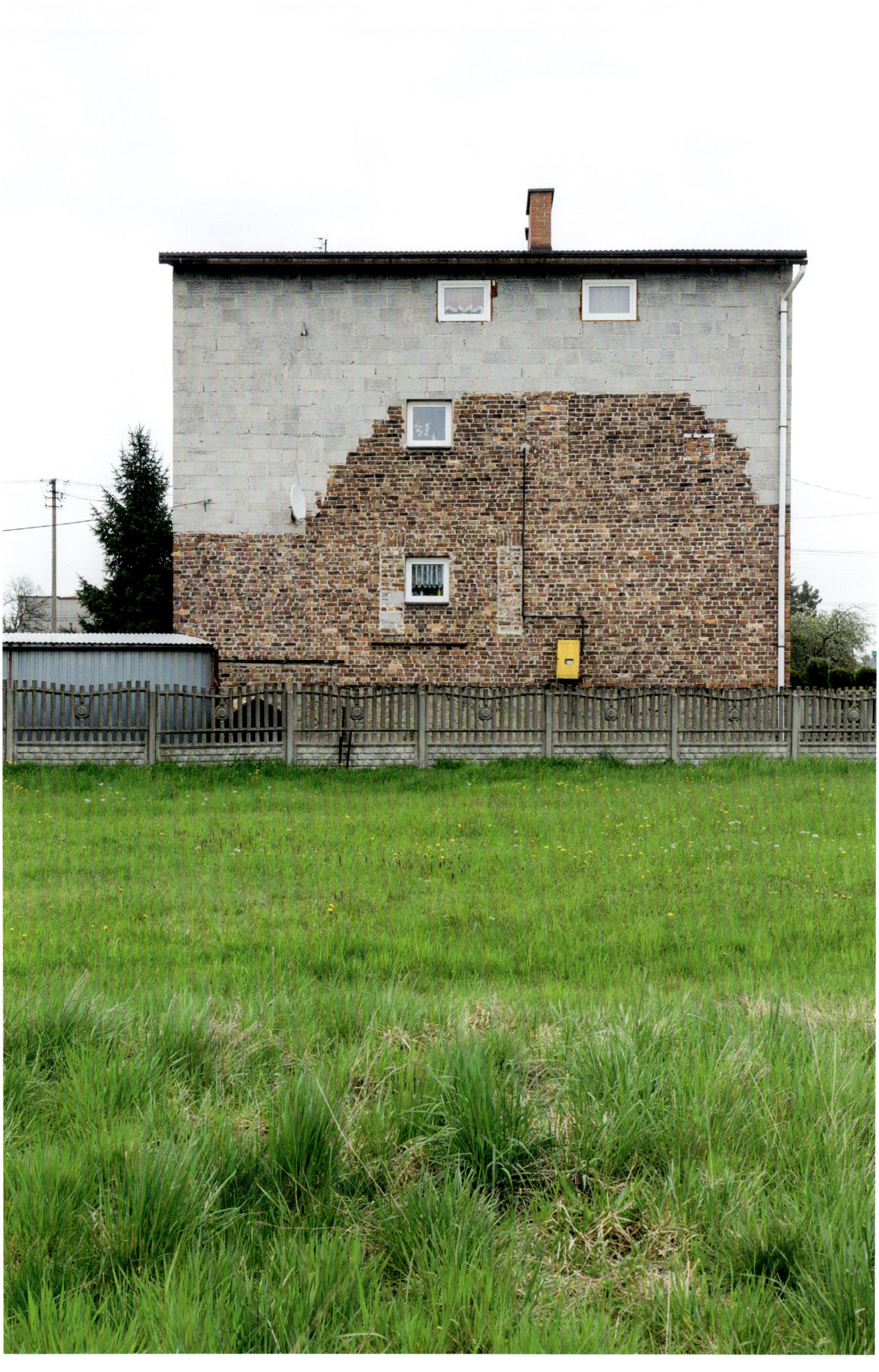

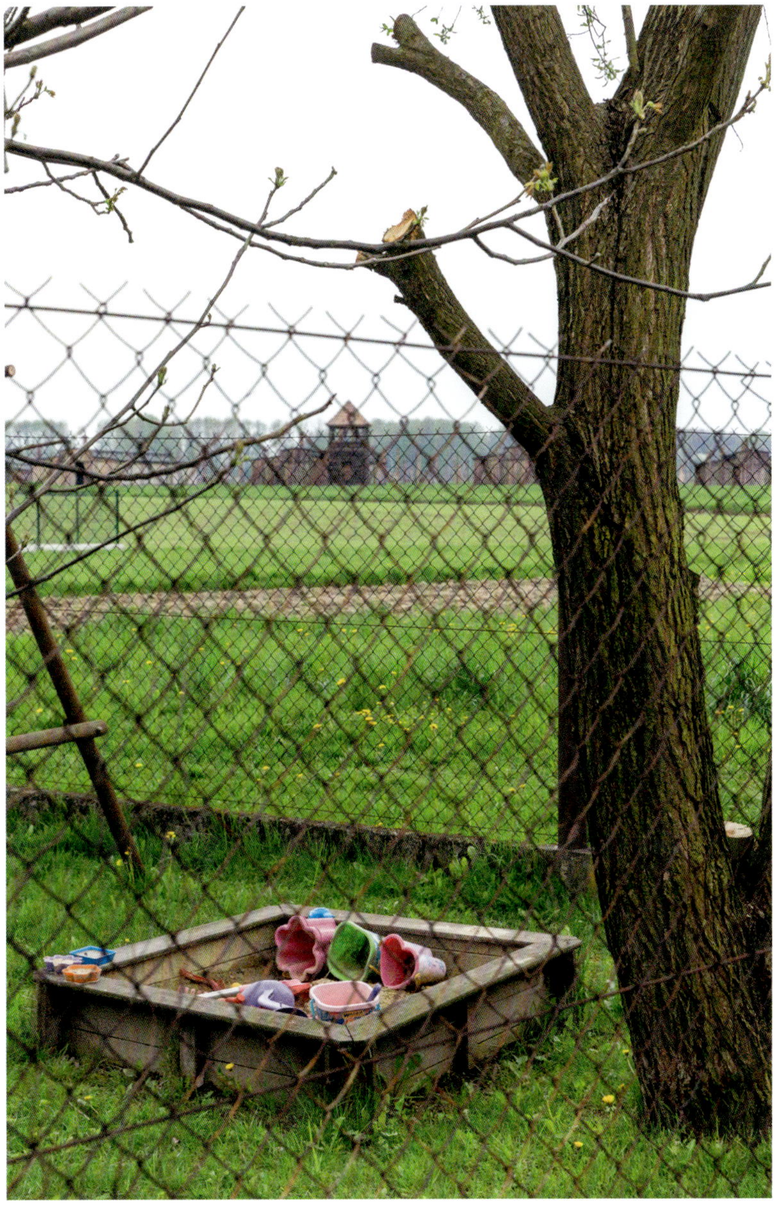

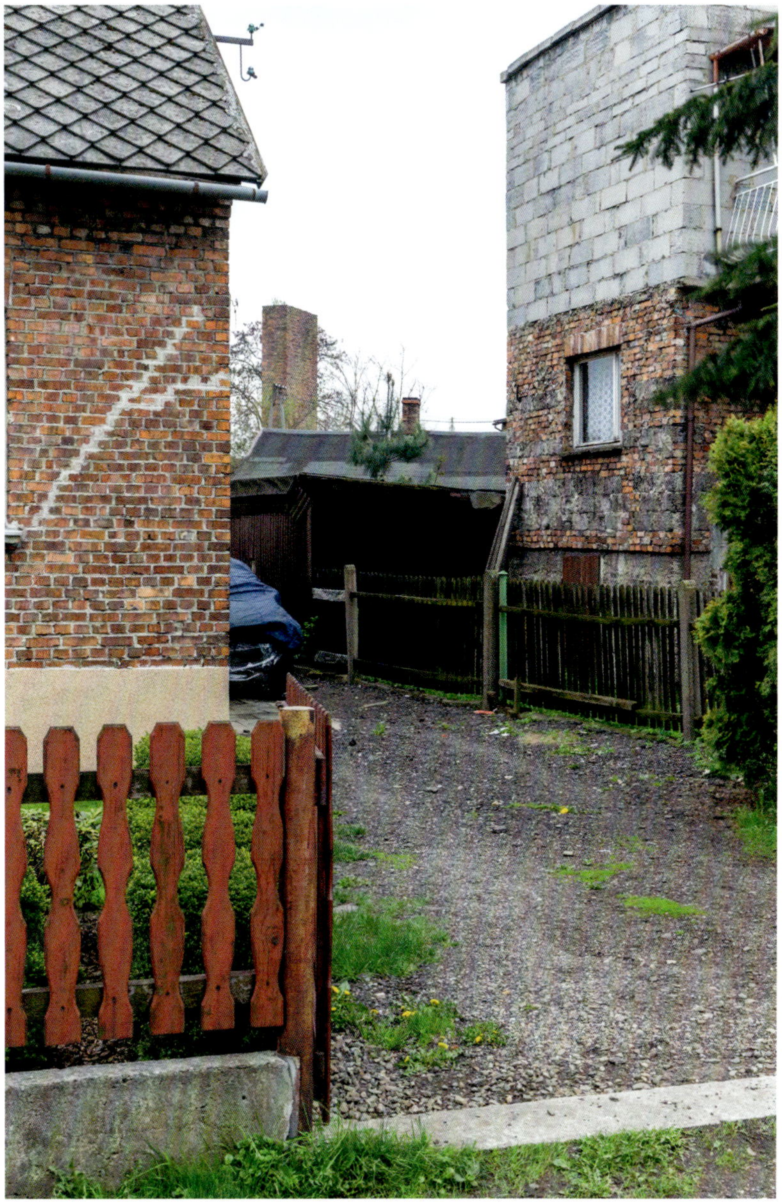

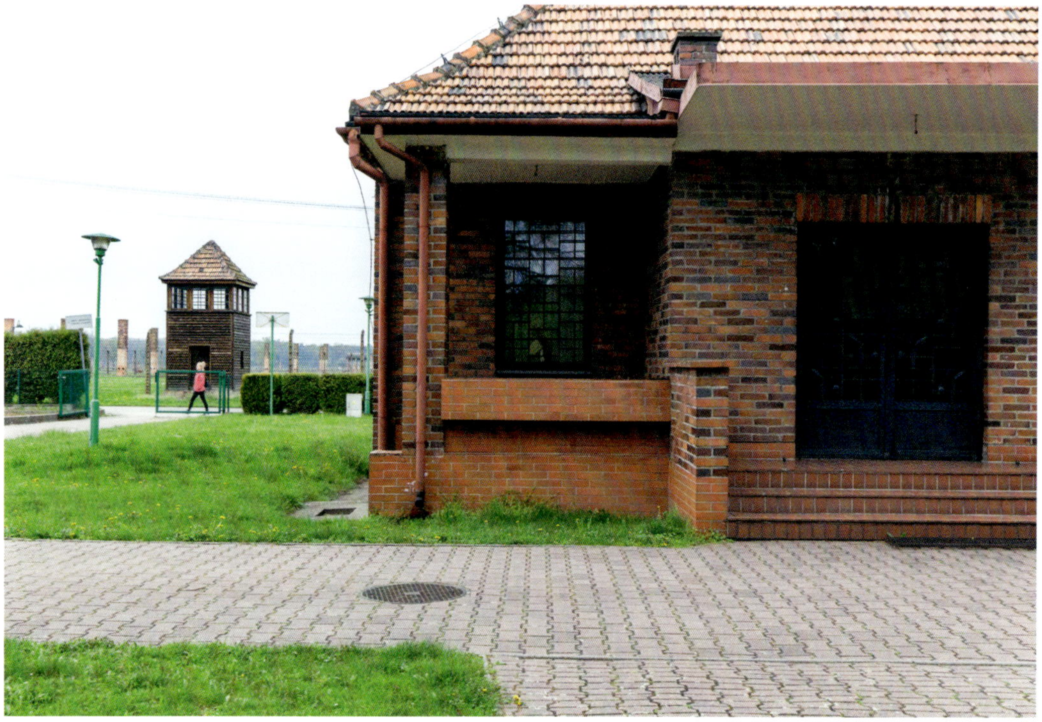

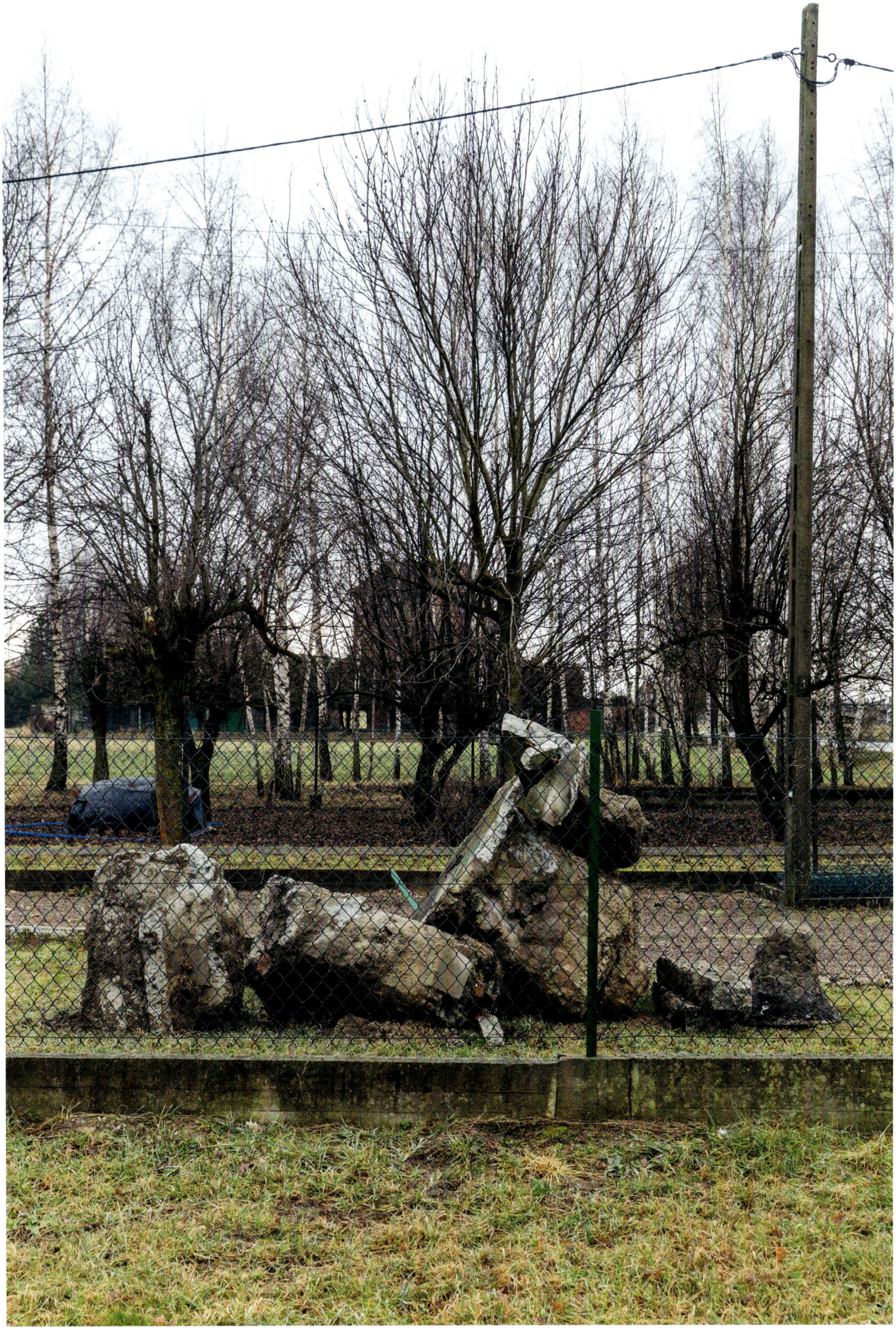

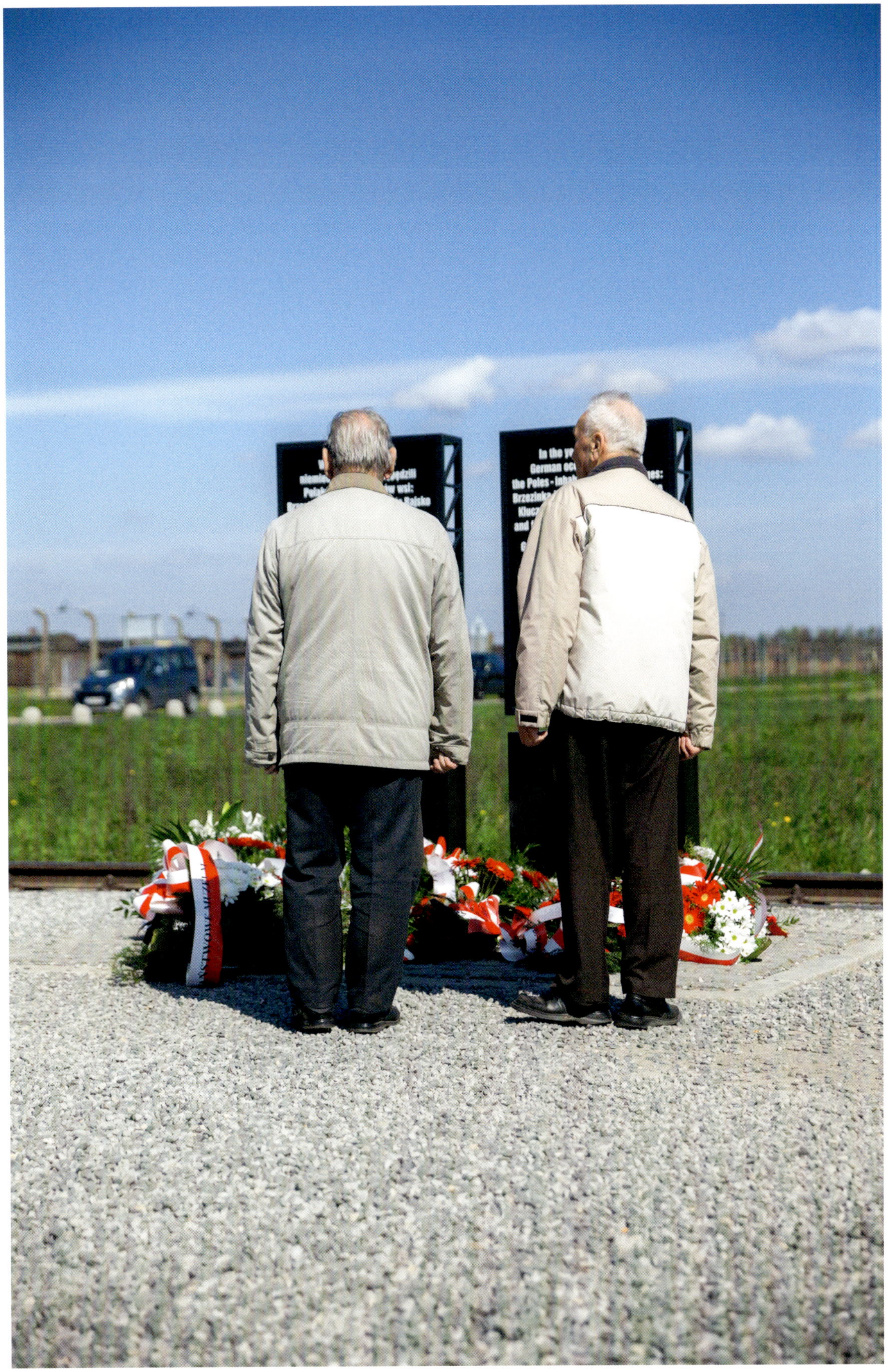

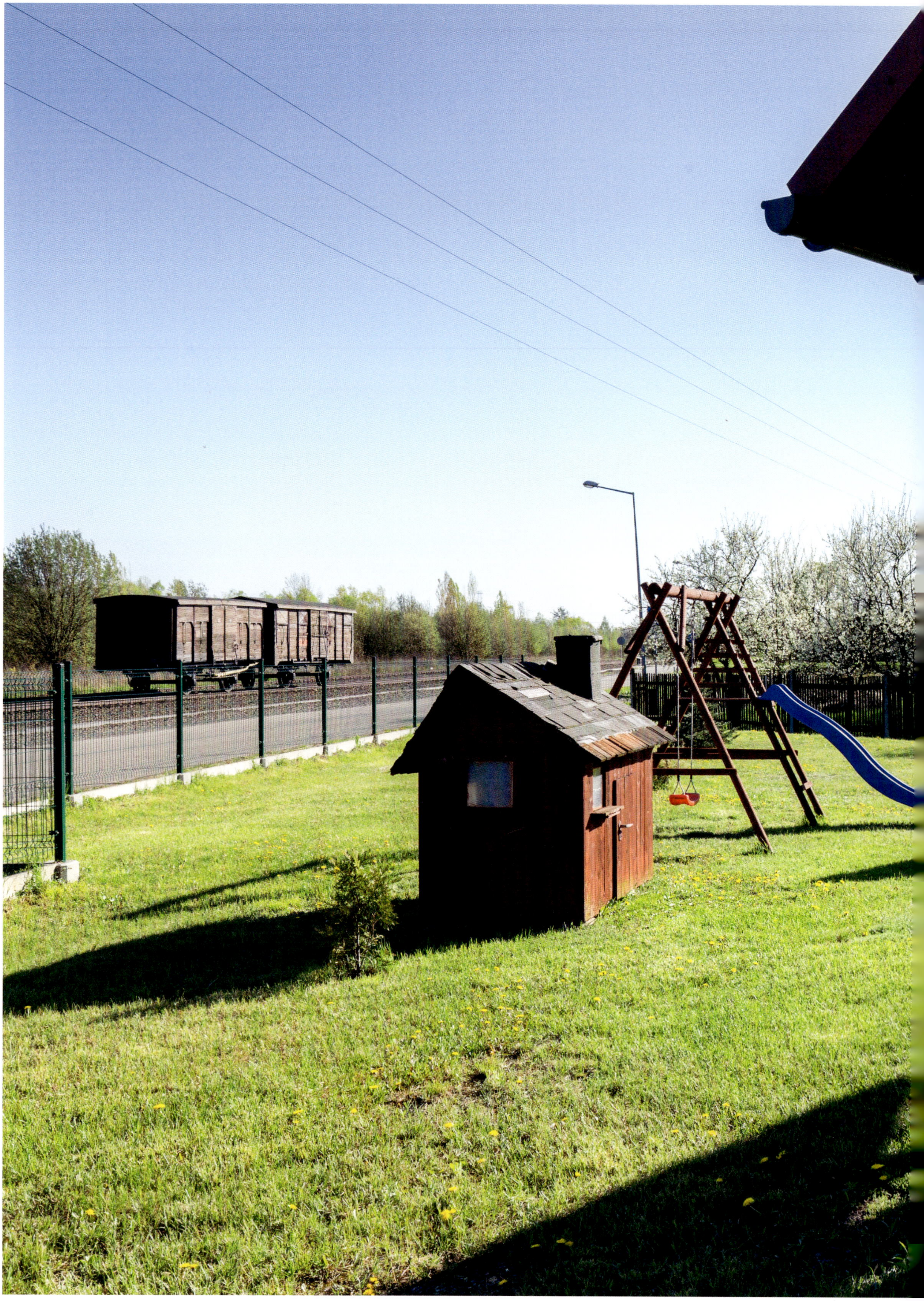

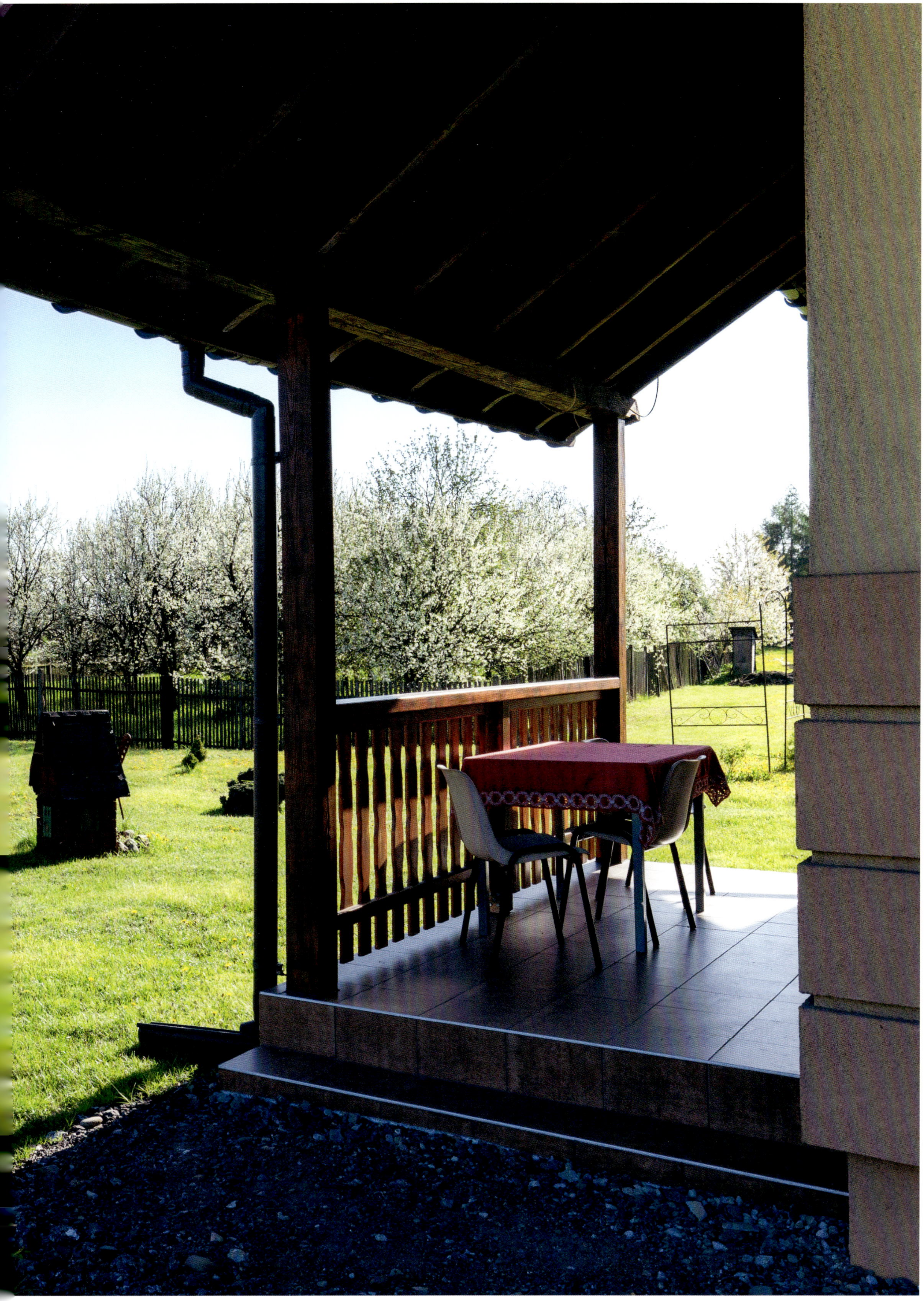

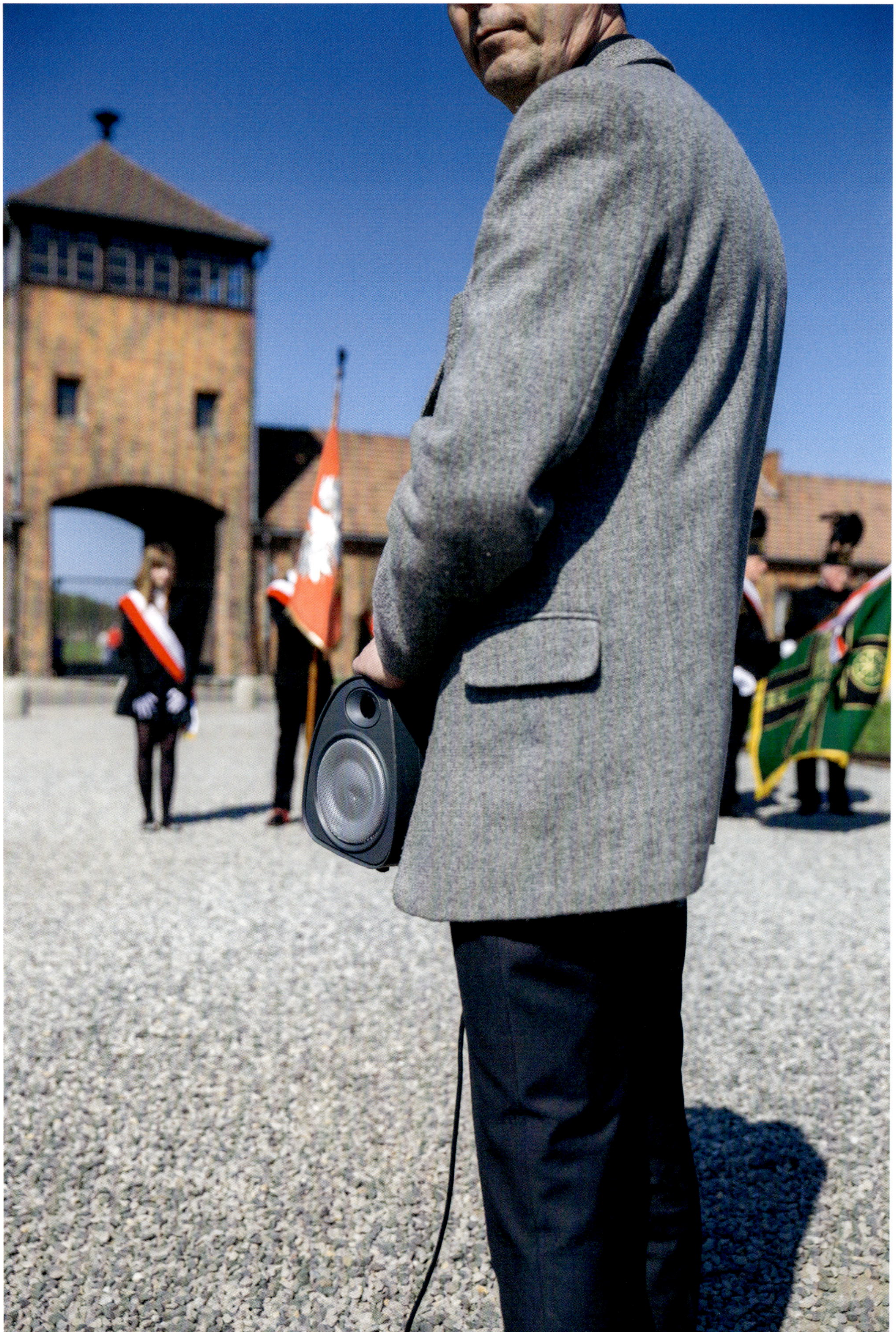

TAK ROZPOCZĘŁA SIĘ HISTORIA
NASZEGO SZTANDARU
W 27 rocznicę
wyzwolenia KL Auschwitz

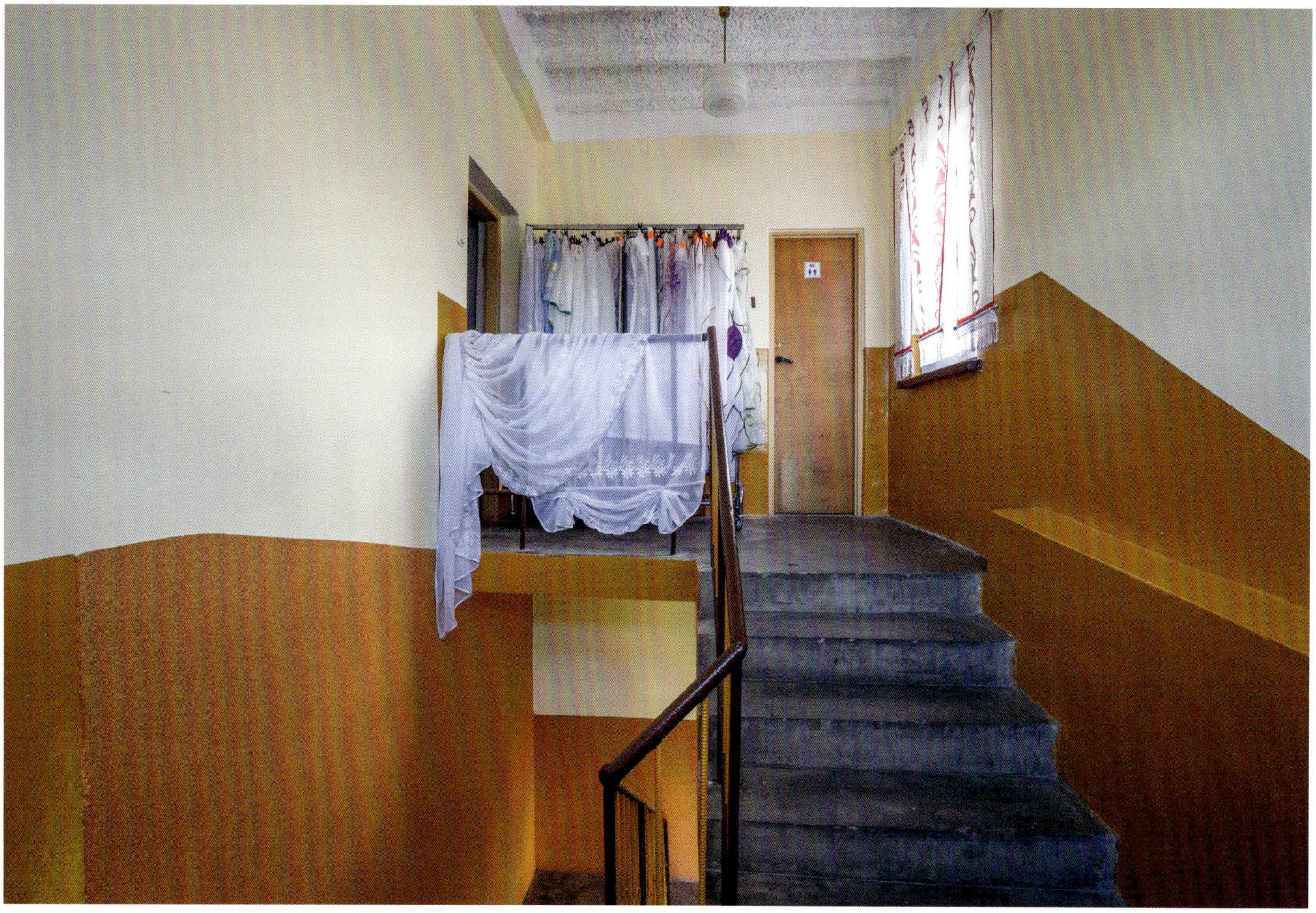

77

60288
62449
60307
Pol.U 57386
K.L.Auschwitz
27018
K.L.Auschwitz
26947
K.L.Auschwitz

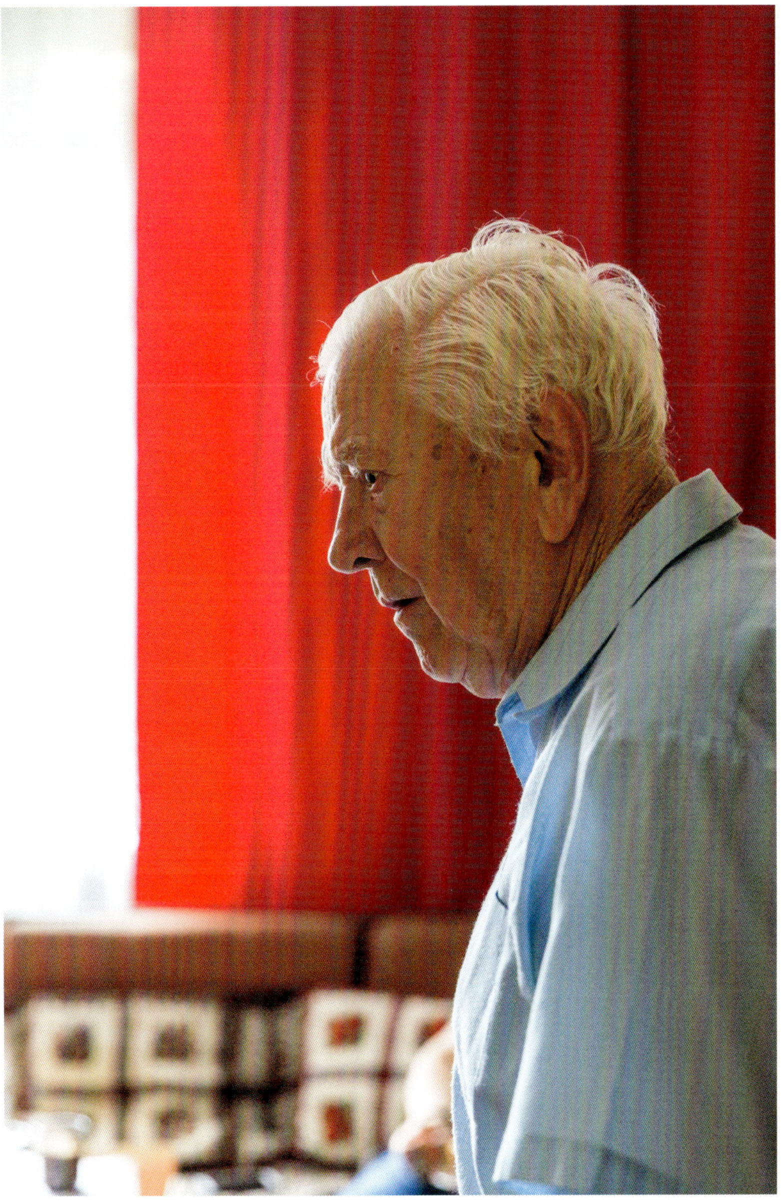

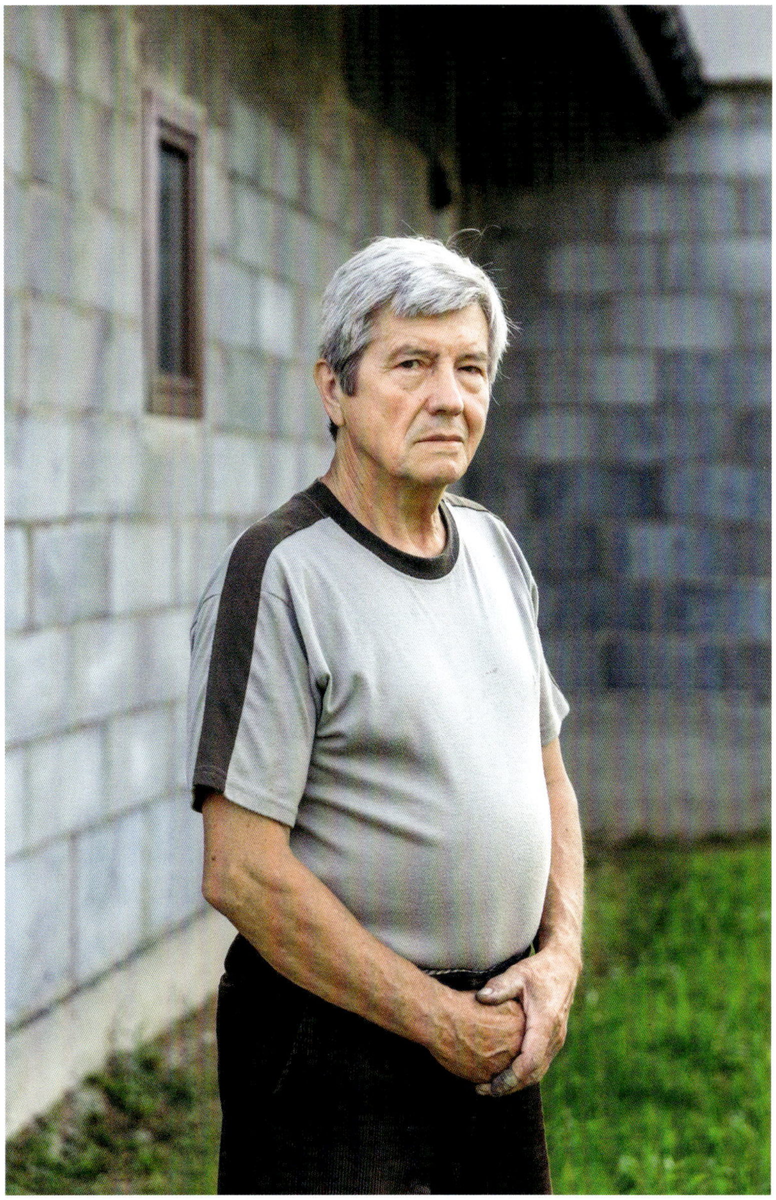

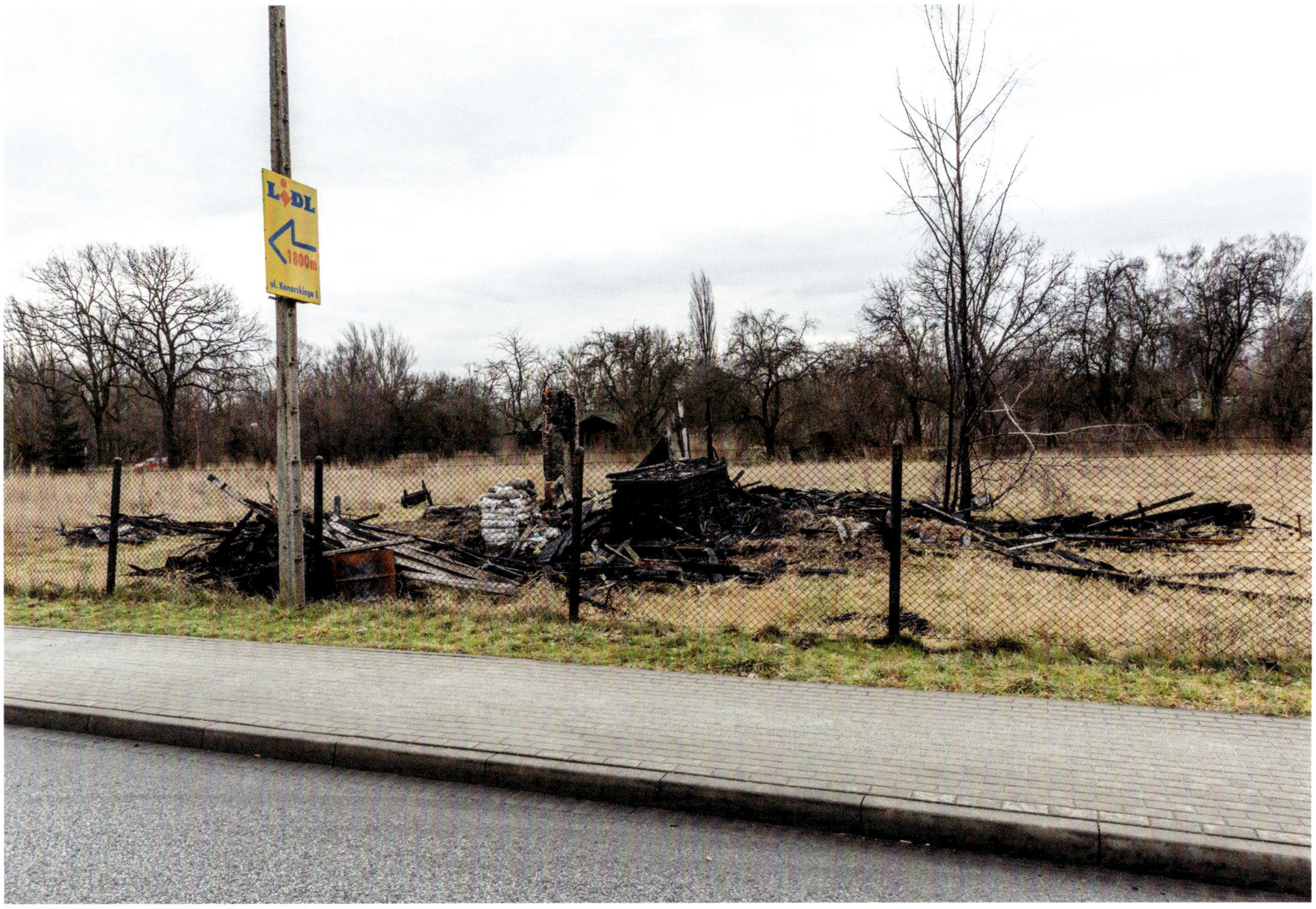

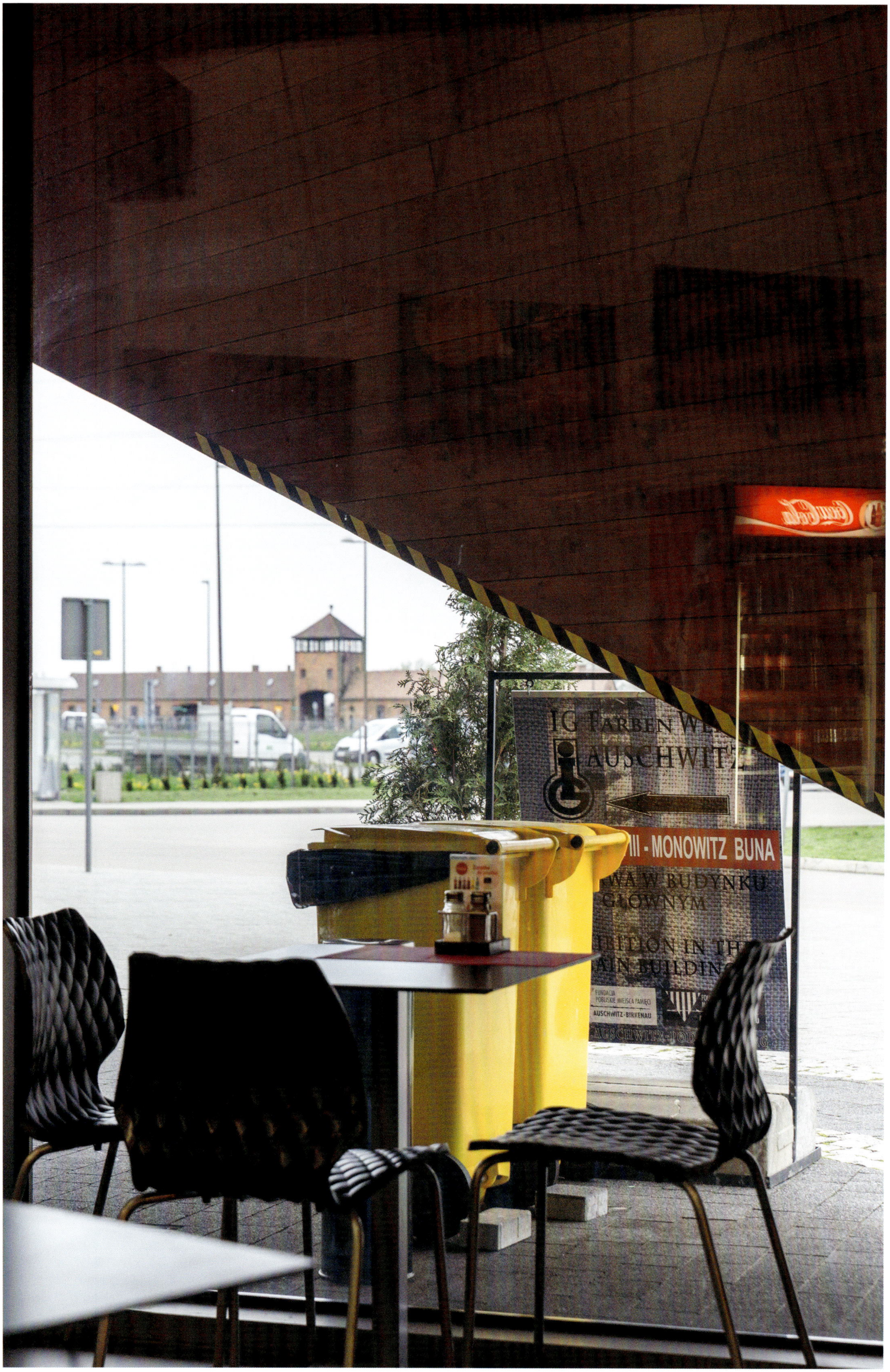
MONOWITZ BUNA
AUSCHWITZ-BIRKENAU

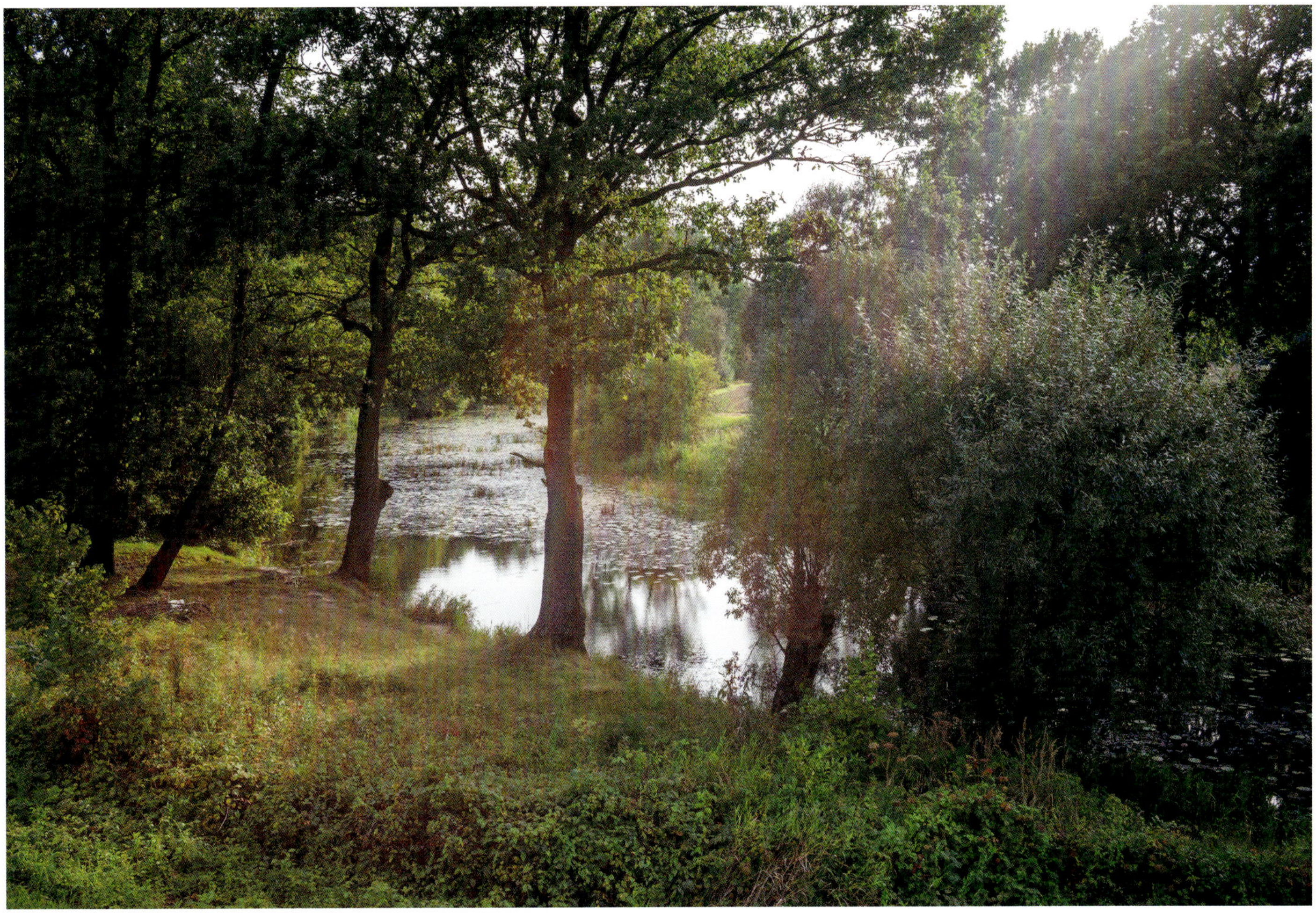

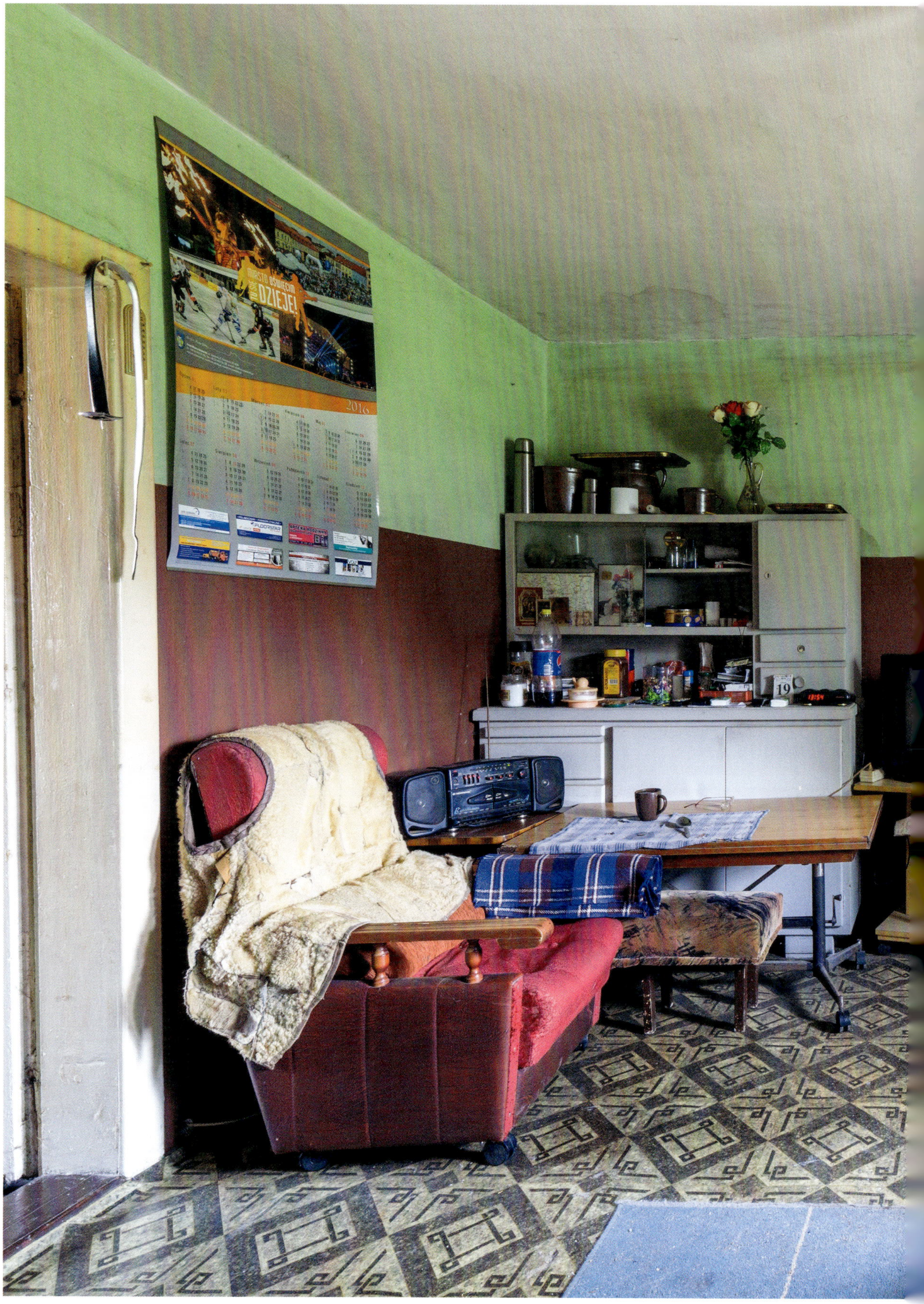

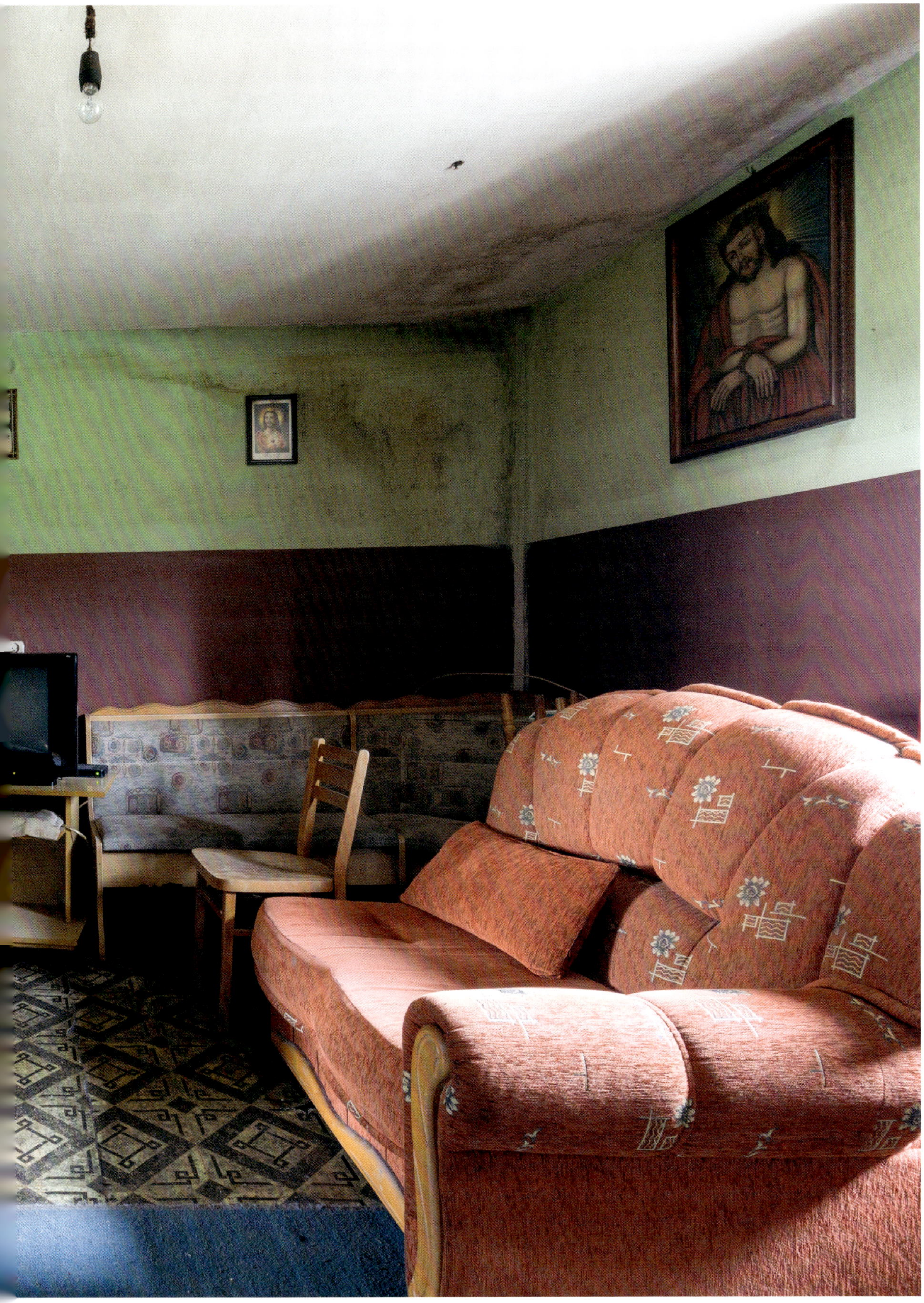

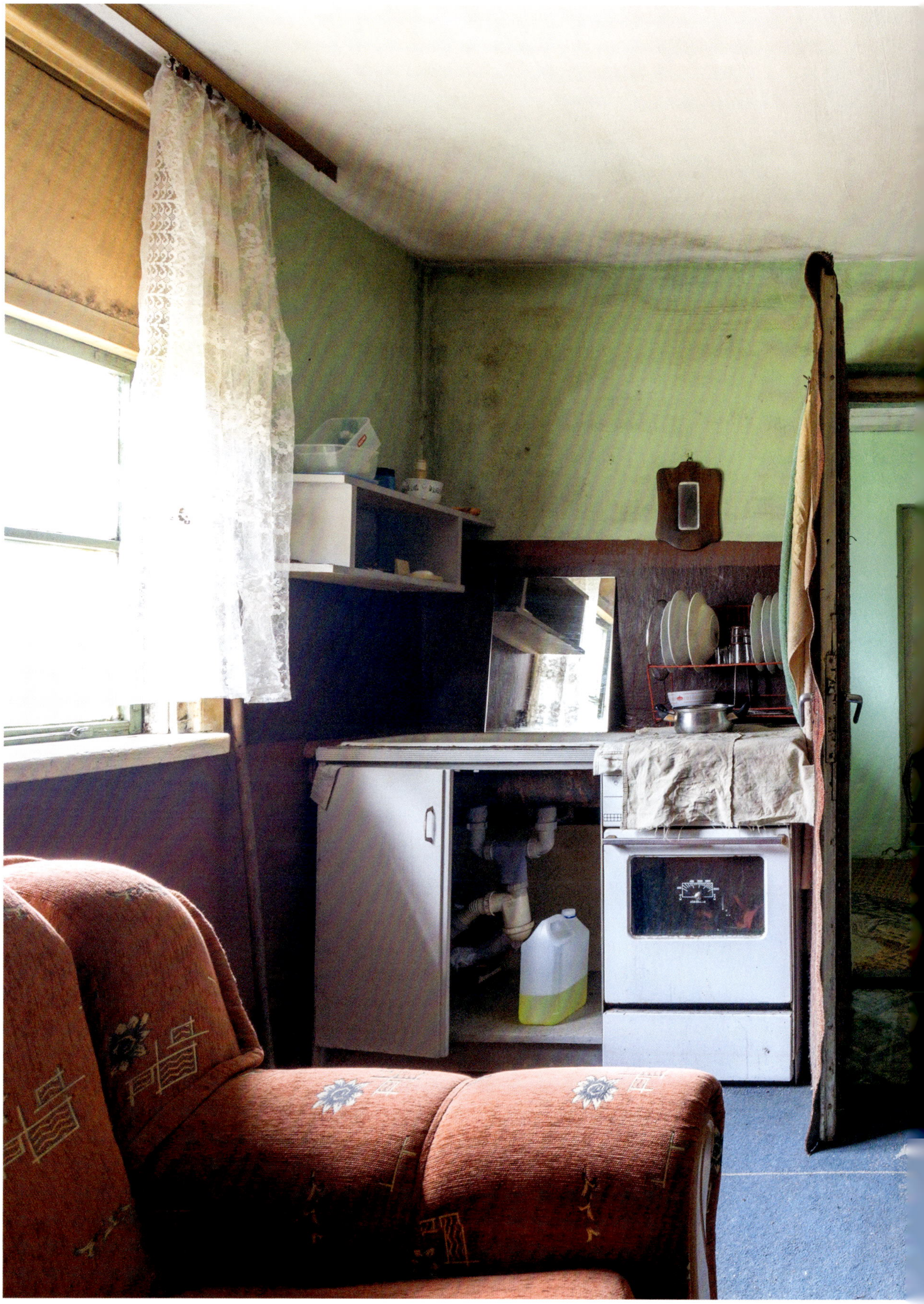

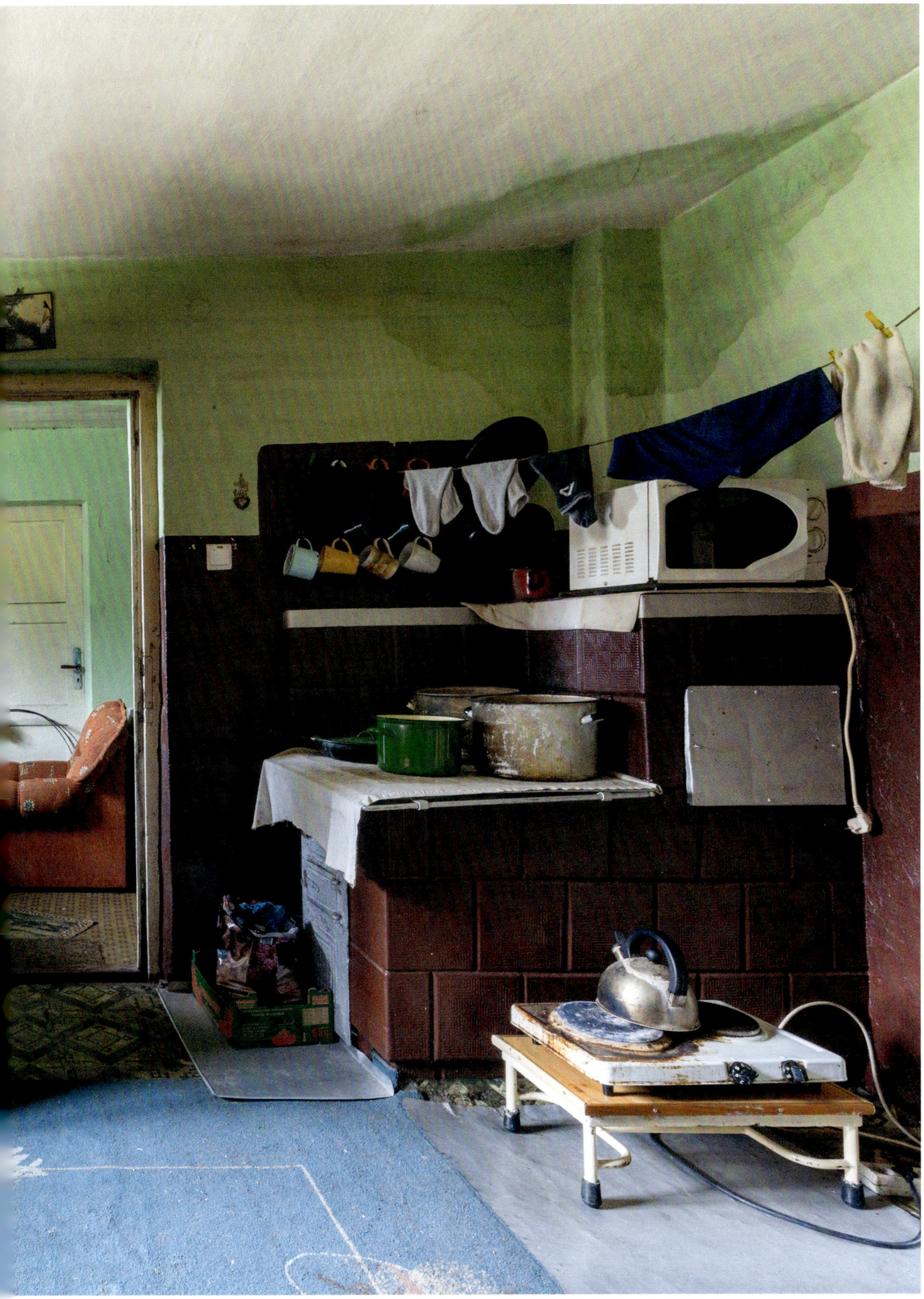

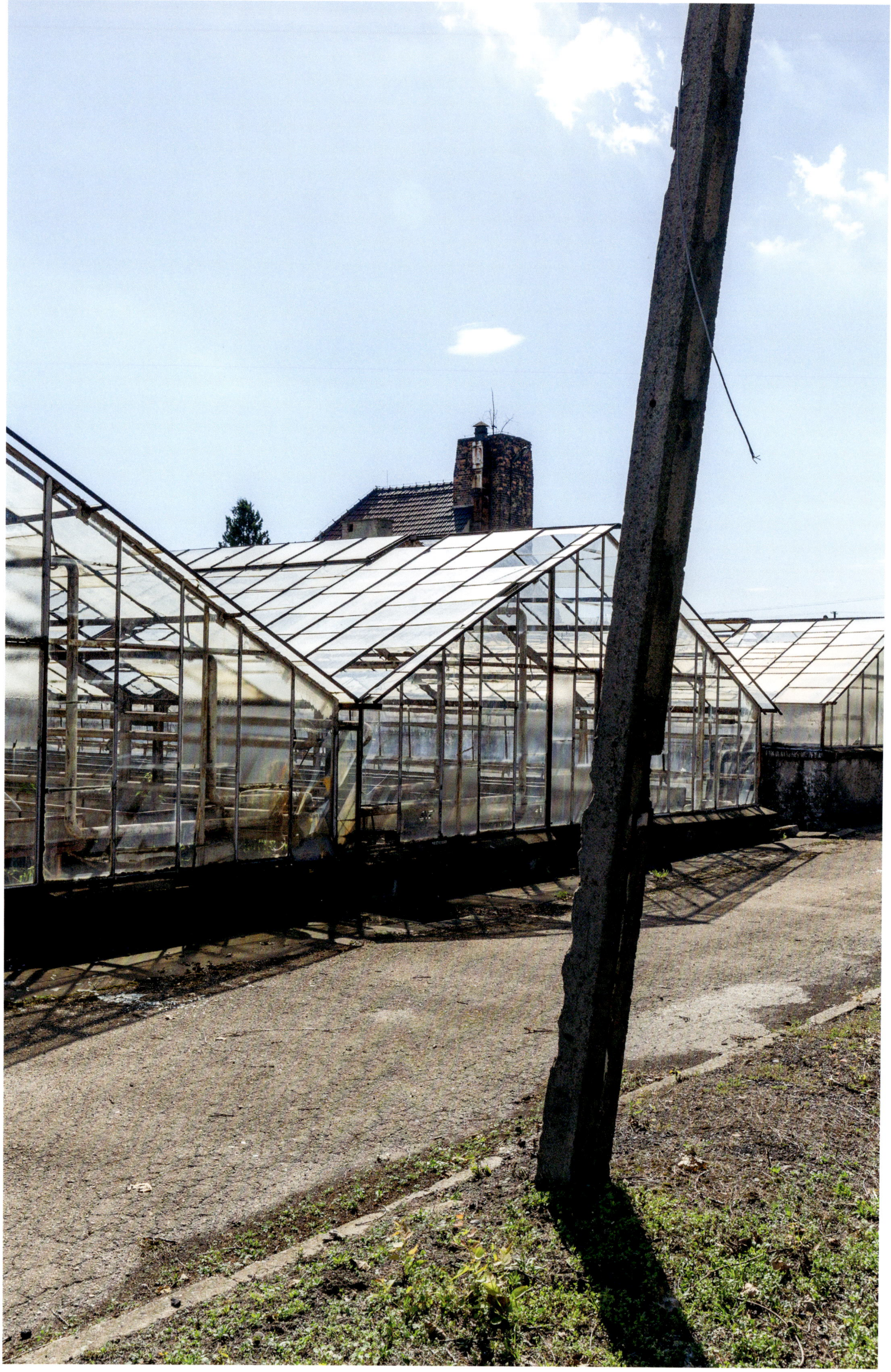

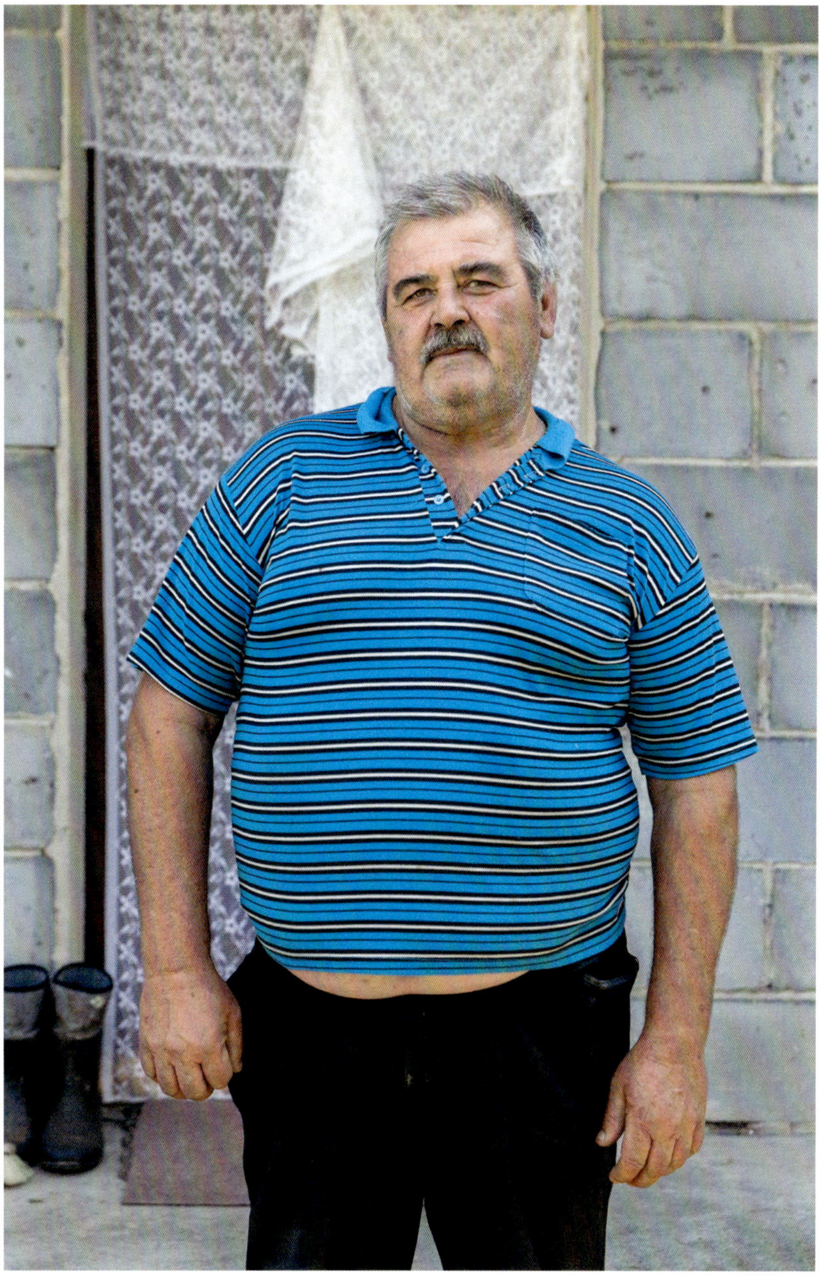

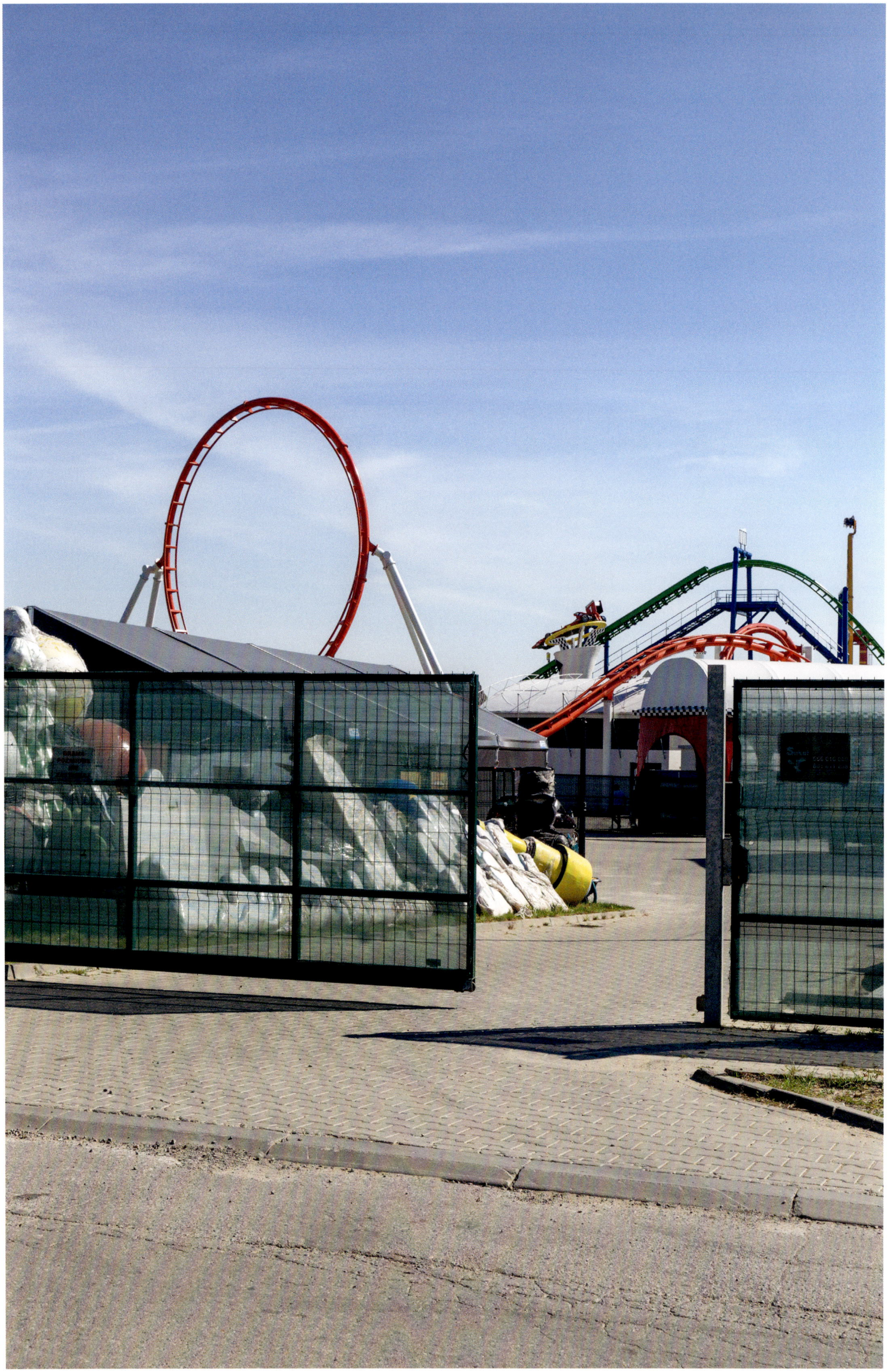

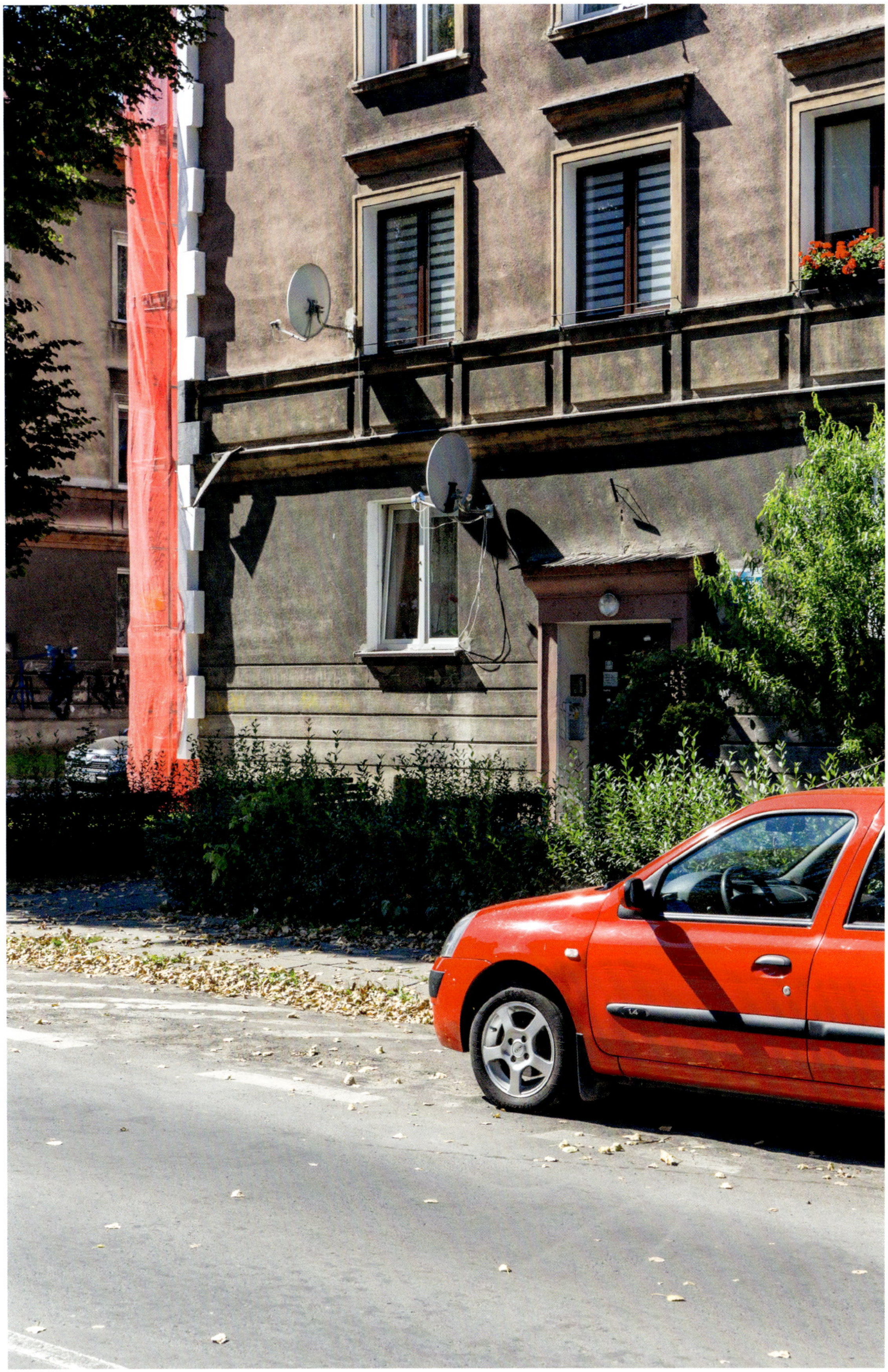

44

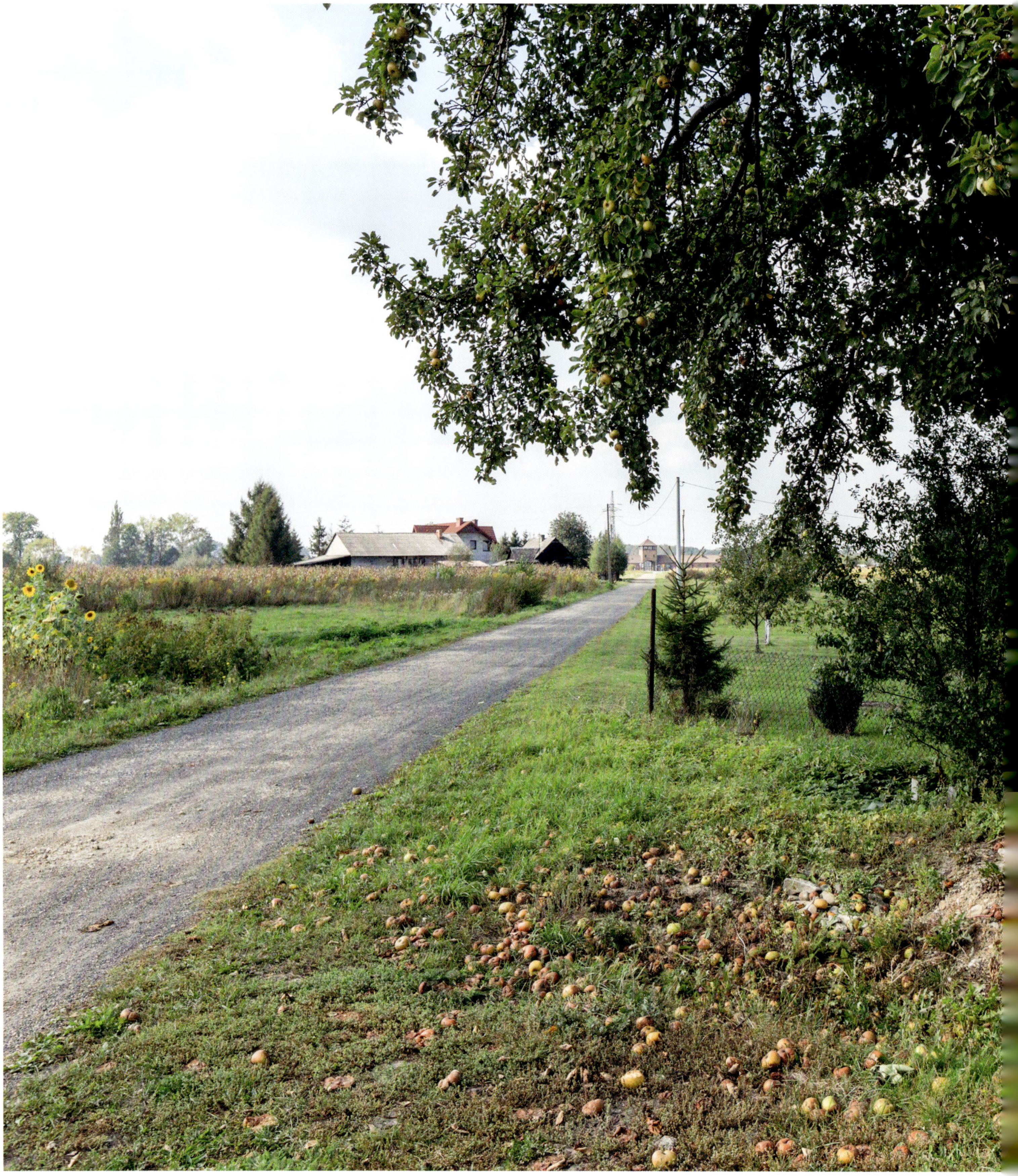

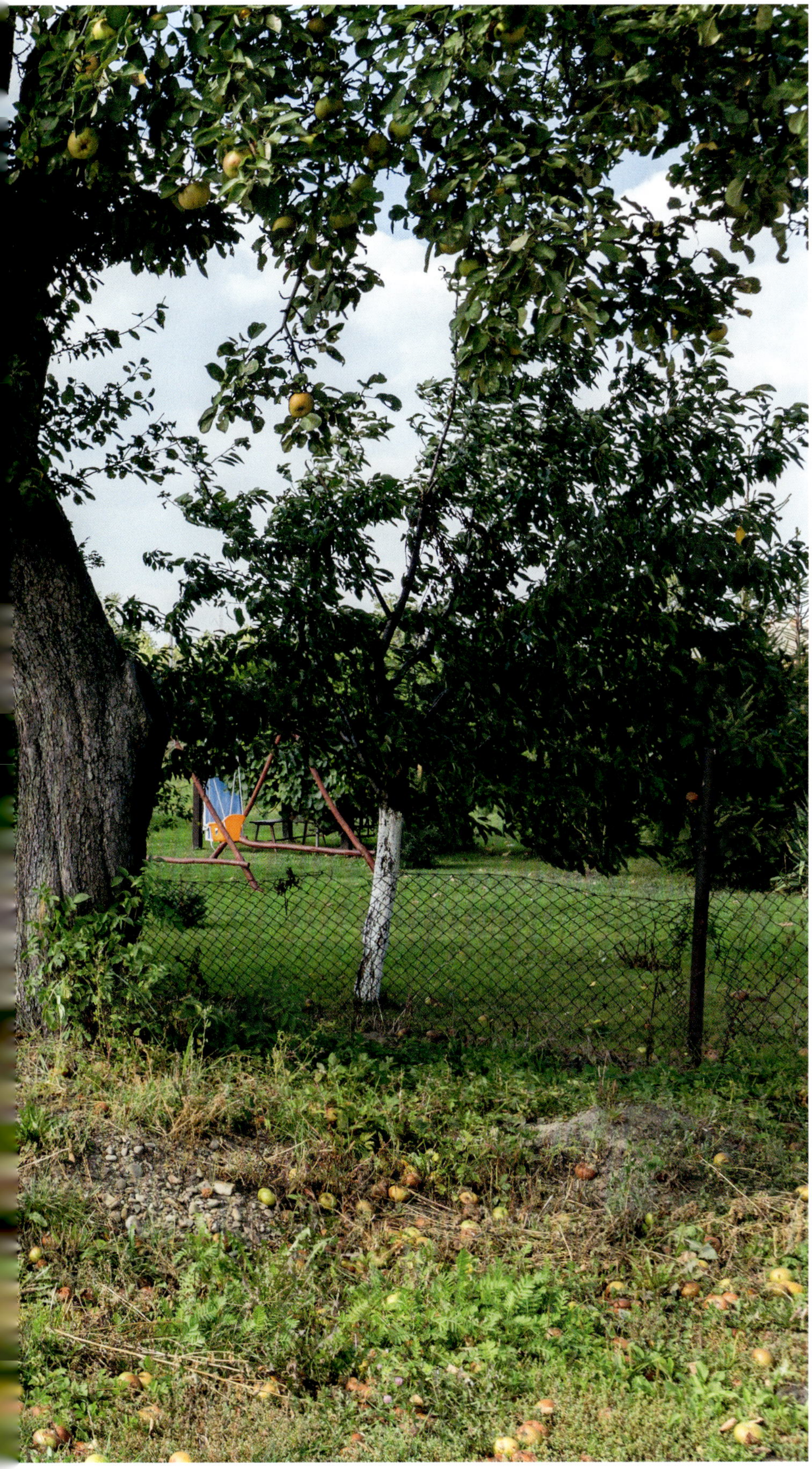

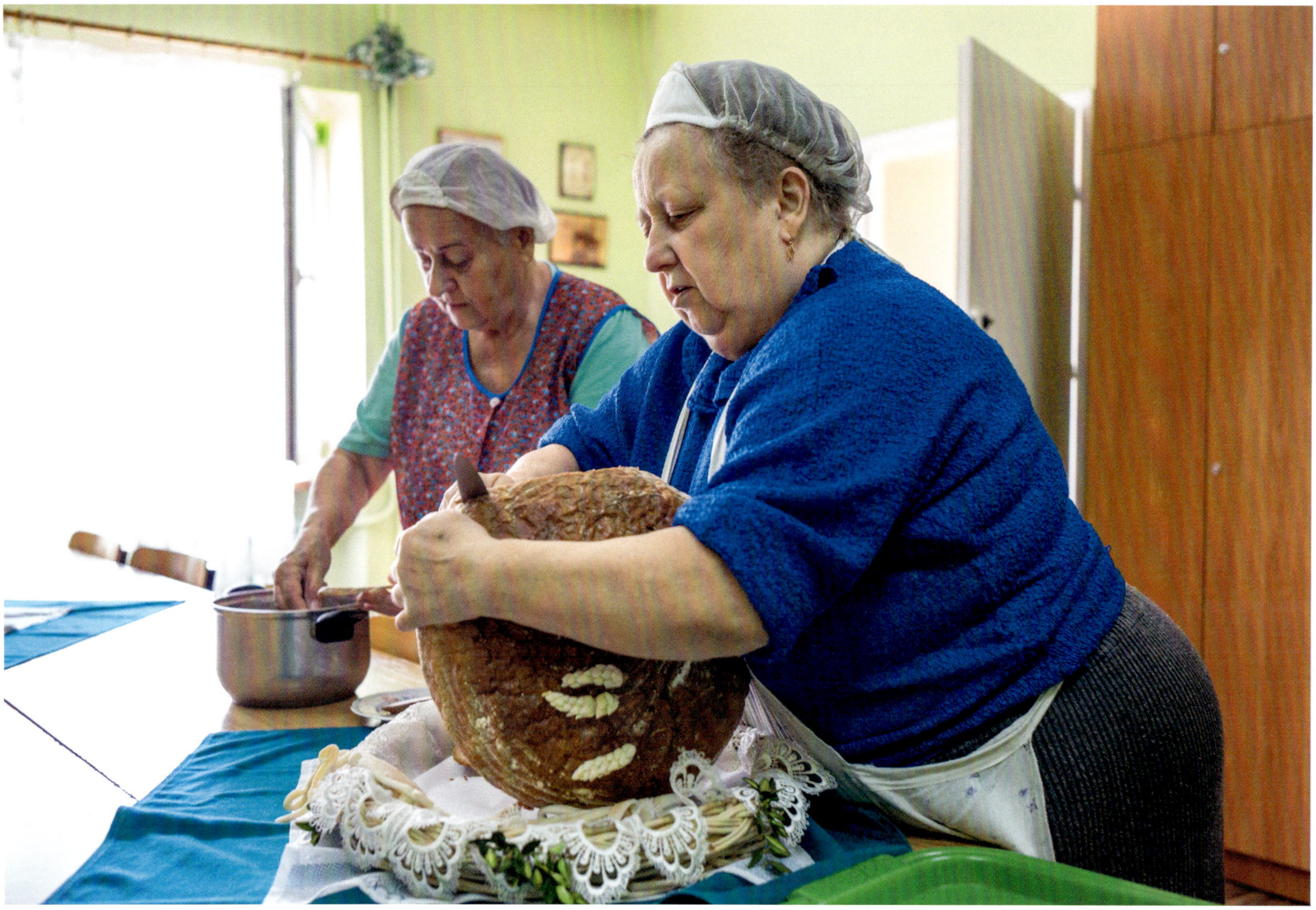

INDEX

2   AUSCHWITZ I / STAMMLAGER, VILLA HÖSS

Das spätere Stammlager war ursprünglich als polnische Kaserne errichtet worden. An deren Rand hatte sich ein Offizier sein Haus bauen lassen, das nach dem deutschen Überfall auf Polen von der SS beschlagnahmt wurde.
Wenige Teile der Inneneinrichtung des Hauses stammen noch aus den Jahren 1941 bis 1945, als der Lagerkommandant Rudolf Höß mit Frau und Kindern hier residierte. Dazu gehört die metallische Verriegelung der Toilettentür, deren Drehknauf beschriftet ist mit »FREI« und »BESETZT«.

2   AUSCHWITZ I/MAIN CAMP, HÖSS VILLA

What later became the main camp was originally built to be Polish barracks. An officer had his house erected on its periphery; after the German invasion of Poland, it was confiscated by the SS.
Only parts of the house's interior still date from the years 1941 to 1945, when the camp commandant Rudolf Höss lived here with his wife and children. Among them are the metal lock on the bathroom door, with a knob labeled FREI ("free") and BESETZT ("occupied").

12   AUSCHWITZ III/MONOWITZ-BUNA

Splitterschutzbunker am Außenrand des ehemaligen Zwangsarbeiterlagers. Die Betonkuppel deckte eine Vertiefung im Boden ab, in der ein SS-Wachmann stand. Er hatte freies Sicht- und Schussfeld ins Lagerinnere und war bei Luftangriffen zumindest teilweise geschützt.

12   AUSCHWITZ III/MONOWITZ-BUNA

A blast protection bunker on the outer edge of what was formerly the forced labor camp. The concrete dome covered a depression in the ground where an SS guard stood. He had a clear field of vision—as well as a clear shot—into the interior of the camp and was at least partially protected in the event of air raids.

13, 14   AUSCHWITZ III/ MONOWITZ-BUNA

Das Zwangsarbeiterlager der IG Farben wurde direkt neben dem chemischen Werk auf dem Gelände des Dorfes Monowice errichtet. In einem rechtwinkligen Raster waren hölzerne Baracken angeordnet, auf stabilen Fundamenten aus Mauerwerk und Beton. Nach der Befreiung 1945 nutzen die zurückgekehrten Einwohner von Monowice diese Fundamente für ihre neuen Häuser. Heute existieren nur noch Teile von zwei hölzernen Baracken aus der Lagerzeit.

13, 14   AUSCHWITZ III/ MONOWITZ-BUNA

The IG Farben's labor camp was constructed right next to the chemical factory on the site where the village of Monowice had been. Wooden barracks were arranged in a rectangular grid on top of a foundation of masonry and concrete. After the liberation in 1945 the residents of Monowice returned and built their new homes on the foundations. Today only parts of two wooden barracks from that era remain.

15 AUSCHWITZ III/ MONOWITZ-BUNA, FUNDAMENTE VON HÄFTLINGSBARACKEN

Vorne die gemauerten Fundamente ehemaliger Häftlingsbaracken, im Hintergrund oben eine der beiden teilweise erhaltenen Baracken aus Holz.

15 AUSCHWITZ III/MONOWITZ-BUNA, FOUNDATION FOR PRISON BARRACKS

Foreground: the masonry foundations of former prison barracks; background: one of the two partially surviving wooden barracks.

16 ZEITZEUGIN STEFANIA WACŁAWEK, MONOWICE

Die Familie von Stefania Wacławek besaß schon vor dem Zweiten Weltkrieg das Grundstück, auf dem die alte Dame heute wohnt. Ab September 1943 befand sich genau dort das Lager E 715 für britische Kriegsgefangene. Weil diese nach der Weltanschauung der Nationalsozialisten keine »Untermenschen« oder »Menschheitsfeinde« waren (wie Slawen, Juden, Kommunisten), wurden sie vergleichsweise gut behandelt. Die Briten konnten durch die Stacheldrahtzäune in das benachbarte Lager Auschwitz III/Monowitz sehen und die Misshandlungen und Tötungen von Gefangenen dort beobachten.

Einer der in E 715 inhaftierten Briten war Denis Avey. Bei der gemeinsamen Zwangsarbeit mit jüdischen Häftlingen lernte er den Deutschen Ernst Lobethall kennen. Avey tauschte zweimal für je einen Tag mit Lobethall die Kleidung, um die Bedingungen für jüdische Häftlinge mit eigenen Augen zu sehen; er wurde auch Zeuge der Erschießung von Häftlingen. Avey schmuggelte Zigaretten und Schokolade ins Lager. Diese begehrten Waren konnte Lobethall gegen lebensnotwenige Güter tauschen. So hat Avey ihm wahrscheinlich das Leben gerettet. Die 1927 geborene Stefania Wacławek erinnert sich, wie sie während der deutschen Besatzung mit gleichaltrigen Teenie-Freunden und -Freundinnen regelmäßig an Sonntagen zum Lager der Briten kam und mit den SS-Wachen Schwarzbier trank. Sie konnte damals auch die Schule besuchen. Stefania berichtet von einer damals wohl weit verbreiteten Taktik der ortsansässigen Bevölkerung, die Häftlinge der Lager mittels Kinder-Kurieren zu unterstützen: »Meine Tante backte Brot und Kuchen und schickte mich mit mehreren Körben los. Einer war für die Bewacher von der SS, einer für die Gefangenen. Einige Male klappte das, aber beim dritten Versuch erwischte mich eine berittene SS-Streife, warf das Essen weg und verscheuchte mich.« Stefania Wacławek hatte großes Glück: Mitsamt ihrer ganzen Familie überstand sie den Krieg unversehrt.

16 STEFANIA WACŁAWEK, EYEWITNESS, MONOWICE

Before World War II, Stefania Wacławek's family owned the property upon which the old lady now lives. From September 1943 onward, camp E 715 for British prisoners of war was located right there. The British were relatively well treated because, according to the Nazis' worldview, they were not "subhuman" or "enemies of humanity" (like the Slavs, the Jews, or communists). The British prisoners were able to see through the barbed wire fences into the neighboring camp of Auschwitz III/Monowitz and witnessed the abuse and killing of prisoners there.

One of the British prisoners in E 715 was Denis Avey. While engaged in forced labor alongside Jewish prisoners, he met Ernst Lobethall, a German. Avey swapped clothes for a day with Lobethall twice, in order to see with his own eyes what the conditions were for the Jewish prisoners; he also witnessed the shooting of prisoners. Avey smuggled cigarettes and chocolate into the camp. Lobethall was able to exchange these coveted goods for necessaries, and so Avey probably saved his life.

Stefania Wacławek, who was born in 1927, recalls that during the German occupation she and her teenage friends regularly went to the British camp on Sundays and drank schwarzbier with the SS guards. She was also able to attend school. Stefania tells of what was probably a widespread tactic employed by the local population, of supporting the camp prisoners using children as couriers: "My aunt baked bread and cake and sent me off with several baskets. One was for the SS guards, one for the prisoners. It worked a couple of times, but on the third try I was caught by a mounted SS patrol, who threw away the food and frightened me off." Stefania was extremely lucky: she and her entire family survived the war unscathed.

17 AUSSENLAGER BUDY

Zum Lagerkomplex Auschwitz gehörten insgesamt 47 Außenlager. Eines davon ist das in Budy, ca. vier Kilometer südlich von Brzezinka. Im ehemaligen Schulhaus des Dorfes war im Juni 1942 ein Frauenstraflager für Häftlinge des Lagers Auschwitz II / Birkenau eingerichtet worden. Die Inhaftierten mussten schwere Arbeiten verrichten, z. B. Gräben ausheben und Fischteiche säubern. Anfang Oktober 1942 töteten deutsche Häftlinge mit Unterstützung der SS ungefähr 90 jüdische Mitgefangene. Sechs der Anführerinnen des Massakers wurden kurz danach von der SS getötet.

Seit 2014 ist im ehemaligen Schulhaus eine kleine Gedenkstätte untergebracht.

17 BUDY SATELLITE CAMP

The Auschwitz complex also included a total of forty-seven satellite camps. One of them is in Budy, about four kilometers south of Brzezinka. In June 1942 a former schoolhouse was turned into a women's camp for prisoners from the Auschwitz II/Birkenau camps. Prisoners had to perform hard labor, such as digging graves and cleaning fishponds. In early October of 1942 German non-Jewish prisoners, with the support of the SS, murdered about ninety of their fellow Jewish prisoners. Shortly afterward, the SS killed six of the massacre's leaders.

There has been a small memorial in the old schoolhouse since 2014.

18 KARPFENTEICHE IN HARMĘŻE

Die Fischzucht in der Umgebung von Auschwitz hat eine große Tradition, von hier aus wurde der polnische Königshof mit Karpfen beliefert. Die SS übernahm die Fischzucht und setzte Zwangsarbeiter aus den Lagern dafür ein. Außerdem verklappte sie einen Teil der Aschen der Ermordeten in den Teichen. Im Oktober 1944 endete der Aufstand des Sonderkommandos aus dem Lager Auschwitz II / Birkenau in der Nähe dieser Teiche. Eine Gruppe von Häftlingen hatte bis hierher fliehen können, wurde aber von der SS gestellt und erschossen. Eine zweite Gruppe geflohener Aufständischer wurde von der SS in einer Scheune bei Rajsko umzingelt und dort bei lebendigem Leib verbrannt. Die genauen Orte, an denen die letzten geflohenen Aufständischen getötet wurden, sind nicht gekennzeichnet.

18 CARP POND IN HARMĘŻE
Fish farming in and around Auschwitz has long been tradition; the area used to supply the Polish royal court with carp. The SS took over the fish farms and used forced labor from the camps to tend them. They also dumped some of the ashes of murdered prisoners in the ponds. In October 1944 the revolt of the "special units" from the Auschwitz II/Birkenau camp ended near these ponds. A group of prisoners had been able to flee to this point but were captured by the SS and shot. A second group of escaped insurgents hiding in a barn near Rajsko were surrounded and burned alive. The exact sites where the last renegades were killed are not marked.

20 PRIVATES WOHNHAUS SÜDLICH DES EHEMALIGEN VERNICHTUNGSLAGERS AUSCHWITZ II / BIRKENAU

Die Eigentümer dieses Hauses haben einen Zaunpfosten des Lagers, den sie in der Nähe fanden, in ihrem Vorgarten neu aufgestellt.

20 PRIVATE HOME SOUTH OF AUSCHWITZ II/BIRKENAU CONCENTRATION CAMP
The owners of this house found a fencepost from the camp nearby and set it up in their front yard.

21 AUSCHWITZ I / STAMMLAGER, EHEMALIGE VILLA HÖSS, WOHNZIMMER

Das ehemalige Wohnhaus der Familie Höß liegt unmittelbar neben den Wachtürmen und Zäunen am nordöstlichen Rand des Stammlagers.
Es wurde kurz vor Kriegsbeginn 1939 als Wohnhaus eines polnischen Offiziers errichtet, der es nach der Befreiung 1945 auch wieder bezog. Ende der Sechzigerjahre verkaufte er es an eine polnische Familie, die es seither bewohnt. Der Großvater der heutigen Besitzerin war selbst im Stammlager inhaftiert. Nach der Befreiung des Lagers starb er im Alter von nur vierzig Jahren an einer Lungenentzündung.

21 AUSCHWITZ I/MAIN CAMP, LIVING ROOM OF THE FORMER HÖSS VILLA
The Höss family's former residence is right next to the guard towers and fences on the northeastern edge of the main camp.
It was built in 1939, just before the war began, as a residence for a Polish officer, who moved back into it after the liberation in 1945. In the late 1960s he sold it to a Polish family, who has been living in it ever since. The grandfather of the current owner was himself a prisoner in the main camp. After the camp was liberated, he died of pneumonia at the age of just forty.

22 AUSCHWITZ I / STAMMLAGER, EHEMALIGE VILLA HÖSS, SPEISEKAMMER

Die Speisekammer war zu Höß' Zeiten immer prall gefüllt mit Köstlichkeiten aus aller Herren Länder. Diese Lebensmittel stammten großen Teils von den Häftlingen, die bei der Einlieferung in das Lager ihren gesamten Besitz abgeben mussten. Gegen die offiziellen Vorschriften beauftragte Hedwig Höß, die Ehefrau des Lagerkommandanten, ihre Untergebenen damit, aus diesem Raubgut ihren Haushalt zu versorgen. Noch bei Kriegsende gehörten zu ihrem Fluchtgepäck, das einen kompletten Lastwagen füllte, Luxusartikel wie französischer Cognac der Marke »Remy Martin«.

22 AUSCHWITZ I/MAIN CAMP, PANTRY IN THE FORMER HÖSS VILLA
During the time Hösses lived there, the pantry was always full of delicacies from all over the world. Most of the food came from the prisoners, who were forced surrender all of their property when they were sent to the camp. Hedwig Höss, the camp commandant's wife, defied official regulations and ordered her servants to supply her household with these stolen goods. Even when fleeing at the end of the war, her supplies, which filled an entire truck, included luxury items such as Rémy Martin cognac from France.

23 AUSCHWITZ I / STAMMLAGER, VILLA HÖSS

23 AUSCHWITZ I/MAIN CAMP, HÖSS VILLA

24 AUSCHWITZ II / BIRKENAU, »ALTE JUDENRAMPE«

Die Deportationszüge, die etwa eine halbe Million Juden aus ganz Europa nach Birkenau brachten, hielten zwischen Frühjahr 1942 und April 1944 an einem Nebengleis der Eisenbahnanlage von Auschwitz, etwa einen Kilometer vom Tor des Vernichtungslagers entfernt. Die exakte Lage der ersten Rampe, an der die Deportationszüge endeten, ist nicht bekannt. Sie befand sich unter oder hinter dem Gestrüpp auf diesem Bild.
Erst am 29. April 1944 fuhr erstmals ein Zug bis zur neuen Rampe auf dem Lagergelände. Weil Fotos von der Ankunft ungarischer Juden im Sommer 1944 vielfach publiziert wurden, wird fälschlicherweise oft angenommen, diese Rampe sei die einzige gewesen.

24 AUSCHWITZ II/BIRKENAU, "OLD JEWISH RAMP"

Between spring 1942 and April 1944, the deportation trains, which brought around half a million Jews from all over Europe to Birkenau, halted at a siding of the Auschwitz rail system about a kilometer away from the gate of the extermination camp. The exact location of the first platform where the deportation trains came to a halt is unknown. It was either under or behind the brush shown in this picture.

It was not until April 29, 1944, that a train went all the way to the new platform on the campgrounds. Because photos of the arrival of Hungarian Jews in the summer of 1944 were published frequently, it has been often wrongly assumed that this platform was the only one.

26 ZEITZEUGE JAN SIKORA, BRZEZINKA

Jan Sikora wurde 1937 am nordwestlichen Rand von Brzezinka geboren, wo er heute noch wohnt. Als er drei Jahre alt war, bauten seine Eltern auf dem Grundstück ein neues Haus, in dem sie gerade mal ein Jahr lebten. Dann wurde die siebenköpfige Familie von den deutschen Besatzern vertrieben. Die Sikoras hatten zwei Stunden Zeit, ihre beweglichen Besitztümer auf einen Pferdewagen zu packen, überwacht von einem deutschen Soldaten. Der kleine Jan – zu jung, um zu verstehen, was vor sich ging – nahm vor allem eine hölzerne Flöte mit, die ihm sein Vater geschnitzt hatte. Etwa sieben Kilometer entfernt kamen die Sikoras im Dorf Dwory in einem Viehstall unter, den sie mit zwei weiteren Familien teilen mussten – fast vier Jahre lang, bis zur Befreiung im Januar 1945. Die Sikoras improvisierten, so gut es ging: Hinter einer doppelten Holzwand hielten sie trotz Verbots heimlich eine Ziege, um mit der Milch des Tieres ihre kärgliche Nahrungsversorgung aufzubessern. Vater Sikora baute eine kleine Mühle, um selber Brot backen zu können. Und Jans Mutter schickte ihren kleinen Sohn trotz aller Knappheit ein bis zwei Mal pro Woche abends mit ziegelgroßen Portionen von Obst, Karotten und Brot, in Lappen oder Papier gewickelt, auf Baustellen in der Umgebung. Jan deponierte die Pakete dort, um den Zwangsarbeitern aus den Lagern zu helfen. Er wurde nie erwischt.
Nach der Vertreibung bekam Jans Vater eine Arbeit als Schreiner im Werk der IG Farben; sein kleiner Sohn Jan durfte ihn dort manchmal besuchen. Während der häufigen Bombenangriffe auf die Fabrik mussten beide in der ungeschützten Werkstatt bleiben, die Deutschen suchten Unterschlupf in Bunkern. Auch in der Stallwohnung im nahen Dwory verfolgte der kleine Jan oft mit Schrecken die alliierten Luftangriffe, bis heute erinnert er sich an Feuer und Detonationen.
Besonders in Erinnerung ist ihm ein Besuch im »Interessengebiet«, dem streng abgeriegelten Sperrbezirk rings um die Lager. 500 Meter vom elterlichen Grundstück hatte ein Freund seines Vaters wohnen bleiben dürfen, als Einziger in Brzezinka – weil er Deichwart der Weichsel war. Diesen Bekannten durfte Sikora Senior einmal besuchen, in Begleitung zweier Nachbarn und seines Sohnes. Die kleine Gruppe wurde vom Deichwärter mit einem Boot abgeholt. Eine SS-Wache trank Wodka mit den Besuchern, dann schauten die Vertriebenen nach ihren Grundstücken und stellten fest, dass ihre Häuser vollständig abgetragen waren. Gut zu sehen waren Feuer im nahe gelegenen Lager Birkenau. Der Deichwärter erklärte, dass es sich um die Verbrennung von Leichen handelt. Jan wusste über das Schicksal der Juden bereits Bescheid: Nahe des Stalls, in dem er lebte, hatte er oft Deportationszüge gesehen, aus denen die Gefangenen bei Regen Hände und Becher herausstreckten, um ihren Durst zu lindern. »Wenn die Gefangenen am Abend in Kolonnen zurück ins Lager gingen, trugen sie immer Tote auf den Schultern«, erinnert sich Jan Sikora.
Nach der Befreiung Ende Januar 1945 wollte er sofort ins Lager Birkenau, doch die sowjetischen Militärs erlaubten den Anwohnern erst nach ein bis zwei Wochen den Zutritt. Jan ging mit seiner Mutter und einigen Nachbarn hinein, begleitet von sowjetischen Militärs. Was Jan im Lager sah, verfolgt ihn bis heute. Während die Erwachsenen miteinander sprachen, entwischte der Junge und streifte unbeaufsichtigt umher. Er sah die Ruinen der Krematorien II und III, die »Sauna« genannte Desinfektion, die Verbrennungsgruben und Duschen, die Haare und Kleidung der Toten und das brennende Effektenlager, »Kanada« genannt. In Baracken lagen in Decken gewickelte Leichen und in einem Graben neben dem Krematorium V erblickte Sikora eine nackte Frauenleiche, »weiß wie Schnee«.
Sikoras Vater wird wenig später von den sowjetischen Aliierten gezwungen, Leichen aus Birkenau ins Stammlager zu bringen und sie dort zu waschen; Jan erinnert sich an den Gestank in der Kleidung seines Vaters.
Jahrzehnte später hatten die Sikoras eine weitere besondere Begegnung mit der historischen Erblast ihrer Heimat. Bei einem Besuch der Frauenbaracken im ehemaligen Vernichtungslager Birkenau entdeckten sie Dachziegel aus ihrem 1941 abgetragenen Haus, erkenntlich am großen »S«, mit dem Sikora Senior die selbst gebrannten Ziegel einst versehen hatte.
Das heutige Haus der Familie haben die Sikoras Ende der Sechzigerjahre gebaut; eine

Reparation in Höhe von 8.000 Euro erhielten Jan Sikora und seine vier Geschwister erst 2001. Die düstere Nachbarschaft des Ortes, an dem er geboren wurde und bis heute lebt, hat ihn nie losgelassen. Zeitlebens hat er darüber gesprochen, mit Freunden, Familie, Kollegen; jedes Jahr nimmt er am 22. April an der Gedenkfeier anlässlich des Jahrestags der Vertreibung der Bevölkerung von Brzezinka teil. In seinem Buchregal steht eine kleine, vom vielen Blättern zerknitterte Handbibliothek zum Thema Auschwitz, und während er sein Leben rekapituliert, sitzt eine seiner Enkelinnen auf dem Sofa und hört zu. »Man muss darüber reden«, sagt Jan Sikora, »aber ich wünschte, ich hätte all das nie mit eigenen Augen gesehen!«

26 JAN SIKORA, EYEWITNESS, BRZEZINKA

Jan Sikora was born in 1937 on the northwestern periphery of Brzezinka, where he lives to this day. When he was three years old, his parents built a new house on their property, where they lived for just one year. Then the family of seven was driven from their home by the German occupiers. The Sikoras had two hours to pack their movable possessions onto a horse-drawn cart, under the supervision of a German soldier. Jan, who was too young to understand what was happening, chose to take a wooden flute his father had carved for him. The Sikoras went to the village of Dwory, around seven kilometers away, where they lived in a cowshed, which they had to share with two other families, for nearly four years, until the liberation in 1945. The Sikoras got by as best they could: behind a double wooden wall they secretly kept a goat, despite the ban, in order to supplement their meager food supply with the animal's milk. Jan's father built a small mill so that they could bake bread. And despite the shortages, once or twice a week in the evenings Jan's mother sent him with brick-sized portions of fruit, carrots, and bread, wrapped in rags or paper, to construction sites in the area. Jan deposited the packets there, to help the prisoners in the labor camps. He was never caught.

After being forced to leave the family home, Jan's father got work as a carpenter at the IG Farben factory. Jan was allowed to visit him there sometimes. During the frequent air raids on the factory, both had to remain in the unprotected workshop, while the Germans sought cover in the bunkers. Even in their stable home near Dwory, Jan often witnessed the allied air raids with horror; to this day he remembers the fires and explosions.

He particularly recalls a visit to the "interesting area"—the tightly sealed, restricted zone surrounding the camp. A friend of his father's—the only remaining resident of Brzezinka—had been permitted to remain in his home about five hundred meters from his parents' house, because he was a dike keeper on the Vistula River. Jan senior was allowed to visit this friend once, accompanied by his son and two neighbors. The dike keeper picked up the little group in a boat. An SS guard drank vodka with the visitors; then the displaced people took a look at their property and saw that their houses had been completely demolished. It was easy to see fire burning in the nearby Birkenau camp. The dike keeper explained that they were burning corpses. By then, Jan already knew about what was happening to the Jews: near the shed in which he lived, he had often seen deportation trains, from which, when it rained, the prisoners held out their hands or cups to catch the rain and quench their thirst. "When the columns of prisoners returned to the camp at night, they were always carrying corpses on their backs," Jan remembers.

After the liberation in late January of 1945, he wanted to go to the Birkenau camp right away, but the Soviet army did not admit locals for a week or two. Jan went with his mother and a few neighbors, accompanied by Soviet military personnel. What he saw in the camp haunts him to this day. While the adults talked to each other, the boy went off on his own and wandered around unsupervised. He saw the ruins of Crematoria I and II, the "sauna" (the disinfection room), the incineration pits and showers, the hair and clothing of the dead, and the burning storehouse of personal effects, known as "Canada." In the barracks lay corpses wrapped in blankets, and in a pit near Crematorium V, Jan saw the corpse of a nude woman, "white as snow."

A little later, the Soviet allies forced Jan's father to carry corpses from Birkenau to the main camp and wash them there; Jan recalls the stink that clung to his father's clothing. Decades later the Sikoras had yet another special encounter with the historical legacy of their hometown. While visiting the women's barracks in the old Birkenau death camp, they discovered roof tiles from their house, demolished in 1941; they were recognizable by the large "S" with which Jan's father had once marked the tiles when he fired them. The Sikoras built the house they currently occupy in the late 1960s. Jan and his four siblings waited until 2001 to receive reparations amounting to eight thousand euros. The bleak neighborhood where he was born and still lives has never let him go. Throughout his entire life he has talked about it with friends, families, colleagues; every year on April 22 he attends the ceremony commemorating the day that the residents of Brzezinka were driven from their homes. His bookshelf contains a small reference library of books about Auschwitz, worn from reading, and while he recapitulates his life, one of his granddaughters sits on the sofa, listening. "One has to talk about it," says Jan, "but I wish I had never seen any of it with my own eyes!"

27 LINKS, JAN TOBIAS, BRZEZINKA, ZEITZEUGE DER VERTREIBUNG 1941
RECHTS, LIDIA SKIBICKA-MAKSYMOWICZ, ÜBERLEBENDE DES VERNICHTUNGSLAGERS BIRKENAU UND PATRONIN DER SCHULE VON BRZEZINKA

In der Schule von Brzezinka tobt das Leben. Mit vor Aufregung teils blassen, teils roten Gesichtern flitzen Jungen und Mädchen durch die Eingangshalle, viele von ihnen bunt kostümiert, die anderen festlich herausgeputzt. Eltern nesteln an Videokameras herum, der Bürgermeister plaudert mit Honoratioren, sanft lächelnd bahnt sich ein Priester im schwarzen Habit den Weg durchs Gewühl. Am Eingang begrüßt die Schulleiterin Agata Kowol einige ältere Herrschaften, die das Gebäude am Ortsrand von Brzezinka betreten.

Es ist der 27. Januar, der wichtigste Tag im hiesigen Schuljahr: An jenem Tag im Jahr 1945 wurde das Lager befreit – aus Sicht eines Grundschülers also vor Ewigkeiten, Welten entfernt. Wenn da nicht die graublauen Streifen an der Wand der Eingangshalle wären. Wenn da nicht gleich neben dem Klassenzimmer Vier der kleine Gedenkraum wäre, wo die gleichen Streifen im zerschlissenen Stoff einer alten Uniform wiederkehren, einer Uniform in Kindergröße. Und wenn da nicht die schwarzweißen Passbilder von Kindern in ebensolchen Uniformen wären, vor allem nicht die kleine Urne, gefüllt mit etwas, das ganz in der Nähe eingesammelt wurde, irgendwo bei den Krematorien des Vernichtungslagers Birkenau.

All das gehört zur Schule von Brzezinka. Von den Klassenzimmern braucht ein Erstklässler zu Fuß vielleicht eine knappe Viertelstunde, um an die Stelle zu gelangen, die sein Heimatdorf weltweit zum Inbegriff eines unfassbaren Menschheitsverbrechens gemacht hat. Der Weg führt erst an Feldern entlang, dann entweder links ab am Kiosk und der Feuerwehr vorbei oder geradeaus bis zur »Straße der Opfer des Faschismus«. Von dort aus fällt der Blick auf die Zäune und die Wachtürme des Vernichtungslagers Auschwitz-Birkenau.

Wie erklärt man einem Kind, was es da sieht? Ist das alles nicht viel zu groß, zu dunkel, zu unbeschreiblich und unfassbar, um es ausgerechnet Kindern nahezubringen? Und wie nahe darf man es ihnen überhaupt bringen, ohne ihre Seelen zu verdüstern?

Die Schulleiterin Agata Kowol kennt die Fragen, auch die Zweifel. Vielleicht hat sie sich nie davon abschrecken lassen, ihren Schülern das Lager zu zeigen, weil schon ihre eigene Biografie untrennbar damit verbunden ist, in unvermuteter Weise: Ihre Familie hat den Zweiten Weltkrieg und das brutale Besatzungsregiment erlitten wie alle hier. Ihre Mutter aber wurde während der Okkupation ausgerechnet von einem Deutschen gerettet – als sie lebensbedrohlich erkrankte, war es ein Apotheker namens Doktor Komraus, der die polnische Patientin entgegen aller Verbote mit Medikamenten versorgte.

Agata Kowol ist also nicht die ungeeignetste Person, um Geschichte klischeefrei zu vermitteln. »Natürlich nehmen wir Rücksicht auf das Alter der Kinder«, sagt sie, »aber irgendwann führen wir sie alle an das Thema heran.« Es ist für die Schüler ohnehin unausweichlich, spätestens dann, wenn sie lesen können – zum Beispiel den Schriftzug an der gestreiften Wand der Eingangshalle: »Denkmal der Kinderhäftlinge von Auschwitz« steht dort. Wenn es je ein lebendiges Denkmal gab, dann ist es diese Schule beziehungsweise der Alltag, der hier stattfindet – pauken, schummeln, Pickel kriegen und Zahnspangen tragen, schwärmen, nachsitzen, turnen, kicken, grübeln und andere blöd finden. Und keinen Bogen ums Lager machen.

»Wir besuchen die Kinderbaracken im Lager, haben Friedensprojekte mit internationalen Partnerschulen, vor allem aber begehen wir die beiden Jahrestage von Vertreibung und Befreiung«, berichtet die Vizedirektorin Beata Herman.

Die Vertreibung ist kaum bekannt. Kein Wunder, wenn direkt nebenan eines der größten Verbrechen aller Zeiten stattfand. Wen interessiert dann das vergleichsweise glimpfliche Schicksal einiger tausend Vertriebener aus Brzezinka? Wahrscheinlich ist diese Mischung aus Entsetzen und Scham der Grund, warum die Entvölkerung der Lagerumgebung erst seit wenigen Jahren öffentlich thematisiert wird. 2001 wurde ein offizieller Gedenkstein vor dem »Todestor« von Birkenau errichtet. 2016 kam auf Privatinitiative eine Blechtafel in Brzezinka hinzu.

Am 22. April 1941 wurde Brzezinka von der SS zwangsgeräumt, ebenso wie sieben weitere Dörfer mit insgesamt etwa 8.500 Einwohnern. Die Nationalsozialisten wollten keine Augenzeugen. Gleichzeitig verschleppten die Deutschen die gesamte jüdische Bevölkerung der Stadt Oświęcim, etwa 6.000 Männer, Frauen und Kinder, in Ghettos. Die jüdischen Einwohner wurden fast alle ermordet; die meisten Dorfbewohner kamen zurück.

An jedem 22. April dürfen drei Schüler aus Brzezinka, die sich durch besondere Leistungen diese Ehre verdient haben, die Fahne der Schule vor das »Todestor« von Birkenau tragen. Es ist ein schweres Stück Stoff. Auf der einen Seite prangt als silberne Stickerei der polnische Adler auf rotem Grund, die andere Seite besteht aus dem billigen Drillich der Häftlingsuniformen. Eingestickt ist eine Mahnung, das Schicksal der Kinderhäftlinge von Auschwitz möge nie zur Legende werden, sondern auf immer als Warnung dienen. Diese Fahne hängt normalerweise im Flur des ersten Obergeschosses, wo in den Pausen zwischen den Schulstunden die Tischtennisplatte aufgeklappt wird.

Gegenüber befindet sich der schmale fensterlose Raum mit der Urne. Über der Vitrine sind Fotos von Kinderhäftlingen aufgereiht, die in der Registrierstelle des Lagers angefertigt wurden. Die Abzüge sind klein, manche verknickt, sie vergilben. Man muss ihnen nahekommen, um Details zu erkennen – die glatte Haut der Gesichter, die grob rasierten Schädel, die schreckensstarren kleinen Körper, die panischen Blicke. Alles ist eingefroren an diesen Bildern, bürokratisch exakt und gleichgültig, ein leerer Hintergrund, die harten Schatten von Scheinwerfern und deren Reflexe in den Augen der Kinder. Wer das sieht, dem kriecht Entsetzen ins Gemüt. Und man versteht, was die ehemalige Schülerin Gosia Musielak, Mitte der Achtzigerjahre in Brzezinka geboren, erzählt: »Jedes Mal, wenn ich ins Lager gehe, überkommt mich das heulende Elend; sobald ich aber wieder draußen bin, ist dieser Ort hier meine Heimat.«

Am 27. Januar 2017 ist sie eine der ersten, die am Eingang der Schule einer älteren Dame um den Hals fallen: Lidia Skibicka-Maksymowicz, Jahrgang 1939, überlebte ein Jahr Vernichtungslager. Sie ist eine Art Patronin der Schule, sie war schon bei der Einweihung im Jahr 1968 zugegen und kommt seitdem jedes Jahr zur Befreiungsfeier hierher. Neben Lidia Skibicka-Maksymowicz hat auch Stefania Wernik den Weg hierhergeschafft. Sie kam im November 1944 im Lager Birkenau zur Welt und entging dem Wassereimer, der dort für Neugeborene bereitstand, um sie zu ertränken. Lidia und Stefania waren zwei von 200.000 Kindern in den Lagern von Auschwitz. Überlebt haben nur einige Dutzend.

Anders als die kurz vor der Befreiung geborene Stefania hat Lidia das Lager bewusst erlebt. Sie stammt aus der weißrussisch-polnischen Grenzgegend, wo sie im Dezember 1943 als Kleinkind mitsamt ihren Eltern und Großeltern von Deutschen gefangen genommen wurde. Nach ein paar Wochen Gefängnis folgte der Transport nach Auschwitz: Einige Tage im Viehwaggon, ohne Wasser, ohne Essen, ohne Toilette. Von der »Selektion« in Birkenau erinnert Lidia Hundegebell, Geschrei, SS-Uniformen und ein babylonisches Sprachenwirrwarr. Sie fand sich schließlich mit ihrer Mutter in einer Menschenkolonne, in einer anderen sah sie ihre Großeltern weggehen – in die Gaskammer, wie später klar wurde.

Gesunde Mütter und Kinder wurden in einen Quarantäneblock gebracht, die Frauen entkleidet und kahlgeschoren; ein Zustand, in dem Lidia ihre Mutter zunächst nicht erkannte. Dann wurde beiden eine Häftlingsnummer tätowiert. Lidia saß erstarrt auf dem Schoß ihrer Mutter, zuckte beim Stechen nicht, daher ist ihre Nummer regelmäßig und klar zu lesen, in blauen, einige Zentimeter hohen Ziffern: 70072.

Nach dem Tätowieren wurden die Kinder gewaltsam von ihren Müttern getrennt. »Weggerissen wie Tiere«, sagt Lidia. Weibliche SS-Wachen prügelten die Mütter mit Stöcken weg, Lidia kam zusammen mit vielen anderen Kindern aus verschiedenen Ländern in eine separate Baracke. Sie erinnert sich, dass alles extrem schnell ablief, ohne Gegenwehr, unter Schock, geschwächt von Hunger und Angst. Die Baracke war dunkel, Licht kam nur von den Wachtürmen, nachts fielen die Temperaturen auf 20 Grad unter null, die dünnen Decken auf den Pritschen waren voller Dreck und Läuse. Kaum jemand verstand sie, nur wenige Kinder kannten ihre Sprache.

Lidias Mutter war damals 22. Sie wurde zur landwirtschaftlichen Zwangsarbeit im benachbarten Harmęże eingeteilt. Dort fand sie immer wieder Lebensmittel, die polnische Zivilisten für die Häftlinge versteckten. Jeden Abend riskierte es die junge Frau, im Dunkeln zur Kinderbaracke zu schleichen. Von draußen rief sie ihre Tochter und reichte ihr das geschmuggelte Essen durch eine Klappe. Lidia sah von ihrer Mutter nichts als Hände, die Nahrung brachten. Ihre Pritsche war nahe der Tür, ganz unten. Von dort aus blickte sie direkt auf die blank polierten Stiefel der SS, wenn Wachleute hereinkamen.

Der Alltag der Kinderhäftlinge war infernalisch. Sie froren und hungerten. »Wir benahmen uns wie Tiere«, sagt Lidia. Jeden Morgen mussten sie zum Apell antreten, und die Toten ihrer Baracke, die während der Nacht gestorben waren, dorthin mitschleppen. Die Leichen wurden auf einen Wagen geworfen, die entsprechenden Nummern aus der Liste gestrichen.

Kinder unter zwölf Jahren waren, anders als die erwachsenen Häftlinge, nicht zur »Vernichtung durch Arbeit« bestimmt; sie dienten den Lagerärzten als Versuchsobjekte. Die Kinder wussten, dass besonders Dr. Josef Mengele gefährlich war. Sein Kabinett lag nahe der Krematorien. Oft kamen Kinder von Mengeles Versuchen nicht zurück, daher versuchten sie, sich vor ihm zu verstecken. Dennoch nahm er Lidia immer wieder mit. Mengele verabreichte ihr Injektionen, nahm ihr Blut ab, tröpfelte Flüssigkeiten in ihre Augen. Ihr Gesundheitszustand verschlechterte sich. Hilfe kam von einer Gefangenen, die im Lager entbunden hatte, deren Kind aber von der SS sofort nach der Geburt getötet worden war. Diese Frau gab Lidia von ihrer Muttermilch.

Dann trafen neue Häftlinge ein, die auf andere Weise halfen: Überlebende des Warschauer Aufstands wurden im Oktober 1944 nach Birkenau gebracht, Frauen in die Kinderbaracken. Lidia erinnert sich gut an die Warschauerinnen: Sie sangen und spielten liebevoll mit den Kindern, eine im Lager völlig ungewohnte und umso wertvollere Zuwendung.

Dann hörten die medizinischen Versuche auf. Lidia meint, die Absicht der Deutschen gespürt zu haben, alle Spuren zu verwischen. Im Spätherbst 1944 wurden die Gaskammern und Krematorien demontiert, Lidia sah ihre Mutter nur noch selten. Vor der Räumung des Lagers kam sie ein letztes Mal zu Lidia und schärfte ihr ein: »Vergiss nicht deinen Namen, dein Alter und wo du herkommst! Ich hole dich später!«

Dann blieben Lidia und etwa 60 andere Kinderhäftlinge unbeachtet im Lager zurück. Nach der Befreiung kam ein ihr unbekanntes Paar zu Lidia. Die Fremden umarmten sie. Die Frau und der Mann nahmen sie mit in ihren polnischen Alltag, nahe Oświęcim. Lidia war zunächst völlig verstört. Sie fragte, wann Mengele käme und ob es keine gefährlichen Hunde gebe. Was ein Bad oder ein Bett ist, musste ihr erklärt werden. Fast ein halbes Jahr brauchte Lidia täglich medizinische Behandlung, um die körperlichen Folgen des Lagers zu heilen. Die seelischen Spuren sitzen ungleich tiefer. »Ich hatte keine Identität, nur die Nummer, hatte Angst vor Nähe, Trost, Umarmungen. Als meine Pflegeeltern mir eine Puppe schenkten, hatte ich keine Ahnung, was ich damit tun sollte. Mit anderen Kindern spielte ich Selektion. Ich stellte sie in Reihen auf und sagte: ‚Du gehst ins Krankenhaus, du gehst ins Gas!' Die meisten Eltern der Nachbarschaft wollten ihre Kinder fernhalten von dieser ‚Lidia aus dem Lager', wie ich genannt wurde. Nach drei Jahren bei meinen Stiefeltern wurde ich adoptiert, bekam einen neuen Namen, Dokumente, und wurde getauft. Die Tätowierung auf dem Arm habe ich dennoch oft mit Pflaster überklebt, um Fragen zu vermeiden.«

Erst 17 Jahre nach der Befreiung entdeckte Lidia, dass ihre Mutter überlebt hatte. Von Birkenau hatten die Deutschen sie über Ravensbrück nach Bergen-Belsen getrieben. Dort wog sie bei ihrer Befreiung durch die US-Army noch 37 Kilo. Als Lidia ihre Mutter 1962 wiedersah, entschied sie sich, bei ihrem Leben als Polin zu bleiben.

Bis zu ihrer Pensionierung hat sie als Chemikerin in Oświęcim gearbeitet. So ist ihr Weg zur Schule nach Brzezinka nicht weit. Sie macht ihn jedes Jahr am 27. Januar. Der Befreiungstag ist das wichtigste Datum des Schuljahres. Die Turnhalle ist mit Papiergirlanden geschmückt und bestuhlt, der Bürgermeister und ein Historiker halten Reden. Dann sprechen die beiden Überlebenden des Lagers. Lidia Skibicka-Maksymowicz ist die einzige Rednerin des ganzen Vormittags, die kein Mikrofon benötigt. Ihre Stimme füllt den Raum. Energisch spricht sie zu den kostümierten Schülern, schildert den Schrecken der Lager und fordert ihre Zuhörer auf, sich aller Menschenverachtung in den Weg zu stellen.

Danach dürfen endlich die angespannt wartenden Darsteller auf die Bühne. Schüler aller Jahrgangsstufen führen Tänze, Lieder und ein Theaterstück auf, in dem die Liebe und das Leben über den Schrecken und die Finsternis siegen. Lehrer assistieren, Eltern und Schüler strahlen, Displays blinken, Blitze zucken, Applaus prasselt. Am Ende gibt es selbstgenähte Herzen aus flauschigem Stoff für alle Ehrengäste. Für ein Gespräch hat Lidia Skibicka-Maksymowicz nun keine Zeit mehr. Eine Meute strahlender, aufgekratzter Kinder umringt die alte Dame. Sie muss jetzt viele Autogramme geben.

27 *LEFT,* **JAN TOBIAS, BRZEZINKA, EYEWITNESS TO THE DISPLACEMENT OF 1941** *RIGHT,* **LIDIA SKIBICKA-MAKSYMOWICZ, SURVIVOR OF BIRKENAU DEATH CAMP AND PATRON OF THE SCHOOL IN BRZEZINKA**

The school in Brzezinka teems with life. With faces pale or flushed with excitement, boys and girls dash down the entrance hall, many of them in colorful costumes and others in their Sunday best. Parents fiddle with video cameras, the mayor chats with dignitaries, a priest in a black habit smiles gently as he makes his way through the crowd. At the door, the principal, Agata Kowol, greets a few elderly gentlemen as they enter the building on the edge of Brzezinka.

It is January 27, the most important day in the local school year. It was on that day in 1945 that the camp was liberated—from the elementary students' perspective, an eternity, worlds away. If it weren't for the gray and blue stripes on the wall of the entrance hall. If it weren't for the small memorial space next to classroom four, where the same stripes appear on the tattered fabric of an old uniform—a child-size uniform. And if it weren't for the black-and-white passport photos of children wearing the same kinds of uniforms. Above all, if it weren't for the small urn filled with something that was collected very close by, somewhere near the crematoria of the Birkenau death camp.

All of that belongs to the school in Brzezinka. From the classrooms, a first grader would need just about fifteen minutes to walk to the place that has long made his home town the embodiment of an inconceivable crime against humanity around the world. At first, the path takes you past fields, then you either turn left after the kiosk and the fire department or go straight until you reach the "Street of the Victims of Fascism." From there, you can see the fences and the guard towers of the Auschwitz-Birkenau death camp.

How do you explain to children what they are seeing? Isn't it all too big, too dark, too indescribable and incomprehensible to be brought to the attention of children especially? And how close can you take them without dimming their souls?

The school principal, Agata Kowol, is familiar with these questions and doubts. Perhaps she has never been deterred from showing her pupils the camp because her own life is inextricably tied up with it, in unexpected ways: her family suffered through World War II and the brutal occupation, just like everyone here. During the occupation, however, her mother was saved by a German, of all people; when she fell desperately ill and her life was in danger, it was a pharmacist by the name of Doctor Komraus who supplied his Polish patient with medicine, despite all prohibitions.

Kowol is, therefore, not the least suitable person to teach history without stereotyping. "Of course, we take the ages of the children into consideration," she says, "but at some point, we introduce them all to the topic." It is unavoidable for the students, anyway, especially by the time they can read the writing on the striped wall of the entrance halls: "Memorial to the Child Prisoners of

Auschwitz." If ever there was a living memorial, then it is this school, or rather, the everyday life that takes place here: cramming for tests, cheating, getting pimples, wearing braces, daydreaming, sitting in detention, doing gymnastics, playing ball, pondering, finding other people stupid. And not circumventing the camp.

"We visit the children's barracks in the camp, collaborate on peace projects with partner schools around the world, but above all, we mark the two anniversaries of the displacement and the liberation," says the vice-principal Beata Herman.

The fact of the displacement is hardly known. No wonder, when one of the greatest crimes of all time took place right next door. Who then could really care about the relatively mild fate of a few thousand displaced persons from Brzezinka? This mixture of horror and shame is probably the reason why the displacement of people in the area surrounding the camp has only recently been publicly addressed. In 2001 an official commemorative stone was set up in front of Birkenau's "gate of death." In 2016, a private initiative gave a brass plate to Brzezinka, as well.

On April 22, 1941, the residents of Brzezinka were forcibly evicted, along with around 8,500 other inhabitants of seven other villages. The Nazis did not want any witnesses. At the same time the Germans sent the entire Jewish population of the city of Oświęcim—around 6,000 men, women, and children, to ghettos. Nearly all of the Jewish residents were murdered; most of the villagers returned.

Every April 22, three schoolchildren from Brzezinka who have earned the honor through their special achievements are allowed to carry the school flag in front of the "gate of death" in Birkenau. It is a heavy piece of cloth. On one side is the Polish eagle embroidered in silver against a red ground; the other side is made out of the kind of cheap ticking once used to make the prisoners' uniforms. A warning is embroidered on it: may the fate of the child prisoners in Auschwitz never become legend but serve as a warning forever. This flag usually hangs in the second-floor hallway, where the ping-pong table is opened up during breaks between classes.

Across from that is the narrow, windowless room containing the urn. Above the display case, old photos of child prisoners taken in the camp's registration office are lined up. The prints are small, some of them are creased, and they are yellowing. You have to get close to see the details—the smooth skin of their faces, the roughly shaved heads, the little bodies paralyzed with fear, the panic-stricken looks. Everything is frozen in these pictures, bureaucratically precise and indifferent; a blank background, the hard shadows of spotlights and their reflections in the children's eyes. Horror creeps into the minds of anyone who sees them. And you understand what the former schoolchild Gosia Musielak—born in Brzezinka in the mid-1980s—tells you: "Every time I go to the camp I am overcome with howling misery, but as soon as I am out, this place here again is my home."

On January 27, 2017, she was one of the first to hug an elderly lady at the entrance to the school. Lidia Skibicka-Maksymowicz, born in 1939, survived a year in the death camp. She is a kind of patron of the school; she was present at its dedication in 1968 and since then she has attended the liberation ceremony every year. Besides Lidia Skibicka-Maksymowicz, Stefania Wernik was also in attendance. She was born in Birkenau in November 1944 and escaped the water bucket that stood ready to drown the newborn. Lidia and Stefania were two of the two hundred thousand children in the camps at Auschwitz. Only a few dozen of them survived.

Unlike Stefania, born just before the liberation, Lidia consciously experienced the camp. She came from the Belarusian-Polish border region, where she—a toddler—along with her parents and grandparents were taken prisoner by the Germans in December 1943. After a couple of weeks in prison they were transported to Auschwitz; spending a few days in a cattle car, without water, food, or toilets. Of the "selection" in Birkenau, Lidia recalls dogs barking, screaming, SS uniforms, and a Babylonian confusion of languages. Ultimately, she and her mother found themselves in one line, and she saw her grandparents leaving in another line—to the gas chamber, as they later realized.

Healthy mothers and children were brought to a quarantine block; the women were undressed and had their heads shaved—at first, Lidia did not recognize her mother. Then both were tattooed with their prisoner numbers. Lidia sat frozen on her mother's lap and did not flinch at the prick of the needle, which is why her number, in blue numerals a few centimeters tall, is even and clearly legible: 70072.

After being tattooed, the children were forcibly separated from their mothers. "Torn away, like animals," says Lidia. Female SS guards beat the mothers away with clubs; Lidia went to a separate barrack, along with many other children from different countries. She recalls that everything went extremely fast, without any resistance, in shock, weak with hunger and fear. The barracks were dark; the only light was from the guard towers. At night the temperatures fell to twenty degrees below zero Celsius; the thin blankets on the bunk beds were filthy and louse-ridden. Hardly anyone understood her; only a few children knew her language.

Lidia's mother was twenty-two at the time. She was assigned to forced farm labor in neighboring Harmęże. There she always managed to find the food that Polish civilians hid for the prisoners. Every night the young woman took the risk of sneaking over to the children's barracks in the dark. From outside, she called to her daughter and gave her the food she had smuggled through a hatch. Lidia saw nothing of her mother but the hands that brought her food. Her cot was near the door, all the way down near the floor. From there she could look directly at the perfectly polished boots of the SS when the guards came in.

As prisoners, the children's days were hellish. They froze and starved. "We behaved like animals," says Lidia. Every morning they had to appear for roll call and bring the bodies of those who had died in their barracks during the night. The bodies were thrown on a wagon and their numbers crossed off the list.

Unlike adult prisoners, children under twelve years old were not fated to be "exterminated through work"; the camp doctors used them for medical experiments. The children knew that Dr. Josef Mengele in particular was dangerous. His office was near the crematoria. Often, children did not return from Mengele's experiments, and so they tried to hide from him. Nevertheless, he always managed to take Lidia with him. Mengele gave her injections, took her blood, and put drops in her eyes. Her health began to fail. Help came from one of the prisoners who had given birth in the camp, but whose child had been murdered by the SS right after it was born. This woman gave Lidia the milk from her breasts. Then new prisoners arrived who helped in different ways: survivors of the Warsaw Uprising were brought to Birkenau in October 1944, and the women were sent to the children's barracks. Lidia remembers the women from Warsaw well: they sang and played lovingly with the children, giving them the kind of attention that was completely unusual in the camp, and therefore all the more valuable.

Then the medical experiments stopped. Lidia thinks that she sensed the Germans' intention: to erase all of the traces. In the late autumn of 1944, the gas chambers and crematoria were demolished. Lidia saw her mother only rarely. Before the camp was cleared out, she came to Lidia one last time and reminded her: "Don't forget your name, your age, and where you come from! I'll get you later!"

Lidia and around sixty other child prisoners remained in the camp, neglected. After the liberation a couple of strangers came to her. The strangers embraced her. The woman and the man took her to live an ordinary Polish life near Oświęcim. At first, Lidia was completely distraught. She asked when Mengele was coming and wanted to know that there were no dangerous dogs. She had to be told what a bath was, and a bed. For nearly six months Lidia needed daily medical treatments in order to heal from the physical torture she underwent in the camp. The psychological wounds were much deeper. "I had no identity, just the number, was afraid of intimacy, comfort, hugs. When my foster parents gave me a doll, I had no idea what to do with it. I played 'Selection' with other children. I put them in rows and said, 'You go to the hospital, you get the gas!' Most of the parents in the neighborhood wanted to keep their children away from this 'Lidia from the camp,' as I was called. After three years with my stepparents I was adopted, given a new name, papers, and was baptized. Still, I often covered the tattoo on my arm with an adhesive bandage, in order to avoid questions."

It was not until seventeen years after the liberation that Lidia discovered that her mother had survived. The Germans marched her from Birkenau to Ravensbrück to Bergen-Belsen. When she was liberated by the American army there, she weighed just thirty-seven kilos. When Lidia saw her mother again in 1962, she decided to carry on with her life as a Pole.

She worked as a chemist in Oświęcim until she retired. So for her it is not far to the school in Brzezinka. She makes the trip every year on January 27. Liberation day is the most important day of the school year. The gymnasium is decorated with paper garlands and filled with chairs; the mayor and a historian give speeches. Then the two camp survivors talk with each other. Lidia is the only speaker that day who does not need a microphone. Her voice fills the space. Energetically, she talks to the costumed pupils, describing the horrors of the camp and challenging her listeners to stand in the way of all contempt for humanity.

Finally, at the end, the nervously waiting actors stand on stage. Students of all ages perform dances, songs, and a play, in which love and life are victorious over terror and darkness. Teachers help out, parents and students beam, displays blink, flashes go off, applause resounds. At the end, all of the guests of honor receive cuddly hearts sewn by hand. Lidia Skibicka-Maksymowicz has no more time for conversation. Because a pack of beaming, excited children surround the old lady. She has to sign a lot of autographs now.

28, 29 BRZEZINKA
Schülerin und Schüler der Schule von Brzezinka in Festkleidung am Tag der Befreiung, 27. Januar

28, 29 BRZEZINKA
Schoolchildren in party clothes in Brzezinka on Liberation Day, January 27

30 AUSCHWITZ I / STAMMLAGER, KOMMANDANTUR
Die ehemalige Kommandantur wird seit Jahrzehnten als Wohnhaus für langjährige und ehemalige Mitarbeiter des Staatlichen Museums Auschwitz genutzt.

30 AUSCHWITZ I/MAIN CAMP, COMMAND HEADQUARTERS
For decades, the former command headquarters has been used as a residence for longterm and retired employees of the Auschwitz-Birkenau State Museum.

32 AUSCHWITZ I / STAMMLAGER
Blick aus dem Fenster der Baracke 24, früher Lagerbordell, heute Museumsarchiv.
Der Bordellbesuch war privilegierten Häftlingen vorbehalten, als Prämie für besondere Arbeitsleistung. Weibliche Häftlinge, die als »asozial« eingestuft waren, wurden von der SS zur Prostitution im Lagerbordell gezwungen. Ungefähr sechzig deutsche, polnische und ukrainische Frauen waren davon betroffen, in den beiden Lagern Auschwitz I und III (Monowitz). Wenn sie mit einer Geschlechtskrankheit infiziert wurden, stellte die SS sie für medizinische Versuche zur Verfügung; wurden sie schwanger, folgte Zwangsabtreibung. Das Bordell im Stammlager existierte von Juni 1943 bis wenige Tage vor der Befreiung im Januar 1945.
Nach dem Zweiten Weltkrieg wurden die Lagerbordelle tabuisiert. Aus Scham verschwiegen die zwangsprostituierten Frauen ihre Leiden. Sie wurden in beiden deutschen Staaten nicht als NS-Opfer anerkannt und erhielten bis in die Neunzigerjahre keine Entschädigungen.

32 AUSCHWITZ I/MAIN CAMP
View from the window of barracks 24, formerly the camp brothel, now housing the museum's archives.
A visit to the brothel was reserved for privileged prisoners, as a reward for certain achievements at work. Female prisoners who were assessed as "antisocial" were forced into prostitution in the camp brothel by the SS. Around sixty German, Polish, and Ukrainian women in the two camps Auschwitz I and III (Monowitz) were affected. If they contracted sexually transmitted diseases, the SS sent them to be used in medical experiments; if they became pregnant, they were forced to abort. The brothel in the main camp existed from June 1943 until just a few days before the liberation in January 1945.
After World War II, the camp brothels were a taboo subject. Out of shame, the women forced into prostitution kept silent about their suffering. Neither West Germany nor East Germany recognized them as victims of the Nazis, and they received no reparations until the 1990s.

34 AUSCHWITZ I / STAMMLAGER, MAGAZIN

Im Magazin des Stammlagers wurde u. a. das Giftgas Zyklon B zur Tötung der Häftlinge gelagert. 1984 hatten deutsche und belgische Katholiken die Gründung eines Karmelitinnenklosters im ehemaligen Magazingebäude betrieben. Sie nannten es »eine geistige Festung, Unterpfand für die Bekehrung unserer verirrten Brüder«. Neben dem Kloster stellten Unbekannte dann 1998 das acht Meter hohe Kreuz auf, das für den Besuch von Papst Johannes Paul II. 1979 im ehemaligen Konzentrations- und Vernichtungslager Auschwitz-Birkenau errichtet worden war. Daraufhin entbrannte ein erbitterter Streit über die angemessene Form des Gedenkens zwischen jüdischen Organisationen und nationalkonservativen polnischen Katholiken. Nachdem der Jüdische Weltkongress drohte, die Gedenkveranstaltungen anlässlich des 50. Jahrestags des Aufstands im Warschauer Ghetto zu boykottieren, lenkte die katholische Seite ein. Der Papst ordnete den Umzug der Karmelitinnen und den Abbau des Kreuzes an.

34 AUSCHWITZ I/MAIN CAMP, STOREHOUSE

In 1984 German and Belgian Catholics opened a Carmelite convent in a building that had once served as a storehouse for, among other things, the poisonous gas Zyklon B used to murder prisoners. They called it "a spiritual fortress, a pledge to convert our erring brethren." In 1998 unknown persons installed an eight-meter-tall cross near the convent; it had been erected in conjunction with the visit of Pope John Paul II at the former concentration and extermination camps at Auschwitz-Birkenau in 1979. There ensued a bitter dispute between Jewish organizations and nationalist, conservative Polish Catholics over the appropriate form of commemoration. After the World Jewish Congress threatened to boycott the commemoration of the fiftieth anniversary of the Warsaw Uprising, the Catholics relented. The pope ordered the removal of the Carmelite nuns and the cross.

35 AUSCHWITZ II / BIRKENAU

Zugangsweg von einem Nebengleis der Eisenbahnanlage Auschwitz zum Torhaus (»Todestor«) des ehemaligen Vernichtungslagers Birkenau. Die Deportationszüge, die etwa eine halbe Million Juden aus ganz Europa nach Birkenau brachten, hielten zwischen Frühjahr 1942 und April 1944 an einem Nebengleis der Eisenbahnanlage »Bahnhof West/Auschwitz«, etwa einen Kilometer vom Tor des Lagers entfernt. Von dort mussten die Deportierten zu Fuß weitergehen. Ab Ende April 1944 fuhren die Züge direkt in das Vernichtungslager nahe der Gaskammern/Krematorien II und III.

35 AUSCHWITZ II/BIRKENAU

The path leading from the siding at the Auschwitz railroad to the gatehouse ("gate of death") of the former Birkenau death camp. Between spring 1942 and April 1944, the trains that deported around five hundred thousand Jews from all over Europe to Birkenau halted at a siding of the Bahnhof West/Auschwitz station, about a kilometer away from the gate of the camp. The passengers had to walk from there. In late April 1944 the trains went directly to the camp, stopping near the gas chambers and Crematoria II and III.

37 AUSCHWITZ II / BIRKENAU, GLEISANLAGE

Das Gleis zum Vernichtungslager Birkenau führt heute von der Gedenkstätte nahe der »Alten Judenrampe« in einem Bogen über öffentlichen sowie privaten Grund. Es kreuzt mehrere Straßen und Felder. Auf dem letzten Stück vor dem Lagertor verläuft das Gleis auf einem flachen Schotterdamm über freies Feld, wo es unter Buschwerk und jungen Bäumen allmählich verschwindet.

37 AUSCHWITZ II/BIRKENAU, TRAIN TRACKS

The train track leading to the Birkenau death camp now runs in an arc from the memorial site near the "Alte Judenrampe" (Old Jewish Ramp) across public and private land. It crosses several streets and fields. On the last stretch before the gate to the camp, the track runs on a flat, gravel embankment across an open field, then gradually disappears into the bushes and young trees.

38 AUSCHWITZ II / BIRKENAU, HAUS UND GARTEN VON EMILIA KRAMARCZYK

In unmittelbarer Nachbarschaft des Vernichtungslagers Birkenau liegt die Ortschaft Brzezinka. Zu Beginn des Lagerbaus im Frühjahr 1941 wurde Brzezinka durch die deutschen Besatzer zwangsgeräumt, ebenso die benachbarten Dörfer Pławy, Babice, Broszkowice, Budy, Harmęże und Rajsko. In Budy bekam die Bevölkerung 15 Minuten Zeit, ihre Häuser zu verlassen; Brzezinka wurde am 22. April geräumt, und danach bis auf einige wenige Gebäude in der Ortsmitte abgetragen. Das anfallende Material wurde zur Errichtung des Lagers verwendet. Nach Kriegsende vier Jahre später fand der umgekehrte Transfer statt: Die vertriebenen Einwohner kehrten zurück und bauten neu, teils mit Material aus dem leerstehenden Lager. Die Familie von Emilia Kramarczyk hatte Glück. Sie hatte überlebt und durfte die gut erhaltenen Fundamente ihres Hauses, das beim Abriss noch keine fünf Jahre alt war, wieder bebauen. Das Grundstück befindet sich genau außerhalb einer Sperrzone rund um das ehemalige Lagergelände, auf dem nach der Befreiung jede Bebauung verboten wurde. Heute hat das Haus dieselbe Größe wie der Vorgängerbau von 1937, allerdings untersagt die Bauordnung Fenster in Richtung Schutzgebiet, also zum ehemaligen Lager hin. Emilia Kramarczyk wurde als jüngste von drei Schwestern kurz nach Kriegsende geboren, nahe des Bahnhofs, der zwischen Brzezinka und Oświęcim liegt; ihr Vater war Eisenbahner. Diese Arbeit war angesehen und gut bezahlt, Eisenbahner konnten sich damals größere Häuser leisten als die traditionellen Holzbauten der Bauern, zudem vornehmere, weil aus Ziegeln gemauert. Etliche Verwandte von Emilia profitierten ebenfalls vom wirtschaftlichen Aufschwung am Eisenbahnknotenpunkt. Sie bauten sich Mitte der Dreißigerjahre entlang derselben Straße ihre Eigenheime, eine kleine Großfamiliensiedlung. Vor dem deutschen Überfall auf Polen arbeitete die Mutter von Emilia als Hausmädchen bei einer der vielen wohlhabenden jüdischen Familien von Oświęcim. Ihr Vater wurde auch während der Okkupation weiter im kriegswichtigen Eisenbahnwesen beschäftigt, er musste bombardierte Gleise ausbessern. Die dazu gehörende Fachvokabel spricht Emilia Kramarczyk als einziges Wort in ihrer langen Erzählung auf Deutsch aus: »Bauzug«. Obwohl sie selbst den Zweiten Weltkrieg nicht erlebt hat, sind ihr dessen Schrecken präsent, als traumatische Erfahrungen in der Familie. Emilias Großvaters starb 1944 bei einem Luftangriff wenige hundert Meter von seinem Grundstück bei den Eisenbahngleisen. Nur durch Zufall überlebte Emilias Vater, der ganz in der Nähe war. Kurz nach dem Angriff kam er an den Ort der Bombeneinschläge, rannte heim und vergrub sich weinend in seinem Bett. Die Überreste des toten Großvaters konnten von Emilias Großmutter nur durch einen Ring am Finger und Teile der Beinbekleidung identifiziert werden.

Auch von den Erlebnissen einer 1930 geborenen Tante berichtet Emilia Kramarczyk im Detail. Das Mädchen sah während des Krieges immer wieder Tote auf den Straßen, bekam aber von seinen Eltern nur die allzu durchsichtige Beschwichtigung zu hören, dass diese Leute schliefen. Emilia hatte als Kind solche Angst vor dem Thema Krieg, dass sie sich die Ohren zuhielt, wenn ihr Vater davon erzählte. Sie weigerte sich auch, das ehemalige Lager zu betreten, das sie wie viele Leute hier »das Museum« nennt; aber sie erinnert sich, mit ihren Eltern zum Pilze sammeln in die Wälder ringsum gegangen zu sein. Erst seit sie erwachsen ist, hat sie das ehemalige Lager ab und zu besucht. Im Turm über dem »Todestor«, das man vom Garten aus sieht, war sie nur ein einziges Mal. Auch ihre Kinder und Enkel befassen sich nicht intensiv mit dem Areal, es ist schließlich in ihren Augen immer schon da gewesen. Vor einigen Jahren aber kam das Thema unversehens ganz nah: Eine Gruppe russischer Überlebender besuchte das ehemalige Lager, zufällig lernten sie Emilia Kramarczyk kennen. Da sie eine gastfreundliche Person ist, lud sie alle ein, brachte einige zum Übernachten bei ihrer Tochter unter, bügelte die gestreiften Häftlingsuniformen, sah die tätowierten Nummern auf faltigen Armen, und bewirtete die ganze Gruppe mit guten hausgemachten Koteletts. Emilia Kramarczyk strahlt, wenn sie davon berichtet. Es muss eine herzliche Begegnung gewesen sein.

38 AUSCHWITZ II/BIRKENAU, EMILIA KRAMARCZYK'S HOUSE AND GARDEN

The community of Brzezinka is located right next to the Birkenau extermination camp. In spring 1941, when construction began on the camp, Brzezinka was forcibly evacuated by the German occupiers, as were the neighboring villages of Pławy, Babice, Broszkowice, Budy, Harmęże, and Rajsko. In Budy residents had fifteen minutes to leave their houses; Brzezinka was evacuated on April 22, and afterward most of it was demolished, apart from a few buildings at the center of the village. The ruins were used to construct the camp. After the end of the war four years later, the reverse occurred: the displaced villagers returned and rebuilt, using some of the materials from the deserted camp. Emilia's family was lucky. They had survived and were able to rebuild their house, which was not yet five years old at the time it was demolished, on its well-preserved foundations. The property is just outside the restricted zone surrounding the camp, where, after the liberation, all construction was forbidden. Today the house is the same size as its 1937 predecessor, although building regulations forbid having any windows that look out onto the protected zone, that is, the old camp.

The youngest of three sisters, Emilia Kramarczyk was born just after the war's end near the train station that lies between Brzezinka and Oświęcim; her father was a railway man. His was a respected and well-paid job; at the time railroad employees could afford houses that were not only bigger than the farmers' traditional wooden structures but also more distinguished, because they were masonry houses. Many of Emilia's relatives also benefitted from the economic boom at the railway junction. In the mid-1930s they built their own homes along the same street, creating a smaller large family settlement. Before the German invasion of Poland, Emilia's mother was a housemaid for one of the many well-to-do Jewish families in Oświęcim. During the occupation her father continued to be employed on the railroad, which was important to the war effort; his job was to repair tracks that had been bombed. In her long narrative, Emilia's only German word is a technical one: Bauzug ("work train"). Even though she herself did not experience World War II, its horrors are still present for her, owing to her family's traumatic experiences. Her grandfather died in 1944 during an air raid just a few hundred meters from his property near the train tracks. Her father, who was close by, survived only by chance. Shortly after the attack he arrived at the site where the bomb hit, ran home, and buried himself in his bed, crying. Emilia's grandmother was only able to identify her husband's remains from the ring on his finger and parts of his trousers.

Emilia also reports in detail the experiences of her aunt, who was born in 1930. During the war, the girl kept seeing dead people on the streets, but her parents simply gave her the all-too-transparent reassurance that these people were just asleep. As a child, Emilia was so afraid of the war as a topic of conversation that she covered her ears when her father talked about it. She also refused to enter the former camp, which she calls "the museum," as many people here do; but she recalls that she and her parents gathered mushrooms in the surrounding woods. Now that she is an adult, she visits the old camp every now and then. She has only been inside the tower above the "gate of death" once, even though it can be seen from the garden. Neither her children nor her grandchildren are particularly interested in the area, either; after all, in their eyes, it has always been there. A few years ago, however, the topic unexpectedly seemed closer: a group of Russian survivors visited the old camp and happened to meet Emilia. Because she is a hospitable person, she invited them all to her place; some spent the night at her daughter's house. She ironed their striped prison uniforms, saw the numbers tattooed on their wrinkled arms, and fed the entire group well with her homemade cutlets. Emilia beams when she talks about it; it must have been a warm encounter.

40 LINKS, **BRZEZINKA/BIRKENAU, HAUS DER FAMILIE RYDZOŃ**
Kein anderes Haus liegt so nahe am »Todestor« des ehemaligen Vernichtungslagers

Birkenau wie das der Familie Rydzoń. Es steht auf den Betonfundamenten des deutlich größeren Wohnsitzes, den die Vorfahren von Adam Rydzoń 1938 in Brzezinka errichtet hatten. Im Jahr darauf begann der Zweite Weltkrieg mit dem Überfall der deutschen Wehrmacht auf Polen. Die Rydzońs wurden im Dezember 1939 von den Besatzern vertrieben, sie durften nur Handgepäck mitnehmen. Wie die meisten Gebäude des Dorfs wurde später auch das Haus der Familie Rydzoń auf Befehl der Nationalsozialisten abgerissen, um das Lager Birkenau zu errichten.

Der überwiegende Teil des sieben Hektar großen Grundbesitzes der Familie Rydzoń liegt auf dem Gelände des ehemaligen Lagers. Da sich ihr Grundstück innerhalb der Bauverbotszone befand, die nach der Befreiung von Auschwitz-Birkenau am 27. Januar 1945 rund um das Lager festgelegt wurde, erhielt die Familie zunächst nur die Genehmigung für dieses kleine Holzhaus. Darin lebten fünf Personen vier Jahrzehnte lang auf engstem Raum. Erst 2005 gestatteten die Behörden den Bau eines größeren Hauses direkt daneben.

40 *LEFT,* **BRZEZINKA/BIRKENAU, THE RYDZOŃ FAMILY'S HOUSE**
No other house is so close to the Birkenau camp's "gate of death" as the one belonging to the Rydzoń family. It is built on the concrete foundation of what was once a much bigger house, erected in Brzezinka in 1938 by Adam Rydzoń's ancestors. The following year World War II began when the Germans invaded Poland. The Rydzońs were evicted from their home by the German occupiers in December 1939; they were only allowed to take hand luggage. Like most of the buildings in the village, the Rydzoń family's house was also torn down on the orders of the National Socialists in order to build the Birkenau camp.

Most of the Rydzoń family's seventeen acres of land is part of the site of the former camp. Because their property was inside of the no-construction zone that was set up around the Auschwitz-Birkenau camp after it was liberated on January 27, 1945, the family initially received a permit for nothing more than this small wooden house. Five people lived in very close quarters there for four decades. It was not until 2005 that the authorities granted permission for the construction of a larger house right next door.

40 *RECHTS,* **AUSCHWITZ II / BIRKENAU, »ALTE JUDENRAMPE«**
Die Deportationszüge, die etwa eine halbe Million Juden aus ganz Europa nach Birkenau brachten, hielten zwischen Frühjahr 1942 und April 1944 an einem Nebengleis der Eisenbahnanlage von Auschwitz, etwa einen Kilometer vom Tor des Vernichtungslagers entfernt. Die exakte Lage der ersten Rampe, an der die Deportationszüge endeten, ist nicht bekannt. Sie befand sich unter oder hinter dem Gestrüpp auf diesem Bild.

40 *RIGHT,* **AUSCHWITZ II/BIRKENAU, "OLD JEWISH RAMP"**
Between spring 1942 and April 1944, the transport trains that deported around five hundred thousand Jews from everywhere in Europe to Birkenau halted at a siding at the Auschwitz station, around a kilometer from the gate of the extermination camp. The exact location of the first platform where the trains stopped is unknown. It was either below or behind the bushes in this picture.

41 AUSCHWITZ I / STAMMLAGER, GARTEN DES LAGERKOMMANDANTEN RUDOLF HÖSS
Für Garten- und Hausarbeit hatte Höß beliebigen Zugriff auf Häftlinge des unmittelbar nebenan liegenden Konzentrationslagers. Einen Teil des Gartens ließ Höß von einem inhaftierten polnischen Landschaftsarchitekten entwerfen.

Für den Haushalt wählten er und seine Frau Hedwig bevorzugt Zeugen Jehovas, da sie diese als ehrlich und friedlich einschätzten. Etwa 15 bis 20 weitere Häftlinge leisteten im Garten Zwangsarbeit. Die Bedingungen waren vergleichsweise gut, stellten für die Häftlinge aber keine Überlebensgarantie dar. Höß' Schwager Gerhard Fritz Hensel, der seine Ferien bei der Familie des Lagerkommandanten verbrachte, berichtet von der Erschießung eines Gärtners durch den Sicherheitsdienst der SS. Höß selbst stellt in seinen Memoiren fest: »Meine Familie hatte es in Auschwitz gut. Meine Frau hatte ihr Blumenparadies. Immer hatten die Kinder im Garten besonderes Viehzeug, stets gab es etwas Interessantes.«

41 AUSCHWITZ I/MAIN CAMP, GARDEN BELONGING TO THE CAMP COMMANDANT RUDOLF HÖSS
For gardening and housework, Höss was able to make discretionary use of prisoners from the concentration camp right next door. He had part of the garden designed by an imprisoned Polish landscape architect.

Höss and his wife, Hedwig, preferred Jehovah's Witnesses to do their housework, because they considered them honest and peaceful. Around fifteen to twenty other prisoners were forced to labor in the garden. The conditions were comparatively good but did not guarantee survival for the prisoners. Höss's brother-in-law, Gerhard Fritz Hensel, who spent his holidays with the camp commander's family, reported that the SS security service shot one of the gardeners. In his memoirs, Höss himself stated: "My family had it good in Auschwitz. My wife had her floral paradise. The children always had special livestock in the garden; there was always something interesting."

42 AUSCHWITZ II / BIRKENAU
Zufahrt zum neuen Parkplatz und Besucherzentrum am ehemaligen Vernichtungslager Birkenau. Der Pfosten des Hinweisschildes steht im Gleisbett, über das von April 1944 an die Deportationszüge direkt in das Lager bis dicht vor die Gaskammern fuhren.

42 AUSCHWITZ II/BIRKENAU
Entrance to the new parking lot and visitor's center at the old Birkenau extermination camp. The signpost stands in the track bed that, from April 1944 onward, took the transport trains directly into the camp right up to the gas chambers.

43 AUSCHWITZ I / STAMMLAGER, KOMMANDANTUR
Die ehemalige Kommandantur wird seit Jahrzehnten als Wohnhaus für langjährige und ehemalige Mitarbeiter des Staatlichen Museums Auschwitz genutzt.

43 AUSCHWITZ I/MAIN CAMP, COMMAND HEADQUARTERS
For decades, the former command headquarters has been used as a residence for longterm and retired employees of the Auschwitz-Birkenau State Museum.

45 AUSCHWITZ I / STAMMLAGER, EHEMALIGE VILLA HÖSS
45 AUSCHWITZ I/MAIN CAMP, FORMER HÖSS VILLA

46, 48, 49 OŚWIĘCIM, BEREITSCHAFTSSIEDLUNG
Für die deutschen Zivilangestellten der IG-Farben-Fabriken Auschwitz sowie für deren Familien mussten KZ-Häftlinge 1942/43 östlich des historischen Zentrums einen Stadtteil für ca. 6.000 Menschen errichten, die sogenannte »Bereitschaftssiedlung«. Die solide gebauten Wohnblocks werden noch heute bewohnt und derzeit umfassend saniert.

46, 48, 49 OŚWIĘCIM, ON-CALL SETTLEMENT
To house the German nonmilitary employees of the IG Farben factory in Auschwitz and their families, concentration camp prisoners had to build an entirely new quarter of the city, known as the Bereitschaftssiedlung or "on-call settlement," for around six thousand people, east of the city's historic center in 1942–43. The solidly constructed apartment blocks are still occupied today and are currently undergoing thorough renovation.

50 BRZEZINKA, ORTSMITTE
Ein von der SS genutztes Gebäude in der Ortsmitte. Nach dem Zweiten Weltkrieg wurde hier die provisorische Schule des Dorfes eingerichtet. Außerdem fanden in dem Gebäude die Entschädigungsverhandlungen statt. Heute dient es als Bürgermeisterbüro. Im Gemeindesaal halten lokale Vereine wie die Landfrauen ihre Treffen und Feiern ab.

50 BRZEZINKA, CENTER OF TOWN
A building used by the SS in the center of town. After World War II a village school was temporarily set up here. In addition, reparations negotiations took place in this building. Today it is the mayor's office. Local clubs like the Women's Farm Club hold their meetings and celebrations in the community hall.

51 BRZEZINKA, ORTSMITTE
51 BRZEZINKA, CENTER OF TOWN

52 AUSCHWITZ I / STAMMLAGER, SS-KOMMANDANTUR
Im Obergeschoss der SS-Kommandantur des Stammlagers befand sich das Büro des Kommandanten. Der großzügige Raum enthält Teile der originalen Ausstattung: die halbhohe dunkle Holzvertäfelung an allen Wänden, den Kachelofen, die gefliese Wandnische für ein Handwaschbecken, einige massive Holzmöbel wie Tisch, Schränkchen und kleine Kommoden sowie die wuchtigen Leuchter aus Holzbalken. Diese Deckenleuchten sind auch auf den einzig bekannten historischen Fotografien des Raums kurz nach der Befreiung zu sehen.
Heute wird der Raum als Schlafstätte für internationale Wissenschaftler und Freiwillige

genutzt, die im Staatlichen Museum Auschwitz-Birkenau arbeiten.

52 AUSCHWITZ I/MAIN CAMP, SS COMMAND OFFICE

The upper floor of the SS Command Office in the main camp contained the commandant's office. The generously sized space contains some of the original décor: the dark wooden wainscoting on all of the walls, the tiled stove, the tiled niche for a sink, some bulky wood furniture including a table, cupboards, and small chests of drawers, as well as the massive chandeliers made of wooden beams. These ceiling lights can be seen in the only known historical photograph of the room, taken shortly after the liberation.

Today the space is used as a bedroom for international scientists and volunteers working at the Auschwitz-Birkenau State Museum.

54, 55 AUSCHWITZ I / STAMMLAGER, SS-KOMMANDANTUR, NUTZGARTEN HÖSS

Im ersten Stock der ehemaligen Kommandantur liegen Räume mit Blick ins Lager. Dort wurden nach dem Zweiten Weltkrieg Wohnungen für Mitarbeiter des Museums eingerichtet. Seit 1966 lebt Teodozja Woitas hier. Sie kam damals als junge Frau aufgrund einer Zeitungsannonce zum Staatlichen Museum Auschwitz-Birkenau, das Mitarbeiter für die Gestaltung der Ausstellung suchte. Als Absolventin einer künstlerischen Fachschule in Lublin war sie qualifiziert und wurde umgehend eingestellt. In ihrer Heimat hatte der Großvater sie nach dem Krieg zur Besichtigung des ehemaligen Vernichtungslagers Maidanek mitgenommen, wo ihr Großonkel inhaftiert gewesen war. Die Begehung der Mordstätte hatte Teodozja als Kind kaum verkraftet. Umso wichtiger war es ihr später, den Besuchern des ehemaligen Konzentrations- und Vernichtungslagers Auschwitz-Birkenau diesen Ort erläutern zu können.

Im benachbarten Nutzgarten der Villa Höß hat Teodozja Woitas, wie alle Bewohner der Kommandantur, eine Parzelle zur Verfügung. Dort zieht sie Blumen und Gemüse. Über der Mauer ist der Kamin des Krematoriums zu sehen. Teodozja Woitas geht pragmatisch mit der historischen Hypothek ihres Lebensmittelpunktes um. So meinte sie zwar im Laufe der Jahre, des Nachts gelegentlich etwas wie Pochen an ihrer Wohnungstür zu hören, hielt dies aber stets für Einbildung und ist nie auch nur aufgestanden, um vor der Tür nachzusehen. Das tat sie erst, als Kollegen behaupteten, zwischen den Häftlingsbaracken gehe es nachts nicht mit rechten Dingen zu, man höre dort unheimliche Geräusche wie Wehklagen und Schritte. Kurzerhand machte Teodozja Woitas auf eigene Faust eine Kontrollrunde durchs nächtliche Lager, um den Spuk aufzuspüren, fand aber nichts Geisterhaftes. Über die spezielle Lage ihrer Wohnung sagt sie: »Es ist ruhig, praktisch und preiswert, hier zu wohnen; und wenn ich zum Fenster rausschaue, sehe ich über den Stacheldraht hinweg – im Erdgeschoss würde ich es nicht aushalten.«

54, 55 AUSCHWITZ I/MAIN CAMP, SS COMMAND OFFICE, THE HÖSS KITCHEN GARDEN

On the second floor of the former command office are rooms with a view into the camp. After World War II, apartments for museum employees were set up there. Teodozja Woitas has lived here since 1966. She came as a young women, in response to a newspaper ad seeking employees to design the exhibitions at the Auschwitz-Birkenau State Museum. As a graduate of an applied arts school in Lublin, she was qualified and hence was immediately hired. In her hometown, her grandfather took her to see the old Maidanek extermination camp after the war; her great-uncle had been a prisoner there. As a child, Teodozja could barely cope with the visit to the site of so many murders. It was all the more important to her later to be able to explain the place to those visiting the Auschwitz-Birkenau concentration camp.

Like all of the residents of the command office, Teodozja has use of a small parcel of land in the nearby kitchen garden belonging to the Villa Höss. There, she grows flowers and vegetables. The chimney of the crematorium can be seen above the wall.

Teodozja deals pragmatically with the historic burden of her place that is the center of her life. Over the years, she has thought she heard something like a knock at the door of her apartment occasionally at night, but she has always believed it was her imagination, and has never once gotten up to check outside the door. She did so only when her colleagues insisted that something was not right at night in between the prisoners' barracks; eerie noises, such as wailing and footsteps could be heard. Without further ado, Teodozja took it upon herself to make a nightly round through the camp, in order to track down the specter, but she found nothing ghostly. Talking about the special location of her apartment, she says, "It's quiet, practical, and affordable to live here; and when I look out of the window I can see over the barbed wire fence—I wouldn't be able to stand it on the ground floor."

56 AUSCHWITZ II / BIRKENAU
56 AUSCHWITZ II/BIRKENAU

57 LINKS, AUSCHWITZ II / BIRKENAU, GLEIS INS LAGER RECHTS, BRZEZINKA, WEG ZUM »TODESTOR«

Eine sehr persönliche Reaktion auf das welthistorische Verbrechen von Auschwitz ist, dort hinzuziehen. Diese Option wählen besonders stark religiös motivierte Menschen. Zu ihnen gehören Rick Wienecke und seine Nachbarn Cathy und Mark Warwick. Ihre Häuser liegen einander direkt gegenüber am Weg von der »Alten Judenrampe« zum Tor des Vernichtungslagers Birkenau, so nah am Lager, wie es die Bauordnung gerade noch erlaubt.

Rick Wienecke stammt aus Kanada und ist Bildhauer. 1977 ging er nach Israel und fand

dort zum christlichen Glauben. Der Künstler, der mittlerweile die israelische Staatsangehörigkeit besitzt, begann 2001 mit der Arbeit an der Großskulptur »Fountain of Tears«, die den Holocaust in Beziehung setzt zur Kreuzigung Jesu. Wienecke betont in beiden Geschehnissen die Tötung von Juden und betitelt sein Werk nach einem Zitat des Propheten Jeremiah: »Ach, dass ich Wasser genug hätte in meinem Haupte und meine Augen Tränenquellen wären, dass ich Tag und Nacht beweinen möchte die Erschlagenen in meinem Volk!«
Dass Wieneckes Sichtweise von jüdischer Seite akzeptiert wird, ist nicht selbstverständlich. In Auschwitz gab es jahrelang erbitterte Auseinandersetzungen über Form und Angemessenheit von christlichem und jüdischem Gedenken. Kern des Streits waren die Präsenz eines Karmelitinnenklosters in einem Nebengebäude des ehemaligen Stammlagers und die dortige Errichtung eines großen Kreuzes. 1993 drohte der Jüdische Weltkongress mit einem Boykott der Gedenkveranstaltungen zum 50. Jahrestag des Aufstands im Warschauer Ghetto. Erst die Entscheidung des Vatikans, das Kloster zu verlegen, beendete den Disput.
Das Original von »Fountain of Tears« steht im israelischen Arad, einer Stadt in der Wüste Negev westlich des Toten Meers. Mit Hilfe einer Stiftung und internationaler Unterstützung, unter anderem aus Deutschland, hat Rick Wienecke ein Duplikat in Brzezinka errichtet. Dort ist die Skulptur in einem Gebäude untergebracht, das sich von den anderen Privathäusern in der Umgebung äußerlich nicht unterscheidet. Geplant ist ein Ort der Reflexion, des Gebetes und Trostes für Trauernde. Auf der Website der Stiftung heißt es: »We are looking to the Lord for guidance and direction.«
Auf Gott vertrauen auch Cathy und Mark Warwick, die direkt gegenüber von Wienecke wohnen. Das entschieden christliche Ehepaar aus Großbritannien hat das Haus vor einigen Jahren von einem polnischen Eigentümer übernommen, der sich bereits vor dessen Fertigstellung durch den Andrang der Besucher des ehemaligen Vernichtungslagers gestört fühlte. Eben diesen Besuchern möchte das Ehepaar geistigen Beistand samt Unterkunft und Blick auf das ikonische Tor von Birkenau bieten. »Wir sind hier im Auftrag des Herren«, sagt Mark Warwick und erzählt: »Freunde kennen diesen Ort seit den Neunzigerjahren und berichten, dass es damals grauenhaft war, hier zu sein. Der Anblick ist zwar immer noch schockierend, aber die Atmosphäre ist mittlerweile gut. In Treblinka und Majdanek kann man kaum atmen, doch hier in Birkenau haben die vielen Gebete den Ort gereinigt. Man erlebt es, wenn man Spaziergänge rund ums Lager macht: In den Auenwäldern kann man Wildtiere sehen, und die Vögel sind zurück.«
Die Vögel waren nie weg. Lagerkommandant Höß hatte die Jagd auf sie verboten und den SS-Sturmmann Dr. Günther Niethammer, einen promovierten Ornithologen, zur Erforschung der Vogelwelt von Auschwitz freigestellt. Niethammers Kenntnisse waren auch nach dem Krieg geschätzt. 1957 wurde er Professor in Bonn, von 1968 bis 1973 amtierte er als Präsident der Deutschen Ornithologen-Gesellschaft. Niethammer starb 1974. Ein kollegialer Nachruf nennt den Vogelkundler von Auschwitz »einen liebenswerten und aufrechten Mann, vortrefflichen Forscher, gütigen, warmherzigen Menschen voll unerschütterlichen Frohsinns«.

57 *LEFT,* **AUSCHWITZ II/BIRKENAU, TRACKS LEADING INTO THE CAMP** *RIGHT,* **BRZEZINKA, PATH TO THE "GATE OF DEATH"**

One very personal reaction to the historic crimes committed at Auschwitz is to move there. This option is chosen by those strongly motivated by religion. Among them are Rick Wienecke and his neighbors Cathy and Mark Warwick. Their houses are directly across from each other on the way from the "Old Jewish Ramp" to the gate of the Birkenau extermination camp—as close to the camp as they can legally get.

Rick Wienecke is a sculptor from Canada. In 1977 he went to Israel, where he converted to Christianity. In 2001 the artist, who also now has Israeli citizenship, began working on a large sculpture titled Fountain of Tears, *which relates the Holocaust to the crucifixion of Jesus. Wienecke emphasizes the killing of Jews in both events, and the title of the work is a quote from the prophet Jeremiah: "Oh that my head were a spring of water and my eyes a fountain of tears. I would weep day and night for the slain of my people!"*

It cannot be taken for granted that Wienecke's perspective would be accepted by the Jewish side. In Auschwitz there were bitter disputes for years about the form and appropriateness of Christian and Jewish memorials. At the heart of this discord was the presence of a Carmelite convent in an outbuilding of the old main camp and the erection there of a large cross. In 1993 the World Jewish Congress threatened to boycott the commemoration of the fiftieth anniversary of the Warsaw Ghetto Uprising. Only the Vatican's decision to move the convent ended the dispute.

The original Fountain of Tears *is located in Arad, Israel, a city in the Negev Desert west of the Dead Sea. With the help of a foundation and international support, including from Germany, Wienecke erected a duplicate in Brzezinka. There, the sculpture is in a building whose exterior does not distinguish it from the other private homes around it. A place for reflection, prayer, and comfort for mourners is planned. On the foundation's website, it says, "We are looking to the Lord for guidance and direction."*

Cathy and Mark Warwick, who live right across the street from Wienecke, also trust in God. The decidedly Christian couple from Great Britain took over the house a few years ago from a Polish owner who was disturbed by the crowds of visitors to the former death camp even before work on it was completed. It is precisely to these visitors that the couple want to offer spiritual support, as well as lodgings and a view of Birkenau's iconic gate. "We're here in the name of the Lord," says Mark Warwick. He continues, "Friends knew this place from the nineties and reported that it was ghastly to be here. Although the view is still shocking, the atmosphere is now good. In Treblinka and Majdanek you can hardly breathe, but here in Birkenau many prayers have purified the place. You can experience it when you talk a walk around the camp: you can see wild animals in the forests along the river, and the birds are back." The birds were never gone. Camp commander Höss forbade hunting them and permitted the SS stormtrooper Dr. Günther Niethammer, who had a PhD in ornithology, to research the avian world of Auschwitz. Even after the war, Niethammer's knowledge was treasured. In 1957 he became a professor in Bonn; from 1968 to 1973 he was President of the Society of German Ornithologists. Niethammer died in 1974. A collegial obituary called the ornithologist of Auschwitz "a lovable and upstanding man, an excellent researcher, a good, warm-hearted person full of unshakable cheer."

58 AUSCHWITZ I / STAMMLAGER
Krupp-Halle, später Weichsel-Union-Metallwerke. Wahrscheinlicher Herstellungsort des

Sprengstoffs, der für den Aufstand des Sonderkommandos in das Vernichtungslager Birkenau geschmuggelt

58 AUSCHWITZ I/MAIN CAMP; KRUPP-HALLE, LATER THE WEICHSEL UNION METAL WORKS
Probably the place where the explosives were made before being smuggled into the Birkenau death camp and used in the uprising of the "special units."

59 AUSCHWITZ III/ MONOWITZ – BUNA
Blick von Monowice auf die Chemiefabrik, früher IG-Farben.

59 AUSCHWITZ III/MONOWITZ—BUNA
View from Monowice of the chemical factory, formerly IG Farben.

60 BRZEZINKA
60 BRZEZINKA

61 AUSCHWITZ II / BIRKENAU, STANDORT DER ERSTEN GASKAMMER
Einige hundert Meter nördlich des Lagerareals hatten Adolf Eichmann und der Lagerkommandant Rudolf Höß 1941 ein zwangsgeräumtes, einzeln stehendes Bauernhaus für den Umbau zu einer Gaskammer ausgesucht. Dieser erfolgte Anfang 1942. Das Gebäude wurde »Kleines Rotes Haus« oder »Bunker 1« genannt. Die ländliche Anmutung des Gebäudes in idyllischer Lage sollte die Opfer beruhigen. Ihrer Irreführung diente auch die Beschriftung des Eingangs mit den Worten »Zum Bad«.
Der Raum, in dem bis zu 800 Menschen dichtgedrängt vergast wurden, war ca. 90 Quadratmeter groß. Zunächst wurden die Leichen nach dem Entfernen von Zahngold, Eheringen, Schmuck und Haaren in einiger Entfernung verscharrt, ab September 1942 unter freiem Himmel verbrannt. Weil immer mehr Menschen deportiert wurden, reichte den Nationalsozialsten die Kapazität für den Massenmord im »Kleinen Roten Haus« bald nicht mehr aus, so dass ab Mitte 1942 ein weiteres ehemaliges Bauernhaus zur Gaskammer (»Weißes Haus«/ »Bunker 2«) umgebaut wurde. Diese Tötungsstätte fasste bis zu 1.200 Personen.

61 AUSCHWITZ II/BIRKENAU, SITE OF THE FIRST GAS CHAMBER
In 1941 Adolf Eichmann and the camp commandant Rudolf Höss selected an isolated farmhouse a few hundred meters north of the camp, whose inhabitants had been expelled, and had it turned into a gas chamber in early 1942. The building was known as the "Little Red House" or "Bunker 1." The countrified appearance of the building in an idyllic location was supposed to calm the victims. They were also deliberately misled by the sign at the entrance, which said, "To the bath." The room, in which up to eight hundred people were crowded in and gassed, was around ninety square meters in size. At first, after removing the gold fillings, wedding rings, jewelry, and hair from the bodies, they were buried some distance away. But from September 1942 onward they were burned in the open air. Because more and more people were being deported, the Nazis soon lacked the capacity for mass murder in the "Little Red House," so that in mid-1942 another former farmhouse was rebuilt into a gas chamber ("White House" or "Bunker 2"). This murder site held up to 1200 people.

62 LINKS, (81) AUSCHWITZ I / STAMMLAGER, »SCHUTZHAFTLAGER-ERWEITERUNG«
Seit Oktober 1944 existierende Unterkunft für ca. 6.000 weibliche Häftlinge. Hier wurden u. a. medizinische Versuche an Häftlingen durchgeführt. Das Areal befindet sich in unmittelbarer Nachbarschaft des Stammlagers, ist aber nicht Teil des Staatlichen Museums, sondern normal genutztes Wohnviertel und nicht als ehemaliger Teil des Lagers erkennbar.

62 LEFT, (81) AUSCHWITZ I/MAIN CAMP, "PROTECTIVE CUSTODY CAMP EXPANSION"
From October 1944 onward there were accommodations for around six thousand female prisoners. Here, medical experiments, among other things, were carried out on prisoners. The area is located in the immediate vicinity of the main camp but is not part of the state museum. Instead, it is an ordinary residential quarter and no longer recognizable as part of the old camp.

62 RECHTS, **AUSCHWITZ I / STAMMLAGER, MUSEUMSVERWALTUNG IN EHEMALIGER HÄFTLINGSBARACKE**

62 RIGHT, *AUSCHWITZ I/MAIN CAMP, MUSEUM OFFICE IN FORMER PRISON BARRACKS*

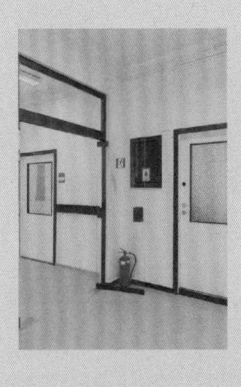

63 **AUSCHWITZ I / STAMMLAGER, MUSEUMSVERWALTUNG IN EHEMALIGER HÄFTLINGSBARACKE**

63 *AUSCHWITZ I/MAIN CAMP, MUSEUM OFFICE IN FORMER PRISON BARRACKS*

65 **AUSCHWITZ I / STAMMLAGER, BETONPFAHL DER LAGERUMZÄUNUNG**
Die »Normpfeiler der Einfriedung« sind auf Konstruktionszeichnungen der »Zentral-Bauleitung der Waffen-SS Abteilung Neubau Auschwitz« genau definiert. Sie wurden zu Hunderttausenden von Häftlingen gefertigt. Die Pfeiler trugen Stacheldrähte, die unter Starkstrom standen. Noch heute befinden sich viele dieser Pfosten in der Region.

65 *AUSCHWITZ I/MAIN CAMP, CONCRETE POST FROM THE FENCING AROUND THE CAMP*
The "standard posts for the enclosure" are precisely defined on the construction drawings for the Central Construction Management of the Waffen SS, New Construction Department Auschwitz. Hundreds of thousands of them were made by prisoners. The posts supported electrified, barbed wire fencing. Many can still be found in the region.

66 **PRIVATES WOHNHAUS IN BRZEZINKA**
In den 1930er Jahren wurden in Brzezinka viele Wohnhäuser in Ziegelbauweise errichtet. Das galt im bäuerlich geprägten Dorf mit seinen traditionellen Holzhäusern als modern und komfortabel, und es war möglich dank des wirtschaftlichen Aufschwungs seit dem Bau der nahe gelegenen Eisenbahn. Im April 1941 wurden die Einwohner von der SS vertrieben. KZ-Häftlinge mussten die Häuser abtragen. Das Material wie Ziegel, Balken, Dachpfannen etc. wurde für den Bau des Vernichtungslagers Auschwitz II / Birkenau verwendet. Knapp vier Jahre später befreite die Rote Armee das Lager und die vertriebenen Einwohner von Brzezinka kehrten zurück. Gegen den Widerstand der Behörden bauten sie die Ortschaft wieder auf, teilweise mit Material aus dem Lager. Es ist nicht rekonstruierbar, in welchen Gebäuden von Brzezinka heute wie viele Teile stecken, die vorher im Lager verbaut waren.

66 *PRIVATE HOUSE IN BRZEZINKA*
In the 1930s many brick houses were constructed in Brzezinka. In the rural village with its traditional wooden houses, these buildings were considered modern and comfortable, and it was all made possible by the economic boom that followed the construction of the nearby railroad. In April 1941 the residents were expelled by the SS. Concentration camp prisoners had to demolish the houses. The bricks, beams, roof tiles, and other materials were used to construct the Auschwitz II/Birkenau death camp. Nearly four years later the Red Army liberated the camp and the displaced residents of Brzezinka returned. Despite resistance from the authorities, they rebuilt the town, using some of the materials from the camp. It is impossible to reconstruct which parts of the camp and how much of it are now in buildings in Brzezinka.

67 LINKS, **BRZEZINKA, BIRKENAU / AUSCHWITZ II**
RECHTS, **BRZEZINKA, PRIVATE WOHNHÄUSER**
Wo bis zu seinem Abriss das Dorf Brzezinka gestanden hatte, mussten KZ-Häftlinge 1941 eine SS-Kaserne mit Lazarett errichten. Ferner unterhielten die Nationalsozialisten hier einen landwirtschaftlichen Betrieb, den »Wirtschaftshof Birkenau«. Abgesehen von Fundamenten, auf die man überall im Boden trifft,

ist der einzige Rest dieser Infrastruktur ein massiver Kamin aus Ziegelmauerwerk, der heute mitten im Dorf steht.

67 LEFT, **BRZEZINKA, BIRKENAU/AUSCHWITZ II**
RIGHT, **BRZEZINKA, PRIVATE HOUSES**
On the site where the village of Brzezinka had once stood before it was demolished, concentration camp prisoners had to erect an SS barracks with a military hospital. Furthermore, the Nazis maintained an agricultural operation here, the Wirtschaftshof Birkenau. Apart from foundations, which can be seen everywhere in the ground, the only thing left from this infrastructure is a massive brick chimney, which stands in the middle of the village.

68 BRZEZINKA, PFARRKIRCHE »HEILIGE MUTTER GOTTES, KÖNIGIN VON POLEN«
Die Dorfkirche von Brzezinka befindet sich in einem Gebäude, das als SS-Kommandantur für die nie fertiggestellte Erweiterung des Vernichtungslagers Birkenau »Bauabschnitt III« errichtet wurde. Die Bilder in der Kirche thematisieren die Gegenwart des ehemaligen Vernichtungslagers. In einer Nische befindet sich ein Gedenkort für die Frauenrechtlerin, Philosophin und katholische Ordensfrau Edith Stein. Die Karmelitin, die aus einer jüdischen Familie stammte, wurde am 9. August 1942 in Birkenau ermordet.

68 BRZEZINKA, HOLY MOTHER OF GOD, QUEEN OF POLAND PARISH CHURCH
Brzezinka's church is located in a building that was built as an SS commander's office for the never completed extension of the Birkenau death camp, Bauabschnitt III, or Construction Phase III. The presence of the former death camp is a theme in the paintings inside the church. In a niche is a memorial to the women's rights activist, philosopher, and Catholic nun Edith Stein. The Carmelite nun, who came from a Jewish family, was murdered on August 9, 1942, in Birkenau.

69 BRZEZINKA, AUSGEGRABENE FUNDAMENTE, IM HINTERGRUND PFARRKIRCHE »HEILIGE MUTTER GOTTES, KÖNIGIN VON POLEN«

69 BRZEZINKA, EXCAVATED FOUNDATIONS. IN THE BACKGROUND: HOLY MOTHER OF GOD, QUEEN OF POLAND PARISH CHURCH

71 BRZEZINKA, JAN TOBIAS UND JAN KASPERCZYK, ZEITZEUGEN DER VERTREIBUNG 1941
Die beiden Jans sind Freunde fürs Leben. Sie kamen Mitte der Dreißigerjahre in Brzezinka zur Welt, gingen zusammen zur Schule, spielten im selben Fußballverein und hatten ganz normalen Umgang mit der Kultur der deutschen Minderheit im Dorf – 1939 lebten in Brzezinka etwa 60 Deutsche unter den knapp 4.000 Polen. Unter den Einwohnern waren 160 Juden. Die Familien Tobias und Kasperczyk lebten mit jüdischen Nachbarn zusammen im Haus, jüdische und christliche, polnische und deutschstämmige Kinder besuchten dieselbe Schulklasse. Noch heute kann Jan Kaspercyk aus dem Stand »Fuchs, du hast die Gans gestohlen« singen – auf Deutsch.
Mit dem Kindheitsidyll war es in der ersten Septemberwoche 1939 schlagartig vorbei. Der Zweite Weltkrieg hatte auch Brzezinka sofort erreicht. Die deutsche Luftwaffe bombardierte die Bahnanlagen am Rand des Dorfes. Die Familien Tobias und Kasperczyk waren in vielfacher Weise in die kriegerischen Zeitläufte verwickelt. Jan Kasperczyks älterer Bruder Władysław kannte einige politische Häftlinge, denen die Flucht aus dem Stammlager gelang. Die SS verhaftete und folterte ihn im Block 11, dem sogenannten »Todesblock«, in dessen Hof viele Erschießungen stattfanden. 16 Mitgefangene von Władysław wurden getötet, ihn selber ließen die Deutschen irgendwann gehen. Der Freigelassene war so traumatisiert, dass er lange über die Schrecken seiner Haft geschwiegen hat.

Auch Jan Tobias bekam noch als kleiner Junge bleibende Eindrücke vom Regiment der SS. Am 22. April 1941 hatten die Nationalsozialisten Brzezinka zwangsgeräumt (ebenso wie sieben weitere Dörfer in unmittelbarer Nähe), um das Vernichtungslager Birkenau zu errichten. Die Vertriebenen wussten nichts von diesen Plänen, sie hofften auf Rückkehr, schließlich standen ihre Häuser zunächst noch eine Weile leer. In dieser Phase schlichen sich immer wieder Einzelne ins Dorf, trotz strikter Verbote der Besatzer. Einmal nahm Jans Vater Josef Tobias seinen damals fünfjährigen Sohn bei einem solchen heimlichen Besuch mit. Doch während er dabei war, das Haus zu lüften, erschien eine dreiköpfige deutsche Patrouille. »Wir versteckten uns im Gebüsch, die Soldaten blieben wenige Meter entfernt stehen und steckten sich in aller Ruhe Zigaretten an. Mein Vater hatte höllische Panik. Er zog mich an sich und hielt mir den Mund zu. Seine Hand war nass vom Schweiß. Es dauerte wahrscheinlich nur ein paar Minuten; mir erschien es ewig, in meiner Todesangst.« Die Sache ging glimpflich aus, Vater und Sohn entkamen unentdeckt.

Josef Tobias war vor dem Zweiten Weltkrieg Bürgermeister in Brzezinka und zudem Lokführer. Aufgrund letzterer Tätigkeit wurde er als kriegswichtig eingestuft und durfte das Sperrgebiet rund um das Lager Birkenau betreten. Einmal musste er unter SS-Bewachung einen Deportationszug inspizieren, dessen Bremsen klemmten. Von der Lok aus konnte er sehen, wie die Häuser von Brzezinka abgerissen wurden. Josef Tobias gab Informationen zu Gefangenentransporten und SS-Personalien an die polnische Untergrundarmee weiter. Die Frauen der Familie packten Lebensmittelrationen und schickten ihre Kinder damit zu den Häftlingskolonnen, die tagsüber außerhalb der Lager Zwangsarbeit verrichteten. »Wir Kleinen waren unauffällige Kuriere«, erzählt Jan. »Ich habe oft auf diese Weise Essen zu Gefangenen gebracht, ohne aufzufliegen. Einmal habe ich gesehen, wie ein anderes Kind erwischt wurde. Der SS-Mann schüttete das Essen einfach weg und ließ das Kind laufen.«

Sein Vater Josef Tobias hatte ebenfalls Glück im Unglück. Er war später noch einmal zum leerstehenden Haus in Brzezinka gegangen und wurde dort aufgegriffen. Die SS sperrte ihn in ein nasses Kellerloch im Lager Birkenau. Nach einer Weile öffnete sich die Ausstiegsluke und Josef Tobias erblickte einen ehemaligen Kameraden aus seiner Dienstzeit bei der polnischen Armee – in SS-Uniform. Der Mann sorgte dafür, dass er Stroh in sein Verlies bekam. Drei Tage später brachten ihn die Wachen ins Stadtgefängnis von Auschwitz. Dort wurde Josef Tobias nach weiteren fünf Tagen entlassen, auf Intervention seines deutschen Vorgesetzten.

Die Geschichte seines Heimatdorfes beschäftigt Jan Tobias bis heute intensiv. Vor einigen Jahren veröffentlichte er ein umfangreiches Buch über die Historie von Brzezinka, die bis in das Jahr 1385 zurückreicht. 2015 beherbergte er Besucher aus Israel. Eine Frau seines Alters, Tochter ehemaliger Nachbarn, hatte sich mit dem Wunsch gemeldet, das Fenster zu finden, von dem aus sie als Kind das letzte Mal ihre Mutter gesehen hatte. Jan Tobias fand das Fenster. Über Leben und Sterben unter der deutschen Besatzung sagt der Chronist von Birkenau: »Alles hing davon ab, an wen man gerade zufällig geriet.«

71 BRZEZINKA, JAN TOBIAS AND JAN KASPERCZYK, WITNESSES TO THE EXPULSIONS OF 1941

The two Jans are lifelong friends. They were both born in the mid-1930s in Brzezinka, went to school together, played in the same football club, and had a totally normal relationship to the culture of the German minority in the village. In 1939 around sixty Germans lived among the approximately four thousand Poles. Among the residents were 160 Jews. The Tobias and Kasperczyk families lived in buildings with Jewish neighbors; Jewish and Christian, Polish and ethnic German children were in the same classes in the same school. Even today, Jan Kaspercyk can sing the German children's song "Fuchs, du hast die Gans gestohlen" (Fox, You Stole the Goose) right off the bat—in German.

In the first week of September 1939, this idyllic childhood came to an abrupt end. World War II intruded upon Brzezinka immediately. The German Luftwaffe bombed the train facilities on the edge of the village. The Tobias and Kasperczyk families were involved in many ways with the war era. Kasperczyk's older brother, Władysław, knew a few political prisoners who managed to escape from the main camp. The SS arrested and tortured him in Block 11, the "Death Block," where many were shot in the courtyard. Sixteen of Władysław's fellow prisoners were killed; at some point, the Germans let him go. After being released, he was so traumatized that he kept silent for a long time about the horrors of his imprisonment.

Even as a small boy, Jan Tobias had lasting impressions of the SS regiment. On April 22, 1941, the Nazis expelled the residents of Brzezinka (and seven other villages in the immediate vicinity) in order to build the Birkenau extermination camp. The displaced persons knew nothing of these plans; they hoped to return—after all, their houses still stood empty for a while. During this phase, individuals would sneak into the village again and again, despite the occupiers' strict prohibitions. Once, when Jan was five years old, his father, Josef Tobias, took him along on such a secret visit. But as he was airing out the house, a three-man German patrol appeared. "We hid in the bushes; the soldiers stood a few meters away from us and calmly lit their cigarettes. My father was panicking like hell. He pulled me to him and clapped his hand over my mouth. His hand was damp with sweat. It probably only lasted a couple of minutes, but for me, who was deadly afraid, it seemed like an eternity." The incident ended smoothly; father and son escaped undetected.

Before World War II, Josef Tobias had been the mayor of Brzezinka as well as a locomotive engineer. Owing to the latter position, he was classified as important to the war effort and was allowed to enter the restricted area surrounding the Birkenau camp. Once, under the watchful eye of the SS, he had to inspect a transport train whose brakes were sticking. From the locomotive he could see that the houses in Brzezinka had been demolished. Josef Tobias passed on information about prisoner transports and SS personnel to the Polish underground army. The women in the families packed food rations and sent their children with them to the columns of prisoners who labored outside the camp. "We little ones were inconspicuous couriers," says Jan Tobias. "I often brought food to prisoners this way, without being discovered. Once I saw another child get caught. The SS man simply scattered the food and let the child go."

Josef Tobias was also lucky when misfortune occurred. He had later gone once more to his empty house in Brzezinka and was arrested there. The SS locked him into a damp cellar hole in the Birkenau camp. After a while the exit hatch opened and he saw an old comrade from his days in the Polish army—wearing an SS uniform. The man made sure that he got some straw in his dungeon. Three days later the guards brought him to the city jail in Auschwitz. There, after five more days, he was released, thanks to the intervention of his German superior officer.

To this day, Jan Tobias continues his intensive study of the history of his native village. A few years ago he published an extensive book on the history of Brzezinka, which goes back to the year 1385. In 2015 he hosted visitors from Israel. A woman his own age, the daughter of a former neighbor, came with a request to find the window from which she had last seen her mother. Jan found the window. Talking about life and death under the German occupation, the chronicler of Birkenau says, "Everything depended upon who you happened to run into at the time."

72 AUSCHWITZ II / BIRKENAU, »ALTE JUDENRAMPE«

Die Deportationszüge, die etwa eine halbe Million Juden aus ganz Europa nach Birkenau brachten, hielten zwischen Frühjahr 1942 und April 1944 an einem Nebengleis der Eisenbahnanlage Auschwitz, etwa einen Kilometer vom Tor des Vernichtungslagers Birkenau entfernt. Am 29. April 1944 fuhr erstmals ein Zug bis zur neuen Rampe auf dem Lagergelände.

Im Jahr 2005 ist die Gedenkstätte an der »Alten Rampe« mit zwei historischen Viehwaggons angelegt worden. Sie befindet sich in der Nähe der ehemaligen Entladeplattform, die nicht erhalten blieb. Das benachbarte Grundstück gehört der Familie von Marcin Mozgała, der jahrelang mit den Behörden stritt, um dort bauen zu dürfen. Der Familienvater empfindet es als Zumutung, dass er erst 15 Jahre nach seiner Heirat die Erlaubnis bekam, sich auf dem eigenen Grund ein Haus zu bauen. Er ist froh, das Lagertor nur in der Ferne zu sehen.

72 AUSCHWITZ II/BIRKENAU, "OLD JEWISH RAMP"

Between spring 1942 and April 1944, the trains that deported around five hundred thousand Jews from all over Europe to Birkenau halted at a siding of the Auschwitz railway facilities, about a kilometer away from the gate of the Birkenau death camp. On April 29, 1944, the first train went all the way to the new platform in the camp.

In 2005 the memorial site at the "Old Ramp" was set up with two historical cattle cars.

They are near the area where the unloading platform was once located. The neighboring plot of land belongs to the family of Marcin Mozgała, who fought the authorities for years for permission to build there. This father of a family feels it was unreasonable that he had to wait fifteen years after he was married to get a permit to build a house on his own land. He is glad that only the gate of the camp can be seen in the distance.

74 AUSCHWITZ II / BIRKENAU
Am 22. April gedenken die Bürger von Brzezinka des Jahrestags ihrer Vertreibung 1941. Direkt vor dem »Todestor« von Birkenau findet eine Zeremonie mit Kranzniederlegung statt.

74 AUSCHWITZ II/BIRKENAU
On April 22 the citizens of Brzezinka commemorate the anniversary of their expulsion in 1941. A ceremony, including the laying of a wreath, takes place directly in front of the "gate of death" at Birkenau.

75 BRZEZINKA, SCHULE
75 BRZEZINKA, SCHOOL

76 BRZEZINKA, EHEMALIGES GELÄNDE DER SS-HUNDEZWINGER, TREPPENHAUS DER EHEMALIGEN HUNDEKÜCHE
Nahe der heutigen Ortsmitte von Brzezinka befindet sich das Gelände, auf dem die SS ihre Wachhundestaffel untergebracht hatte. Mit den Hunden wurden die Menschen in die Gaskammern getrieben. Nach dem Willen von Heinrich Himmler sollten sie zu »reißenden Bestien« abgerichtet werden, »die mit Ausnahme ihres Wärters jeden anderen zerreißen«. Mit Hilfe der Tiere sollte zudem der Personalbedarf der SS gesenkt werden. In Birkenau waren etwa 160 Hunde und deren Hundeführer stationiert.

Der polnische Staatsanwalt Jan Sehn veranschaulichte in Kriegsverbrecherprozessen der Fünfzigerjahre die Lebensbedingungen der Häftlinge auch anhand von Unterlagen der »Zentralen Bauleitung« über die Hundestaffel. Demnach hatten die Tiere in den Hundezwingern von Birkenau mehr Platz als die Häftlinge, die zum größten Teil in Wehrmachts-Pferdeställen des Bautyps 260/9 untergebracht waren. Diese Ställe waren für je 52 Tiere konzipiert, wurden in Birkenau aber mit 400 bis 800, in Extremfällen auch mit mehr als 1.000 Menschen belegt.

In der Ortsmitte von Brzezinka hatte die SS eine Gruppe massiver Betongebäude stehen lassen. Darin befand sich unter anderem die Küche der SS-Hundestaffel; heute sind hier ein Frisör und eine Textilienhandlung untergebracht.

76 BRZEZINKA, FORMER SITE OF THE SS KENNELS, STAIRCASE IN THE FORMER "DOG KITCHEN"
Near the center of Brzezinka is the site where the SS kept their "watchdog squadron." The dogs were employed to drive people into the gas chambers. According to the wishes of Heinrich Himmler, they were supposed to be trained as "ripping beasts ... who, with the exception of their keeper, tear everyone else apart." The animals were also meant to reduce the number of personnel required by the SS. Around 160 dogs and their handlers were stationed in Birkenau.

During the war crimes trials in the 1950s, the Polish prosecutor Jan Sehn illustrated the prisoners' living conditions using documents from the Central Construction Management about the dog squadron. According to the plans, the animals had more room in the kennels at Birkenau than prisoners, most of whom were housed in military stables of the 260/9 construction type. These stables were designed to hold fifty-two horses, but in Birkenau, they were occupied by four to eight hundred people, and, in extreme cases, with more than one thousand.

In the center of Brzezinka the SS left a group of massive concrete buildings standing. In them were the kitchen for the SS dog squadron, among other things. Today, they house a hair salon and a fabric shop.

77 BRZEZINKA, BÜRGERMEISTERBÜRO
Der Lageplan der Ortschaft verdeutlicht die Dimensionen. Das heutige Brzezinka hat ungefähr die gleiche Größe wie das Vernichtungslager Birkenau damals, das sich auf einer rechtwinklig strukturierten Fläche ausdehnte.

77 BRZEZINKA, MAYOR'S OFFICE
A map of the town clarifies the dimensions of the site. Brzezinka today is about the same size as the Birkenau death camp back then, occupied a rectangular area.

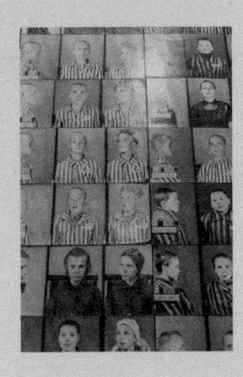

78 BRZEZINKA, GEDENKRAUM DER SCHULE
78 BRZEZINKA, MEMORIAL ROOM IN THE SCHOOL

79 LINKS, **EDWARD NAGY, ZEITZEUGE DER VERTREIBUNG 1941, ZWANGS-ARBEITER DER IG-FARBEN, BRZEZINKA**

Am 2. September 1939, einen Tag nach dem Beginn des deutschen Überfalls auf Polen, erlebte der damals zwölfjährige Edward Nagy das erste Bombardement seines Heimatorts. Der Luftangriff galt dem Bahnhof, jener Infrastruktur, die dem Dorf Wachstum und Wohlstand gebracht hatte (und die später einer der Gründe für die Errichtung des Vernichtungslagers Birkenau war). Edward Nagy erinnert sich an die Flucht mit seinen drei Geschwistern und den Eltern auf dem Pferdefuhrwerk eines Nachbarn. Eine Woche lang irrte die Familie im chaotischen Getümmel der allgemeinen Auflösung umher, dann wagten sich die Nagys zurück nach Hause. Mit Pferden und zwei Kühen durchquerten sie die Soła bei Oświęcim, die Straßenbrücke war zerstört. Ihr Haus war unversehrt, die Familie führte dort noch eine Weile ein relativ normales Alltagsleben, Edwards Vater hatte Arbeit in der örtlichen Dachpappenfabrik. Andere aus der Familie fanden sich einer schlimmeren Lage wieder. Edward erinnert sich an die Ruine eines Hauses, das seinem Onkel gehört hatte. Es stand ganz in der Nähe des Stammlagers Auschwitz I. Als er dort im Juni 1940 mit seinem Bruder auf einer Wiese spielte, beobachteten die beiden Jungen, wie ein Zug vorbeirollte und in der Nähe hielt. Es war der erste Gefangenentransport in das KZ Auschwitz.

Am 22. April 1941 wurde Brzezinka von der SS geräumt, die Familie Nagy floh nach Monowice. Dort wurde Edwards Mutter fast getötet, als SS-Angehörige ohne besonderen Grund um sich schossen; Edward erinnert sich an seine Todesangst. Später wurde er vom »Arbeitsamt«, was er auf Deutsch ausspricht, zur Arbeit im Buna-Werk abkommandiert; den IG-Farben-Ausweis mit eingeschweißtem Passbild hat er noch. Sein direkter Arbeitgeber war die Gleiwitzer Elektrofirma Georg Grabasch, die unter anderem die SS-Kommandantur des Stammlagers Auschwitz mit elektrischen Leitungen ausstattete. Während seiner Arbeit im Buna-Werk erlebte Edward Nagy viele Bombenangriffe. Trotz Überwachung durch die SS hatte er Kontakte zum polnischen Widerstand, war Kurier für geheime Briefe und beteiligte sich an Fluchtvorbereitungen von Häftlingen. Edward Nagy war auch Augenzeuge von brutalen Misshandlungen der Häftlinge bis hin zu Mord. Einmal sah er, wie zwei SS-Männer Wachhunde auf weibliche Häftlinge hetzten, eine der Frauen wurde von den Hunden getötet. Auch die Massentötungen in den Lagern waren ihm bewusst. »Der Geruch der Leichenverbrennungen war in der ganzen Stadt zu riechen, und ich habe auch mit Leuten gesprochen, die das mit eigenen Augen gesehen hatten«, berichtet Nagy.

Alle Angehörigen seiner Familie überlebten den Zweiten Weltkrieg. Sie kehrten im Februar 1945 zurück nach Brzezinka, doch vom gesamten Ort mit seinen etwa 1.000 Häusern war fast nichts übrig. Die SS hatte nur eine Handvoll massiver Betonbauten stehen lassen, Kasernen und ein Lazarett errichtet; der Rest der Gemarkung bestand aus Wiesen. Edwards Vater hatte Land besessen, das nun auf dem Gelände des ehemaligen Vernichtungslagers Birkenau in der Nähe des Krematoriums II lag. Später erhielt er dafür eine Entschädigung aus der Schweiz.

Im ehemaligen Lager selber war Edward Nagy nur einziges Mal: 1979, beim Besuch von Papst Johannes Paul II.

79 LEFT, **EDWARD NAGY, EYEWITNESS TO THE EXPULSION IN 1941, FORCED LABORER AT THE IG FARBEN FACTORY, BRZEZINKA**

On September 2, 1939, one day after the German invasion of Poland began, the twelve-year-old Edward Nagy experienced the first bombardment of his hometown. The target of the air raid was the train station, that piece of infrastructure that had brought growth and prosperity to the village (and was later one of the reasons for the construction of the extermination camp at Birkenau). Edward remembers fleeing with his parents and three siblings in a neighbor's horse-drawn wagon. For a week, the family wandered about amid the chaos of the general disbandment, and then the Nagys decided to risk going home. With horses and two cows, they crossed the Soła River near Oświęcim; the bridge with the road had been destroyed. Their house was untouched, and the family led a relatively normal life there for a while. Edward's father worked in the local roofing paper factory. Others from the family found themselves in a worse situation. Edward recalls the ruins of a house that had belonged to his uncle. It stood very near the main camp, Auschwitz I. When he and his brother were playing in a meadow there in June 1940, the two boys saw a train pass them and stop close by. It was the first prisoner transport to the Auschwitz concentration camp.

On April 22, 1941, Brzezinka was cleared out by the SS, and the Nagy family fled to Monowice. There, Edward's mother was nearly killed when an SS man fired his gun for no particular reason. Edward remembers how deathly afraid he was. Later, the Arbeitsamt (labor office), as Edward calls it, using the German word, assigned him to work at the Buna factory; he still has his IG-Farben identification card with its laminated passport photo. His immediate employer was the Georg Grabasch Electrical Company in Gleiwitz (Gliwice in Polish), which equipped the SS command office, among other places, at the main camp in Auschwitz with electrical wiring. While working in the Buna factory, Edward lived through many air raids. Despite the SS surveillance, he was in contact with the Polish resistance, carried secret letters, and helped in preparing prison breaks. Edward was also an eyewitness to brutal abuses of the prisoners, including murder. Once he saw two SS men set guard dogs on some female prisoners; one of the women was killed by the dogs. He was also aware of the mass murders being committed in the camps. "You could smell the burning bodies all over town, and I talked to people who had seen it with their own eyes," says Edward.

All the members of his family survived World War II. In February 1945 they returned to Brzezinka, but there was almost nothing left of the town and its nearly one thousand houses. The SS had left only a handful of massive concrete buildings, barracks, and a military hospital; the rest of the district consisted of nothing but meadows. Edward's father had owned land close to Crematorium II, in what was now the Birkenau death camp.

Later, he received compensation for it from Switzerland.
Edward himself was only inside the former camp once, during the visit from Pope John Paul II.

79 RECHTS, **ROMAN REZOŃ, BRZEZINKA**
Roman Rezoń ist ein Jahr nach dem Zweiten Weltkrieg geboren und wuchs von 1948 an in Brzezinka auf, der Heimat seiner Familie. Früher hatten die Rezońs ein kleines Haus etwas abseits vom Dorf, in den Flussauen der Weichsel. Dort lebten Romans Eltern mit den älteren Geschwistern und den Großeltern – bis zur Vertreibung durch die Deutschen im Jahr 1941. Das Haus der Familie lag am nordwestlichen Rand des Areals, auf dem das Vernichtungslager Birkenau errichtet werden sollte. Anders als die meisten Gebäude in der Ortschaft Brzezinka ließ die SS das kleine Haus stehen und baute es in eine Gaskammer um. Viele Tausend Menschen wurden hier ermordet. Die Tarnnamen des Gebäudes lauteten »Bunker 2« und »Weißes Haus«. Seine Grundmauern sind bis heute zu sehen. Sie liegen auf dem Gelände des Staatlichen Museums Auschwitz.
1948 kehrten Roman Rezońs Eltern mit ihm und seinen Geschwistern zurück nach Brzezinka. Für den verlorenen Besitz wurde die Familie mit Feldern im Nachbarort Plawy entschädigt. Als Kind hütete Roman Kühe in der Nähe des »Weißen Hauses«, er spielte oft auf dem ehemaligen Lagergelände, und die Kinder badeten in den Wasserbecken des Lagers, in denen einige Anwohner auch Fische züchteten. »Niemand dachte damals über die Lager nach«, sagt Roman Rezoń heute. 1971 baute er in Brzezinka ein eigenes Haus. Es steht auf einem Grundstück, das der Familie schon vor dem Zweiten Weltkrieg gehört hatte. Ein großer Teil dieses Geländes reichte in das später errichtete Lager hinein. Der Rest grenzt direkt an die ehemalige SS-Kommandantur, die nach dem Krieg zur Pfarrkirche des Dorfes umgebaut wurde. Zwischen seinem Haus und dem Lager hat Roman Rezoń vor zehn Jahren einen kleinen Wald angepflanzt, der die Sicht vollständig versperrt. »So ist es besser«, sagt er, »wir müssen das Lager nicht sehen, und von dort aus sieht uns niemand.«
Die nächste Generation der Familie Rezoń geht offensiver mit dem Thema um. Roman Rezońs Sohn Robert ist Geschichtslehrer und Guide an der Gedenkstätte Auschwitz-Birkenau. Er berichtet, dass die ortsansässige Bevölkerung von den deutschen Besatzern 1939 vor die Wahl gestellt wurde, sich entweder auf einer »Volksliste« als Deutsche registrieren zu lassen oder in Arbeitslager deportiert zu werden. Die männlichen Unterzeichner der Volksliste wurden bis zum Alter von dreißig Jahren zum Dienst in der Wehrmacht eingezogen. »Mein Großvater Valentin, dem das ‚Weiße Haus' gehörte, war dafür zwei Jahre zu alt«, berichtet Robert Rezoń. »Mein anderer Großvater, Julian Poloński, wurde zur Zwangsarbeit nach Deutschland deportiert.« Nach dem Krieg kam Poloński zurück und suchte sein Grundstück in Brzezinka. Dort hatte die SS bis auf eine Handvoll Gebäude alle Häuser abgerissen. Wo früher das Dorf stand, hatten die Deutschen ein SS-Lazarett gebaut. Kriegsheimkehrer konnten sich deswegen bei der Suche nach ihren Grundstücken nur an alten Obstbäumen orientieren. In Julian Polońskis Fall kam noch ein skurriles Detail dazu, berichtet Robert Rezoń: »In seinem Garten hinterm Haus hatte mein Großvater ein buntes Vogelhaus in einen Baum gehängt. Das hatte die Okkupation überstanden – und zeigte Opa Julian, wo sein Zuhause war.«

79 RIGHT, **ROMAN REZOŃ, BRZEZINKA**
Roman Rezoń was born a year after World War II ended and from 1948 onward he grew up in Brzezinka, his family's home town. Before the war the Rezońs lived in a small house located a little bit outside the village, on the floodplains of the Vistula River. Roman's parents lived there with his older siblings and grandparents, until they were expelled by the Germans in 1941. The family's house stood on the northwestern edge of the land upon which the Birkenau extermination camp was supposed to be constructed. Unlike most of the other buildings in the town of Brzezinka, the SS allowed the little house to remain standing and turned it into a gas chamber. Many thousands of people were murdered here. The building was nicknamed "Bunker 2" and the "White House." Its foundation walls can be seen to this day; they are located on land belonging to the Auschwitz-Birkenau State Museum.
In 1948 Roman's parents returned to Brzezinka with him and his siblings. The family was compensated for their lost property with fields in the neighboring town of Pławy. As a child Roman tended cows near the "White House" and often played on the grounds of the old camp; the children swam in the camp's water tanks, where some villagers also farmed fish. "Nobody thought about the camp in those days," says Roman now. In 1971 he built his own house in Brzezinka. It stands on a plot of land that had belonged to the family before World War II. Much of this land was incorporated into the camp that was later erected. The rest borders directly on the former SS command office, which was turned into the parish church after the war. Between his house and the camp Roman planted a small wood that completely blocks the view. "It's better this way," he says, "we don't have to look at the camp, and nobody there can see us."
The next generation of the Rezoń family deals with the theme a little more aggressively. Roman Rezoń's son Robert is a history teacher and a guide at the Auschwitz-Birkenau memorial. He says that the German occupiers gave the local population a choice between registering as German on a "people's list," or being deported to a labor camp. Men up to the age of thirty who signed the list were drafted into the German army. "My grandfather, Valentin, who owned the 'White House,' was two years too old," reports Robert Rezoń. "My other grandfather, Julian Poloński, was deported to a labor camp in Germany." After the war Poloński returned to look for his property in Brzezinka. Except for a few buildings, the SS had torn down all of the houses. Where the village had once stood, the Germans had built an SS military hospital. When looking for their homes, those returning from the war could only orient themselves on old fruit trees. In Julian Poloński's case, says Roman, there was an odd detail: "In the garden behind his house my grandfather had hung a colorful birdhouse in a tree. It survived the occupation—and showed Grandpa Julian where his home had been."

81 AUSCHWITZ I / STAMMLAGER
Ruine eines Lagerschuppens unbekannter Funktion nahe des Krematoriums, abgebrannt 2015/16.

81 AUSCHWITZ I/MAIN CAMP
Ruins of a shed, function unknown, near the crematorium; burned down in 2015–16.

82 AUSCHWITZ II / BIRKENAU, NEUES BESUCHERZENTRUM
Unmittelbar nach der Befreiung machten sich ehemalige Häftlinge daran, das Lagergelände als Mahnmal zu erhalten. Im Juli 1947 wurde auf Beschluss des polnischen Parlaments das Staatliche Museum Auschwitz-Birkenau gegründet. Seit 1979 ist es UNESCO-Welterbe. Die Besucherzahlen steigen ständig, auf zuletzt über zwei Millionen im Jahr 2016. Eine langjährige Mitarbeiterin sagt: »Wir hatten mal 1.000 Besucher pro Monat, heute sind es so viele in einer Stunde. Dies hier sollte keine Destination des Massentourismus sein. Es ist ein Friedhof.«

82 AUSCHWITZ II/BIRKENAU, NEW VISITOR CENTER
Immediately after the liberation former prisoners lobbied to maintain the camp as a memorial site. In July 1947 the Auschwitz-Birkenau State Museum was established by a resolution of the Polish parliament. Since 1979 it has been a UNESCO World Heritage site. The number of visitors is constantly increasing; there were more than two million in 2016. A long-time employee says, "We used to have a thousand visitors per month, today we get that many in an hour. This should not be a destination for crowds of tourists. It is a cemetery."

83 AUSCHWITZ II / BIRKENAU, FLUSSAUEN DER WEICHSEL
Um alle Spuren der Massenmorde zu vertuschen, verstreute die SS die Asche der Getöteten in der Umgebung der Lager. Ein Teil dieser Asche wurde in die Weichsel geschüttet.

83 AUSCHWITZ II/BIRKENAU, FLOODPLAINS OF THE VISTULA RIVER
To hide all traces of the mass murders, the SS scattered the ashes of the dead around the camp. Some of the ashes were scattered in the Vistula.

84, 86 AUSCHWITZ III/ MONOWITZ – BUNA
Interieur der letzten erhaltenen Häftlingsbaracke. Sie wird von einem mittellosen Frührentner bewohnt, der sich keine andere Wohnung leisten kann. Eigentümer des Gebäudes ist ein Verwandter, der ihm die Unterkunft sehr günstig überlässt. Der Bewohner nimmt Anteil am Gedenken an die ehemaligen Häftlinge, zum Bespiel durch regelmäßige Besuche von Gottesdiensten und Feiern anlässlich des Jahrestags der Befreiung am 27. Januar.
Das Gebäude ist als einfacher Holzschuppen ausgeführt und nicht auf lange Lebensdauer ausgelegt. Daher ist der Zustand der Bausubstanz sehr schlecht. Der angrenzende Teil der Nachbarbaracke diente bis vor wenigen Jahren als Lagerschuppen. Dann wurde er von einer lokalen Initiative vor weiterem Verfall gesichert und in Einzelteilen eingelagert. Diese Baracke ist von besonderem historischen Wert, weil der italienische Schriftsteller und Holocaust-Überlebende Primo Levi sie exakt beschreibt. In seinem autobiografischen Bericht »Ist das ein Mensch?« schildert Levi die Prozedur des Waschens in der Badebaracke. Er zitiert dabei Wandbeschriftungen des Wortlauts »So bist du rein«, »So gehst du ein«. Diese Wandtexte sind auf den eingelagerten Barackenteilen erhalten.

84, 86 AUSCHWITZ III/ MONOWITZ–BUNA
Interior of the last surviving prisoner barrack. It is inhabited by a poor person who had to retire early and could not afford any other type of home. The owner of the building is a relative who rents it to him at a very affordable price. The tenant takes part in commemorating the prisoners, for instance, by regularly attending worship services and ceremonies centered on the anniversary of the liberation on January 27.
The structure is like a simple wooden shed and not built to last, so its material state is very poor. Up until a few years ago, an adjoining section of the neighboring barrack served as a storage shed. Then a local initiative had it insured against further decay and it was stored in sections. This barrack is of particular historical value, because the Italian author and Holocaust survivor Primo Levi describes it in exact detail. In his memoir, If This Is a Man, Levi describes the process of washing in the bath barrack. He quotes inscriptions on the wall, "This is how you will be clean" and "This is how you die." These inscriptions have survived on the barrack sections in storage.

88 RAJSKO
Heinrich Himmler, Reichsführer SS, hatte angeordnet, in der Umgebung der Lager landwirtschaftliche Betriebe aufzubauen. Wie in allen Sektoren des täglichen Lebens, mussten KZ-Häftlinge auch hier Zwangsarbeit leisten.
In Rajsko entstand eine Versuchsstation für Pflanzenzucht, die unter anderem Stoffe zur Gummiproduktion liefern sollte. Auf der Gemarkung der Ortschaft Brzezinka befand sich ein ähnlicher Betrieb. Er hieß »Wirtschaftshof Birkenau« und ist heute restlos verschwunden.

88 RAJSKO
Heinrich Himmler, the SS Reichsführer, ordered that farms be set up in the area surrounding the camp. As they did in all sectors of everyday life, concentration camp prisoners also had to perform forced labor here. An experimental plant breeding station was set up in Rajsko, which was supposed to supply materials for the production of rubber, among other things. There was a similar operation within the boundaries of the village of Brzezinka. It was known as the Wirtschaftshof Birkenau, or the Birkenau Farmyard, but it has disappeared without a trace.

89 ADAM RYDZOŃ, NÄCHSTER ANRAINER DER LAGERS AUSCHWITZ II/ BIRKENAU

89 ADAM RYDZOŃ, NEIGHBOR NEAREST THE AUSCHWITZ II/BIRKENAU CAMP

90 »ENERGYLANDIA« ZATOR
Der Vergnügungspark »Energylandia« wurde im Sommer 2014 eröffnet, etwa 25 Kilometer östlich von Oświęcim. Er soll unter anderem einen Teil der jährlich über zwei Millionen Auschwitz-Besucher anziehen, die fast ausschließlich Tagestouristen sind. Das funktioniert nur bei Gruppen aus Ländern, die von der Shoah historisch unbelastet sind. Ein kleiner Teil dieser Besucher verlängert den Besuch der Gedenkstätte um einen Aufenthalt im Vergnügungspark.

90 ENERGYLANDIA IN ZATOR
In summer 2014 the amusement park Energylandia was opened around twenty-five kilometers east of Oświęcim. Among other things, it was intended to attract some of the more than two million annual visitors to Auschwitz, the majority of whom are daytrippers. This only works with groups from countries that are not historically burdened by the Shoah. A small number of these visitors supplement their visit to the memorial with a stop at the amusement park.

91 OŚWIĘCIM, BEREITSCHAFTSSIEDLUNG
Für die deutschen Zivilangestellten der IG-Farben-Fabriken Auschwitz sowie für deren Familien mussten KZ-Häftlinge 1942/43 östlich des historischen Zentrums einen Stadtteil für ca. 6.000 Menschen errichten, die sogenannte »Bereitschaftssiedlung«. Die solide gebauten Wohnblocks werden noch heute bewohnt und derzeit umfassend saniert.

91 OŚWIĘCIM, ON-CALL SETTLEMENT
To house the German nonmilitary employees of the IG Farben factory in Auschwitz and their families, concentration camp prisoners had to build new quarter of the city, known as the Bereitschaftssiedlung or "on-call settlement," for around six thousand people, east of the city's historic center in 1942–43. The solidly constructed apartment blocks are still occupied today and are currently undergoing thorough renovation.

93 BRZEZINKA, AUSCHWITZ II/ BIRKENAU
Privates Wohnhaus am Ortsrand von Brzezinka. Im Hintergrund ein Wachturm des Lagers Auschwitz II/Birkenau.

93 BRZEZINKA, AUSCHWITZ II/ BIRKENAU
Private home on the edge of Brzezinka. A guard tower at the Auschwitz II/Birkenau camp is in the background.

94 BRZEZINKA, AUSCHWITZ II/ BIRKENAU
Weg von der ersten Bahnrampe zum Vernichtungslager.
Die Deportationszüge, die etwa eine halbe Million Juden aus ganz Europa nach Birkenau brachten, hielten zwischen Frühjahr 1942 und April 1944 an einem Nebengleis der Eisenbahnanlage von Auschwitz, etwa einen Kilometer vom Tor des Vernichtungslagers entfernt. Die Deportierten mussten diesen Weg zu Fuß

gehen. Wer dazu nicht in der Lage war, wurde auf LKW verladen, die oft direkt an die Leichenverbrennungsgruben fuhren und ihre Passagiere lebend in die Flammen kippten.

94 BRZEZINKA, AUSCHWITZ II/BIRKENAU

Path from the first train platform to the extermination camp.

Between spring 1942 and April 1944, the transport trains that deported around five hundred thousand Jews from everywhere in Europe to Birkenau halted at a siding at the Auschwitz station, around a kilometer from the gate of the extermination camp. The deportees had to walk the rest of the way. Anyone not able to walk was loaded into trucks, which often went straight to the cremation pits and dumped their passengers into the flames while they were still alive.

96 ZEITZEUGINNEN IRENE KRZEMIEŃ UND ANNA KULCZYK, BRZEZINKA

Irene Krzemień wurde im März 1939 in Brzezinka geboren, knapp ein halbes Jahr, bevor die ersten deutschen Bomben fielen. Aus den Erinnerungen ihrer Mutter berichtet sie, dass die Familie an einem Abend im April 1941 vertrieben wurde, bei Fackelschein und unter den Rufen: »Raus, raus!« Irenes Großmutter nahm ihre Tochter, Enkelin Irene, deren Bruder und ihre Schwester mit auf einen Pferdewagen und lenkte das Fuhrwerk ostwärts. Keine zwanzig Kilometer weiter, in Zator, gerät die Familie auf dem Dorfplatz in eine Umzingelung durch die Wehrmacht. Die Soldaten holen Irenes kleine Schwester aus der Gruppe und reichen das Baby herum. Die Frauen und Geschwister sind vor Angst erstarrt, doch die Soldaten tun dem Kind nichts zuleide. Sie reichen die Kleine ihrer Mutter zurück, geben den Flüchtenden zu essen und weisen ihnen einen sicheren Weg aus der Kampfzone.

Menschenfreundlich ist das Besatzungsregime allerdings nicht. Die Frauen und Kinder der Familie Krzemień hausen fortan in einem Schweinestall im Dorf Dwory; Irenes Vater, der von der Familie getrennt worden war, muss Zwangsarbeit bei der IG Farben in Monowitz leisten. Dort riskiert er es, den Häftlingen des KZ Lebensmittel zuzustecken, wird denunziert und von den Deutschen stundenlang verhört. Seine Rettung ist ein Deutscher, der für ihn eine entlastende Falschaussage macht.

Nach Kriegsende legt Irenes Vater sich weiterhin mit den Autoritäten an. Als die sowjetischen Besatzer die Chemiefabrik Monowice in großen Teilen demontierten, protestierte er lauthals, beklagte öffentlich auch das Massaker von Katyn, wo KGB-Leute tausende polnische Offiziere erschossen hatten. Prompt verlor der Mann seinen Job, bekam nur weit entfernt eine andere Arbeit und konnte seine Familie nur noch alle paar Wochen einmal kurz sehen. Die Armut der mittlerweile fünf Kinder und ihrer Eltern war so erbärmlich, dass Irene Krzemień die Lebensbedingungen unter der deutschen Besatzung sogar als besser schildert: »Da hatten wir wenigstens zu essen.«

Ihren Grundbesitz nahe der späteren IG-Farben-Werke hat die Familie fast ersatzlos verloren. Irenes Eltern konnten die erforderlichen Dokumente nicht beibringen; was ihnen ausgezahlt wurde, reichte für zwei Betten. Irenes Eltern erhielten immerhin die relativ gute Wohnung eines ehemaligen Mitarbeiters der IG Farben.

Der Bruder von Irenes Mutter heiratete im zarten Alter von 18 seine zwanzigjährige deutsche Freundin Erika, nicht gerade zum Vergnügen der polnischen Familie. Diese Heirat jedoch rettete die junge Frau vor der drohenden Deportation nach Sibirien.

Irene Krzemień hielt nach 1945 eher Abstand zum Thema Krieg und Shoah. Als Kind war sie ab und zu im Lager, wie alle ihre Spielkameraden. Die direkte Auseinandersetzung kam in ihrer Familie, wie bei vielen, erst Generationen später: Einer ihrer Enkel hat eine Stelle im Staatlichen Museum Auschwitz.

96 IRENE KRZEMIEŃ AND ANNA KULCZYK, EYEWITNESSES, BRZEZINKA

Irene Krzemień was born in Brzezinka in March 1939, just about six months before the first German bombs fell. Recounting her mother's memories, she says that the family was expelled by torchlight one evening in April 1941, among shouts of "Raus, raus!" Irene's grandmother put her, along with her mother, brother, and sister, into a horse-drawn wagon and drove it eastward. Not twenty kilometers on, in Zator, the family found itself at the village square, surrounded by the German army. The soldiers took Irene's little sister away from the group and handed the baby around. The women and children were frozen with fear, but the soldiers did not hurt the child. They gave the little one back to her mother, gave the refugees something to eat, and showed them a safe way out of the battle zone.

The occupying regime, however, was not friendly to people. The women and children of the Krzemień family lived from then on in a pigsty in the village of Dwory. Irene's father, who was separated from the family, was forced to work in the IG Farben in Monowitz. There, he took the risk of feeding concentration camp prisoners, was denounced, and interrogated by the Germans for hours. He was saved by a German, who made a false statement exonerating him.

After the end of the war, Irene's father continued to struggle with the authorities. When the Soviet occupiers began demolishing large parts of the chemical factory in Monowice, he protested loudly and also publicly lamented the massacre at Katyn, where the KGB executed thousands of Polish officers. The man promptly lost his job, was only able to get another job far away, and could only see his family briefly every couple of weeks. The now five children and their parents lived in such miserable poverty that Irene even describes the living conditions under the German occupation as better: "At least we had something to eat then."

The family lost their property near what was later the IG Farben plant without almost any compensation. Irene's parents were not able to produce the required documents; they received exactly enough for two beds. Irene's parents were at least given a relatively good apartment once occupied by a former IG Farben employee.

At the tender age of eighteen, Irene's uncle married his twenty-year-old German girlfriend Erika, not exactly to the great pleasure of the Polish family. This marriage, however, saved the young women from being deported to Siberia.

After 1945 Irene Krzemień preferred to keep her distance from the topics of the war and the Shoah. As a child, she occasionally went to the camp, as did all of her playmates. In her family, the direct confrontation came, as it did for many, with the next generation: one of her grandchildren has a job at the Auschwitz-Birkenau State Museum.

126 AUSCHWITZ II / BIRKENAU, FLUSSAUEN DER WEICHSEL

Flussauen der Weichsel westlich der einstigen Krematorien des Vernichtungslagers Birkenau. Im Vernichtungslager Birkenau wurde mehr als eine Million Menschen ermordet. Die genaue Zahl ist nicht zu ermitteln, da viele Opfer ohne Registrierung direkt aus den Deportationszügen in die Gaskammern getrieben wurden. Um die Spuren des Massenmords zu verwischen, wurden die Leichen verbrannt. Ihre Asche wurde in der Umgebung verstreut, auf Wiesen, in Wäldern, Wasserläufen und Tümpeln.

126 AUSCHWITZ II/BIRKENAU, FLOODPLAINS OF THE VISTULA RIVER

The floodplain of the Vistula River west of what were once the crematoria at the Birkenau death camp. More than a million people were murdered in Birkenau. The exact number cannot be determined, since many of the victims were sent to the gas chambers directly from the transport trains without being registered. To erase any traces of the mass murders, the corpses were burned. Their ashes were scattered in the area, in meadows, forests, rivers, and ponds.

126 AUSCHWITZ II / BIRKENAU

Weg ins ehemalige Vernichtungslager Auschwitz II / Birkenau. Diesen Weg gingen die Deportierten, bevor Ende April 1944 das Eisenbahngleis direkt ins Lager fertiggestellt war.

128 AUSCHWITZ II/BIRKENAU

Path to the former extermination camp Auschwitz II/Birkenau. The deportees walked this path before the train tracks leading straight into the camp were finished in late April 1944.

TAGEBUCH 2012–2017
JOURNAL

Riesige Fläche, hunderte Kamine in allen Stadien der Windschiefheit und des Zerfalls, struppige Wiesen, Stille abseits der Wege, hoher Himmel, Zäune, Wachtürme klein, weit weg. Was würde ein nicht mit NS-Geschichte vertrauter Besucher, sagen wir aus Peru, Vietnam, Indonesien oder von den Osterinseln, an diesem Ort wahrnehmen, wenn man ihn mit verbundenen Augen hierher führte? Gras, Wind, Weite?

Nachts schlafe ich ein wenig unruhig, aber ich schlafe, und frage mich am nächsten Morgen, wo die Alpträume bleiben.

Auf der Fahrt nach Auschwitz ist mein Vademecum die Musik des späten Bob Dylan. Ich höre ihn ohnehin viel, aber bei dieser Reise tut der alte Nörgler meinen Nerven besonders gut. Unser Ziel ist einer der höllischsten Orte aller Zeiten, da beruhigt es ungemein, einem alten Mann zu lauschen, der nuschelnd und heiser die ewigen Geheimnisse des Menschseins umkreist. Die Songs von Dylan sind so entschieden jenseits unseres Themas, dass ich innerlich aufatme, wenn er schrammmelt und näselt. Und da ist noch was: Bob Dylan ist Jude; geboren im Mai 1941, vier Wochen nachdem die verdammten Krauts das bis dahin unbekannte polnische Dörfchen Brzezinka entvölkerten, es abtrugen, und aus seinen Ziegeln und Balken ein Vernichtungslager bauten, wie es die Welt noch nicht gesehen hatte: Birkenau. Gedichte schreiben nach Auschwitz sei barbarisch, sagte Adorno. Dylan lebt, singt und dichtet. Auf seinem vielleicht finstersten Album, »Time out of Mind«, ist einer der finstersten Songs »Not Dark Yet«. Darin heißt es: »*Well, my sense of humanity has gone down the drain / Behind every beautiful thing there's been some kind of pain (...) Sometimes my burden is more than I can bear / It's not dark yet but it's gettin' there.*« Dazu diese trägen, bluesigen Akkorde, der Sound der Loser und Leidenden – gemeinsames Klagen hat schon immer den Schmerz gelindert, also: Play it again, Bob!

Nachts, nach Tagwerk mit Recherche und Fotografie, sehe ich viele Stunden lang auf dem kleinen Laptopbildschirm »Shoah« von Claude Lanzmann, gebückt auf dem niedrigen Plastikhocker, der einzigen Sitzgelegenheit in meinem Pensionszimmer. Irgendwann tut der Rücken weh, brennen die Augen. Exerziere ich hier Bußübungen?

Wie zur Imprägnierung gegen die langsam wachsende Vertrautheit mit dem Dorf, seiner Lage an den Zäunen, mit dem Alltag im Angesicht des »Todestors«, lese ich die Lebensbeichte des Lagerkommandanten Rudolf Höß, und die Berichte von Überlebenden der Sonderkommandos.
Immer wieder Details, die absolut grässlich sind. Wenn ich über unser Projekt mit jemandem rede, habe ich oft den intuitiven Wunsch, diese Horroszenen wiederzugeben; wahrscheinlich wäre es entlastend, den Schrecken zu teilen. Ich habe es mir aber immer verkniffen, um die inneren Bilder jener Grausamkeiten nicht in die Hirne meiner Gegenüber zu transportieren.
Was klüger, richtiger, gebotener oder angebrachter ist, bleibt mir ein Rätsel.
Wird ein Schrecken größer, wenn er als Imagination im Bewusstsein von mehr Menschen vorhanden ist? Oder nimmt er ab, wenn man seine innere Repräsentation teilt und teilt und teilt und teilt – also buchstäblich mitteilt?
In jedem Fall belegt dieser Konflikt, dass es ein Irrtum oder zumindest eine grobe Ungenauigkeit ist, von »unvorstellbar« zu sprechen, wenn es um große Grausamkeit, epochale Verbrechen, massivste Gewalt geht. Das Gegenteil stimmt: Es ist vorstellbar. Vorstellbar bedeutet nicht, dass meine Imagination auch nur entfernt der realen Erfahrung eines Augenzeugen gleicht. Aber wenn Gewalt nicht vorstellbar wäre, würde jede Justiz, jede historische Forschung, jede literarische und auch jede bildnerische Beschäftigung damit sinnlos sein. Es gäbe keine Ahnung von richtig und falsch, von Schuld und Sühne. Schon die Kategorien »Verbrechen« und »gegen die Menschlichkeit« implizieren eine Vorstellung der entsprechenden Taten. Menschen haben die Fähigkeit, sich in andere Personen hineinzuversetzen; also ist Auschwitz vorstellbar.
Wer dem widerspricht, der lese die Berichte der Überlebenden der Sonderkommandos: Wir waren nicht dabei, aber erhalten sehr präzise Vorstellungen dessen, was in den Gaskammern und Krematorien vor sich ging.
Zu diesen Vorstellungen gehört die Einsicht, dass Vorstellung und Erfahrung so verschieden sind wie einen Krimi zu lesen und Opfer eines Mordversuchs zu werden.
Daher gibt es eine unverzichtbare Bedingung, bevor ich daran gehe, mir eine Vorstellung von Auschwitz zu machen: Demut.

Andreas Langen

Huge area, hundreds of chimneys in all kinds of crooked and decaying states, scrubby meadows, silence away from the paths, the sky high above, fences, small guard towers far away. What would a visitor unfamiliar with Nazi history—say, someone from Peru, Vietnam, Indonesia, or Easter Island—perceive in this place, if you led them here blindfolded? Grass, wind, expansive space?

At night my sleep is a little restless, but I sleep and wonder the next morning where the nightmares are.

On the journey to Auschwitz my vade mecum is late Bob Dylan music. I listen to him a lot anyway, but on this trip the old grumbler does my nerves especially good. Our destination is one of the most hellish places of all time, so it's incredibly calming to listen to an old man hoarsely mumbling about the eternal mysteries of being human. Dylan's songs are so decidedly outside of our theme that I inwardly breathe a sigh of relief at his scratchy twang. And there's something else: Bob Dylan is Jewish, born in May 1941, four weeks after the damn krauts depopulated the previously unknown, little Polish village of Brzezinka and carried off its bricks and beams to use in constructing an extermination camp of the kind never before seen in this world: Birkenau.
Writing poetry after Auschwitz is barbaric, says Adorno. Dylan lives, sings, and writes poetry. On what is perhaps his darkest album, Time Out of Mind, is one of his darkest songs, "Not Dark Yet." In it, he says: "Well, my sense of humanity has gone down the drain / Behind every beautiful thing there's been some kind of pain . . . Sometimes my burden is more than I can bear / It's not dark yet but it's gettin' there." Plus those languid, bluesy chords, the sound of losers and wretches—complaining along with others has always eased the pain, so, play it again, Bob!

At night, after working all day doing research and taking photographs, I spend many hours bent over the small laptop screen watching Claude Lanzmann's film Shoah, hunched down on my low plastic stool, the only seat available in my little guesthouse room. At some point my back hurts, my eyes burn. Am I doing penance here?

As if to inoculate myself against my slowly growing familiarity with the village, its location next to the fences, with everyday life in the presence of that gate of death, I read the confessions of the camp commander Rudolf Höss and the reports from the survivors of the special units.
More and more details that are absolutely abominable. When I talk to someone about our project, I often have an intuitive wish to recite these loathsome scenes; it would probably be a relief to share the horror. But I always have to stifle myself, so as not to transport the intimate images of these atrocities to my counterpart's brain.
What would be wiser, more proper, more necessary, or more appropriate remains a mystery to me.
Does a horror become greater when it is present in the imaginations of more people? Or does it decrease when you share and share and share and share these visceral images? In any case, this conflict proves that it is a mistake, or at least a gross inaccuracy to call something "unimaginable," when it has to do with immense cruelty, epic crimes, the most massive violence. The opposite is true: it can be imagined. "Imaginable," however, does not mean that what I imagine is even remotely similar to the real experiences of eyewitnesses. Yet, if violence were unimaginable, then any sort of justice, any historical research, any literary or even visual study of it would be pointless. There would be no notion of right and wrong, of guilt and sin. The very categories of "crime" and "against humanity" imply some idea of the corresponding deeds. People have the ability to imagine what it would be like to be someone else. So Auschwitz is imaginable.
Anyone who disagrees should read the reports of the survivors of the special units; we were not there, but we get very precise ideas of what went on in the gas chambers and crematoria.
These ideas include the insight that imagination and experience are as different as reading a murder mystery and being the victim of attempted murder.
Therefore, before I start forming an idea of Auschwitz, I must take on an indispensable condition first: humility.

Andreas Langen

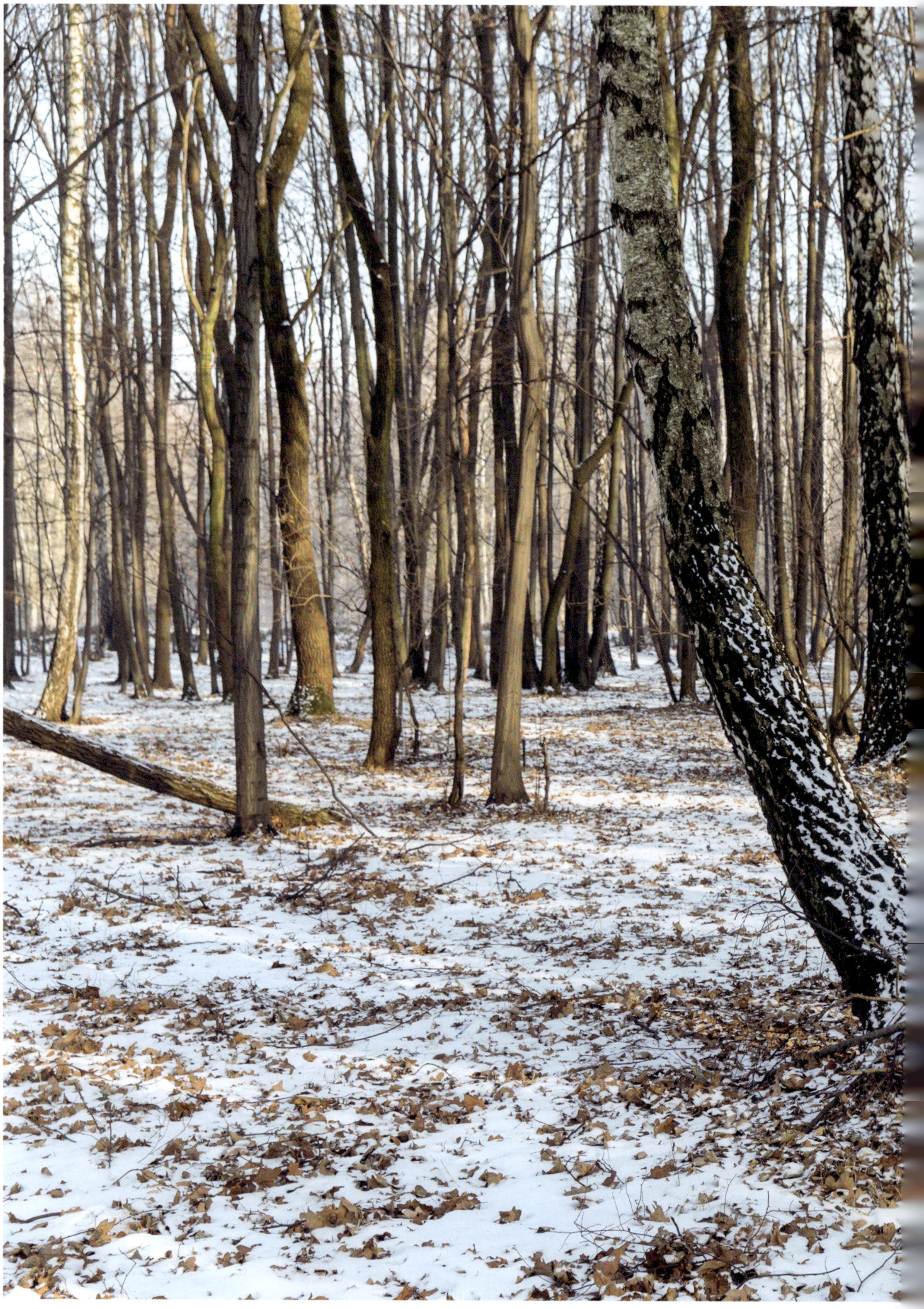

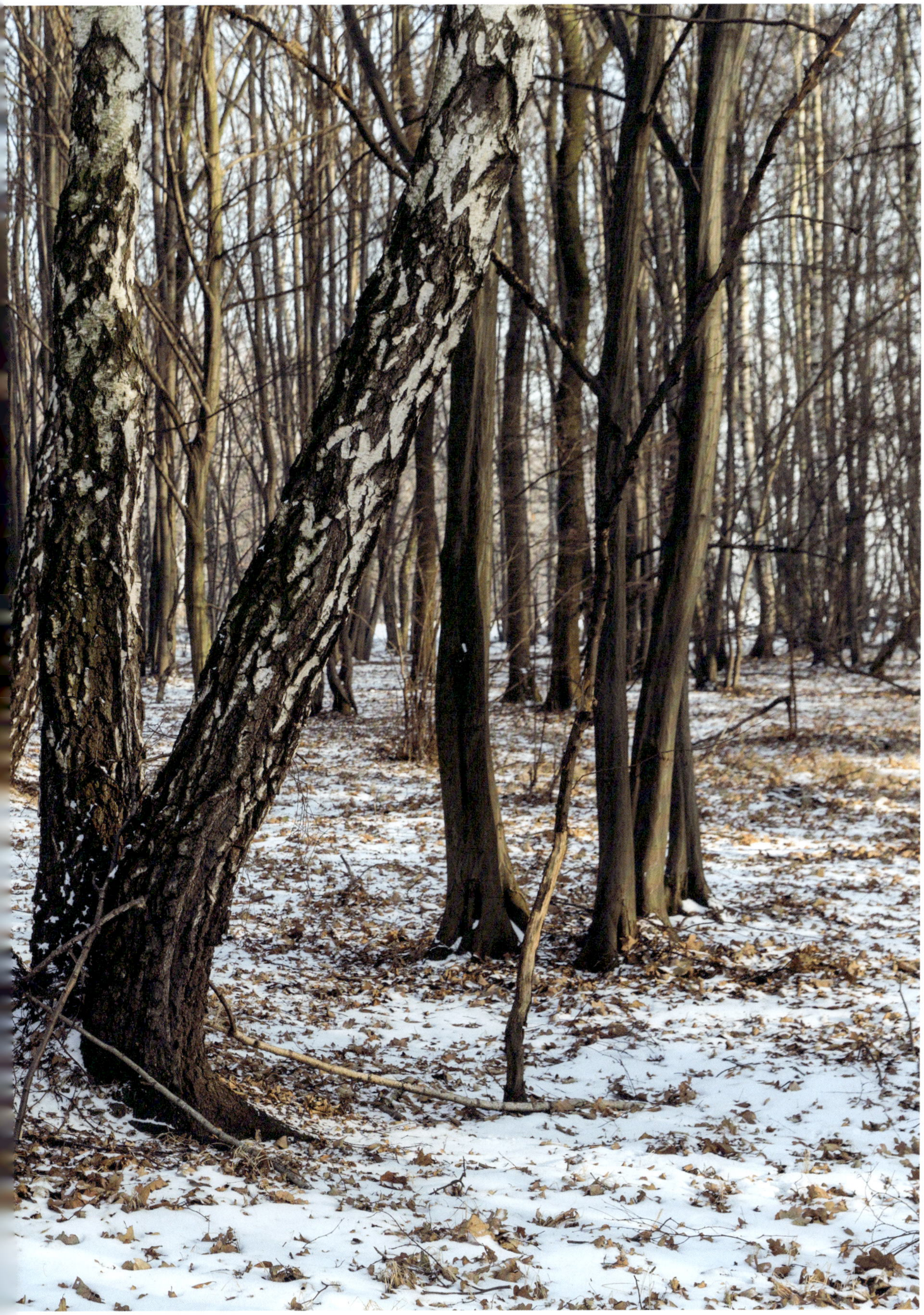

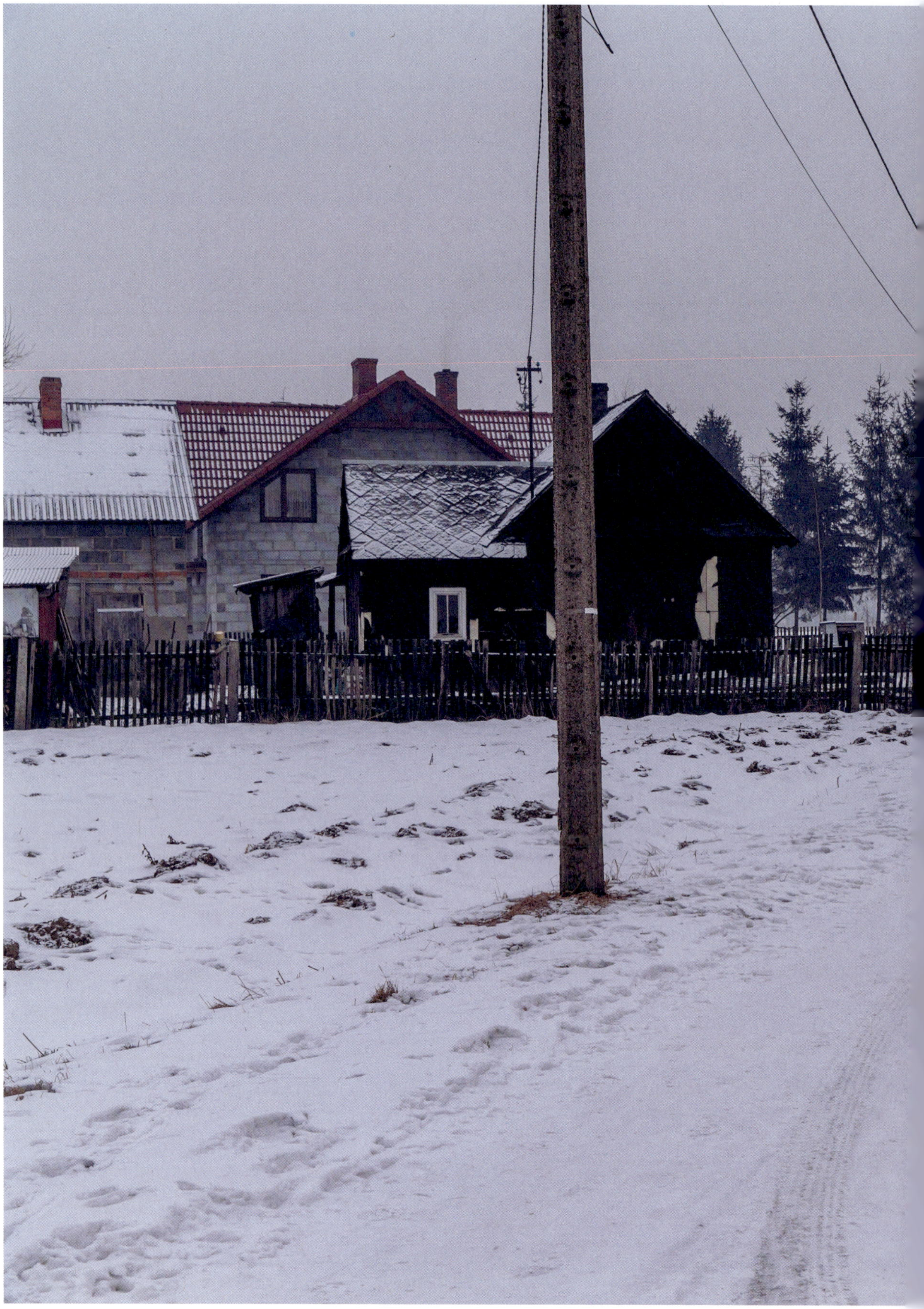

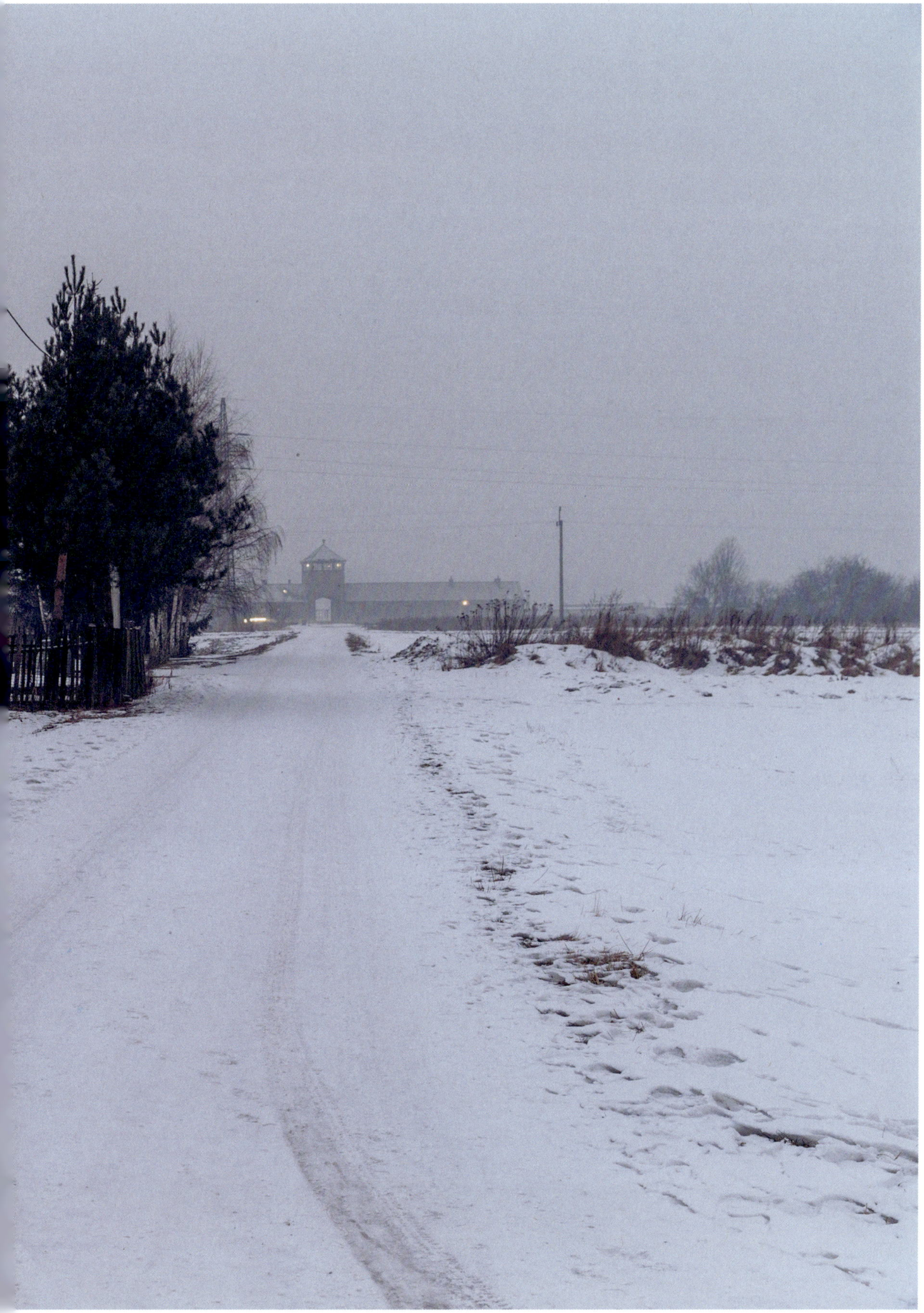

DANK
ACKNOWLEDGMENTS

Wir danken, stellvertretend für alle Menschen vor Ort, die uns Einblick in ihren Alltag gewährt haben, besonders Gosia Musielak aus Brzezinka. Sie war spontan bereit, uns zu helfen, als wir es brauchten. Sie wurde zur wichtigsten Organisatorin hinter den Kulissen. Ohne ihre Geduld, Kenntnisse, Kontakte und Übersetzungen wäre dieses Projekt unmöglich gewesen.

Ein besonderer Dank auch an unseren Assistenten Jakob Trepel, der die Portraits von Jan Sikora und Lidia Skibicka-Maksymowicz fotografiert hat (S. 30/31).

Wir widmen dieses Buch unserem Freund und Kollegen Franjo Tholen (1960–2021), der kurz vor seinem Tod noch einen wichtigen Beitrag zur Bildauswahl geleistet hat.

Dieses Projekt wurde unterstützt durch das Kulturwerk der VG Bild-Kunst, die Landeszentrale für politische Bildung Baden-Württemberg sowie das Landesmuseum Baden-Württemberg/ Museum der Alltagskultur Waldenbuch.

We would particularly like to thank Gosia Musielak of Brzezinka, who is representative of all of the local people who gave us insight into their daily lives. She was instantly ready to help us when we needed it. She became the most important organizer behind the scenes. Without her patience, knowledge, contacts, and translations, this project would have been impossible.

Special thanks also go to our assistant Jakob Trepel, who took the portraits of Jan Sikora and Lidia Skibicka-Maksymowicz (pp. 30–31).

We dedicate this book to our friend and colleague Franjo Tholen (1960–2021), who, shortly before his death, contributed greatly to the process of picture editing.

This project was supported by the Kulturwerk der VG Bild-Kunst, the Landeszentrale für politische Bildung Baden-Württemberg, and the Landesmuseum Baden-Württemberg/Museum der Alltagskultur Waldenbuch.

IMPRESSUM
COLOPHON

Hartmann books

Lektorat / *Copyediting:* Tas Skorupa, Florian Wolf
Übersetzung / *Translation:* Allison Moseley
Grafische Gestaltung / *Graphic design:* musen design, Balingen
Schrift / *Typeface:* Neue Vektor
Bildbearbeitung / *Color separation:* ctrl-s, Stuttgart
Papier / *Stock:* Condat matt Périgord, 150 g/m², Circle Offset Premium White 100 g/m²
Druck / *Printing:* Offizin Scheufele, Stuttgart
Buchbinder / *Binding:* Josef Spinner Großbuchbinderei GmbH, Ottersweier

© 2021 Hartmann Projects, Stuttgart
© 2021 die arge lola für die reproduzierten Bilder/*for the reproduced works*
© 2021 Andreas Langen für den Text/*for the text*

Alle Rechte vorbehalten. Kein Teil dieses Buches darf ohne vorherige schriftliche Zustimmung des Verlags in irgendeiner Form (Druck, Fotokopie, Mikrofilm oder einem anderen Verfahren) reproduziert oder unter Verwendung elektronischer Systeme vervielfältigt oder verbreitet werden.

All rights reserved. No part of this book may be reproduced or transmitted in any form or by any means, electronic or mechanical, including photocopy, recording, or any other information storage and retrieval system, without prior written permission from the publisher.

Erste Auflage / *First edition*
Oktober / *October* 2021

Erschienen bei / *Published by*
Hartmann Books
Breitscheidstraße 48
70176 Stuttgart
www.hartmann-books.com

Hartmann Books ist der Verlag von Hartmann Projects; ein Unternehmen, das Künstler fördert, Ausstellungen organisiert und kuratiert sowie Bücher verlegt.

Hartmann Books is the publishing arm of Hartmann Projects, a company promoting artists, curating and organizing exhibitions, and publishing books.

ISBN 978-3-96070-077-7
Printed in Germany